MEN DON'T CRY . .

Series in Death, Dying, and Bereavement
Consulting Editor
Robert A. Neimeyer

FORMERLY THE **SERIES IN DEATH EDUCATION, AGING, AND HEALTH CARE**
HANNELORE WASS, CONSULTING EDITOR

MEN DON'T CRY . . . WOMEN DO

Transcending Gender Stereotypes of Grief

Terry L. Martin
Kenneth J. Doka

BRUNNER/MAZEL
Taylor & Francis Group

USA	Publishing Office:	BRUNNER/MAZEL
		A member of the Taylor & Francis Group
		325 Chestnut Street
		Philadelphia, PA 19106
		Tel: (215) 625-8900
		Fax: (215) 625-2940
	Distribution Center:	BRUNNER/MAZEL
		A member of the Taylor & Francis Group
		47 Runway Road, Suite G
		Levittown, PA 19057
		Tel: (215) 269-0400
		Fax: (215) 269-0363
UK		BRUNNER/MAZEL
		A member of the Taylor & Francis Group
		11 New Fetter Lane
		London EC4P 4EE, UK
		Tel: +44-171-583-9855
		Fax: +44-171-842-2298

MEN DON'T CRY . . . WOMEN DO: Transcending Gender Stereotypes of Grief

1 2 3 4 5 6 7 8 9 0

Printed by George H. Buchanan, Philadelphia, PA.
Cover design by Joan Wendt
Edited by Beth Schad and Karin McAndrews.

A CIP catalog record for this book is available from the British Library.
∞The paper in this publication meets the requirements of the ANSI Standard Z39.48-1984 (Permanence of Paper).

Library of Congress Cataloging-in-Publication Data available from publisher.

ISBN 0-87630-994-5 (case)
ISBN 0-87630-995-3 (paper)
ISSN 0275-3510

CONTENTS

This book is dedicated to my wife, Nicole, who not only cheerfully tolerated my long bouts with the computer, but edited the initial drafts of the book; and my friend and mentor Dana Cable, who both challenged me to succeed, and equipped me with the tools to do so.

—TLM

To my favorite instrumental grievers: my son, Michael and my godson, Keith; and to Kathy, Angela, and Linda who put up with us.

—KJD

ACKNOWLEDGMENTS

We would be amiss if we failed to recognize all those who, in one fashion or another, left their mark on these pages. Both of us wish to acknowledge our colleagues in the Association for Death Education and Counseling and the International Work Group on Death, Dying, and Bereavement. Many have contributed ideas at these conferences that it is difficult to list all the names. Nonetheless, some names do stand out for special acknowledgment. Without slight to all who helped, we want to acknowledge and thank: Dana Cable, Charles Corr, Donna Corr, Richard Ellis, Neil Heflin-Wells, Gene Knott, John Morgan, Robert Neimeyer, Jane Nicols, Van Pine, Therese A. Rando, Lu Redmond, Catherine Sanders, Sherry Schachter, Judy Stillion, Ron Wilder, and J. William Worden.

Both of us want to acknowledge all those in our own colleges who offered support and encouragement. Terry wishes to thank all his colleagues at Hood College, especially the college administration who affirmed all of his professional activities in thanatology, including lending its organizational and financial support to the Hood College Summer Institute in Thanatology. He wishes to thank his psychology department colleagues for their support and encouragement including: Jeff Arbuckle, Bob Boyle, Dana Cable, Wanda Ruffin, and Linda Scott. In particular, Linda Scott was characteristically unselfish with her time and talents and provided invaluable suggestions to several sections of the book. Terry also wants to thank all of his friends at Hospice of Frederick County for their support, especially Laurel Cucchi and Cathy Walker. Finally, he wishes to thank all of his students who over the years have taught him as much as he has taught them.

Ken wishes to thank those at The College of New Rochelle from whom he has received a high level of organizational support and collegial encouragement. He wishes to give special thanks to President Stephen Sweeney, Vice-President Joan Bailey, Dean Laura Ellis, as well as Jerri Frantzve, Jim Magee, and Claire Lavin. Two student assistants—Eleanora Tornatore and Susan McVicker—were invaluable in this project and two secretaries—Vera Mezzacuella and Rosemary Strobel—were always available.

Ken also wishes to acknowledge the constant support and stimulation he receives from the Hospice Foundation of America. President Jack Gordon, vice presidents David Abrams and Lisa McGahey-Veglahn, as well as the staff provide continuing opportunities to develop and to present new ideas. Their annual teleconference, as well as their publication of books, and the newsletter *Journeys*, provide avenues for the dissemination and evaluation of innovative concepts. In addition, the publication of *She Came to Live Out Loud* by President Gordon's wife, Myra MacPherson, provided a study of a family's journey through illness and loss, which further afforded opportunities to discuss the implications and insights of grief counseling.

Both of us also wish to recognize the support we received from family and friends. Ken wants to thank: his son, Michael; Mike's fiancée, Angela; his Godson, Keith; his Mother, Josephine, and especially Kathy for all their love and companionship. In addition, Ken would like to thank his brother, Frank, his sister, Dorothy, and both of their families. They, and numerous friends, make every project a labor of love.

Terry wants to first thank his wife Nicole, who, in addition to showing the patience of Job over his long hours on the computer, served as the initial editor for all of his work. Her loving support has made this project possible. He also wishes to acknowledge the support of his family who has been faithful in its support of his efforts. Terry wishes to recognize the contributions of Zelda and Spenser—his two dogs—who were always ready with unconditional positive regard when he felt overwhelmed (especially at feeding time). Finally, this book would never have happened without Dana Cable—his friend and mentor—whose wisdom and integrity was invaluable, and whose friendship sustained him.

Finally, we want to thank the editors at Brunner/Mazel for their patience and support. The ideas of our former editor, Elaine Perrone, as well as our current editor, Bernadette Capelle, grace these pages. And we cannot help but thank our production editor, Karin McAndrews, for her help and patience. Finally, we wish to thank all those at Brunner/Mazel—known or unknown to us—who labored over this book.

FOREWORD

In the field of thanatology, we have worked long and hard to explore the experience of bereavement. Building upon ever-increasing empirical and clinical data, at the beginning of the new millenium, we now can point with pride to an impressive accumulation of knowledge about the essential generic processes and/or tasks that must be successfully undertaken to healthily accommodate a major loss. Specifically, we have become able to: identify critically significant issues present in certain types of losses; describe how particular circumstances of the death can impact the survivor; and delineate high-risk factors for predisposing to complicated mourning.

In other words, when it comes to responding to the death of a loved one, we have substantial knowledge about the stimulus (i.e., loss, death), the generic response (i.e., grief, mourning), and many of the influencing variables. What we have had relatively less information about is the major mediator between all of these, that is, the mourner himself or herself. While it would appear intuitively that personality variables are among the most important determinants of adjustment to loss, there is less research on these factors than on others. Thanks to the work of Terry Martin and Ken Doka in this book, a giant step forward has been taken in the conceptual and clinical understandings of the mourner in terms of his or her personality-related pattern of grief and how best to facilitate it.

Unfortunately, too often, in mental health today, only lipservice gets paid to the idiosyncratic meanings, experiences, and needs generated by a loss for a given individual. As a psychologist, I see this played out frequently in scenarios like the following: I am in the initial clinical supervision meeting with a new supervisee. He or she does an expert job presenting the therapeutic case at hand and outlining the treatment concerns that are operating. I will hear all of the relevant details concerning the specifics of the loss, and will be apprised of the current phenomenology of the person's bereavement experience. Then, queries are made about the intervention that is required. In turn, I ask the supervisee several questions in order to be able to address the issues raised: How does this person tend to cope in general? What type of previous loss experiences has he or she had, and in what fashion did the mourner contend with them? What is his or her personality type? What are the individual's social, cultural, ethnic, generational, and spiritual backgrounds? What has their gender socialization been like? In most instances, while the supervisee can tell me much about the loss and the reactions thereto, he or she knows relatively little about the person going through it all.

It is sad to say, but of the 37 sets of factors that influence any individual's grief and mourning—with such factors breaking down into categories that are psychological (including characteristics pertaining to the nature and meaning of the specific loss, characteristics of the mourner, and characteristics of the death), social, and physiological (Rando, 1993)—those that pertain to the individual mourner are typically the most overlooked.

In their discussion of grief patterns, particularly the intuitive and instrumental styles, Martin and Doka identify and account for the majority of mourner-specific variables. However, these authors go further than merely describing grief patterns and pinpointing the impacts of personality, gender, and culture in shaping them. They not only discuss the experience of grief that is associated with each pattern they reveal how the pattern influences the actual expression of the mourner's grief and what types of adaptive strategies tend to be utilized to cope with that grief. Thus, we come to understand not only what each pattern is like, but the underlying dynamics and forces that influence both its manifestations and the mourner's ultimate adjustment to loss.

One of the many strengths of the book is the explicit identification of the general Western bias in mental health that affective expression is necessary for healthy grief and mourning. While this supports the intuitive griever, it actually can hurt the instrumental griever. One need observe just one instance where the counselor engages in a power struggle to wrest tears from an instrumental mourner, in a mistaken belief that only through such expression will that person be able to effectively contend with their loss, to appreciate the countertherapeutic, and often iatrogenic, effects such a myth can have.

Two corollaries stem from this widespread but mistaken belief. The first, the "grief work hypothesis," asserts that it is only by experiencing strong affect and working it through that loss can be accommodated. The second is that the absence of affective expression suggests some type of pathological response. In response to these, Martin and Doka argue cogently that there many different ways to experience, express, and adapt to grief—the latter including cognitive, spiritual strategies—and that no grief pattern is inherently superior or inferior to the others. Rather, it is the person's choice and implementation of effective adaptive strategies, and how these dovetail with their own particular grief pattern that determines how well an individual adjusts to loss.

This linking of grief patterns with particular adaptive strategies brings us into the domain of coping, putting Martin and Doka squarely alongside other contemporary thanatological writers in espousing the value of viewing grief work or mourning as active attempts at coping with and adapting to the loss (see, for example, Corr & Corr, 2000; Rando, 2000). With such a perspective, there is less of a chance that the counselor, if not the mourner himself or herself, will make the all-too-common error of focusing upon the aforementioned stimulus and/or response while ignoring the central protagonist. The focus is placed where it ought to be—upon the individual, who, after appraising the situation, brings what he or she wants, needs, or can to the loss experience and to the specific circumstances created by this particular death at this specific time.

We are continually reminded that while gender influences grief patterns, it does not determine them. Hence, grief patterns may have associations with the genders (i.e., more women than men are intuitive grievers, and more men than women are instrumental grievers), but there are a number of other factors that affect the personal grief pattern adopted. The notion of a continuum of grief patterns is useful for clinicians, enabling us to recognize that actually both styles can offer therapeutic benefit and that a blending of the two may be quite useful in providing additional choices for adaptive strategies.

Certainly, Martin and Doka's Grief Pattern Inventory will be a helpful tool enabling clinicians and concerned others to identify styles of grieving so that grief-related processes of communication, interaction, and intervention are optimized or at least improved.

To me, the greatest contribution of this book lies in what it will do in terms of preventing secondary victimization of those who, already burdened by the loss of a loved one, are additionally adversely impacted by the responses of others to their instrumental or blended patterns of grief. Such persons are often misunderstood, pathologized, traumatized by being coerced to say, do, and endure things that are ego-dystonic to or inappropriate for them; and/or alienated from those from whom they ideally would like support, although often in different fashions from how it is proffered. Thus, the education and psychonormative information provided herein by Martin and Doka essentially can be viewed as a form of primary prevention for those who grieve in other-than-intuitive ways.

Through their specification of the treatment strategies and discussion of interventions that will support the strengths of each individual mourner—whether intuitive, instrumental, or blended—and supplement his or her relative weaknesses, these authors confront "conventional wisdom" and straighten it out with healthy doses of reality, both empirical and clinical. After digesting this book, *no* clinician should ever again believe that there is only one way to grieve. Or that a person's way must the traditionally feminine approach of expression of emotion. *No* man, or *no* woman, who happens to be an instrumental griever, should ever again be made to feel guilty for their particular approach to cope with their grief merely because it conflicts with certain notions about emotionally "working through" or "processing" loss.

Nitty-gritty therapeutic suggestions fill the two treatment chapters and give counselors the tools to reach the mourner with any pattern of grief. There are critically important practical and clinically-oriented discussions about assessment, rationale, interventive intentionality, use of language, engagement of instrumental grievers, pros and cons of the four possible adaptive strategies, the "blended" griever, objections to the call for androgeny, three critical rules for counselors, and the pragmatics for use of five specific vehicles for intervention.

In writing *Men Don't Cry . . . Women Do*, Terry Martin and Ken Doka have not only provided us with efficacious implements to intervene in the grief experiences of persons of varied grief patterns. They also have challenged traditionally held, yet empirically unsupported, notions that have caused varying levels of harm to a significant proportion of bereaved individuals and to their loved ones. With this information before us, no responsible clinician can conceive of himself or herself as ethical if the insights put before us in this book are not appropriately integrated into their practice.

From now on, we need to give at least as much attention to the mourner as we do to the death and to the grief and mourning it generates.

Therese A. Rando, Ph.D.
The Institute for the Study and Treatment of Loss
Warwick, Rhode Island
October 4, 1999

CHAPTER

Introduction and Plan of the Book

When Brad's infant son died, he was surprised and troubled at the extent of his wife's grief. Every night she disconsolately cried herself to sleep. He was also perplexed at his own lack of tears. "Why am I not grieving?" he constantly asked himself. Yet as he asked this question, he would be alone in his workshop sculpting a memorial stone for his child. "What is wrong with me? Why can't I feel grief?" he reflected, as he pounded his hammer on a chisel.

Friends often wondered about Alicia. When her husband John died, she used the insurance to finance her graduate education. She thinks of John frequently, taking comfort that her new job has allowed her to continue to support their family. But friends keep questioning her, wondering, as one put it, "if she is doing too well."

Bob, too, wondered about his grief. When their son, a training pilot, was lost at sea, his wife availed herself of all the counseling the airline provided. All Bob wanted to do was to take his own plane up every afternoon to search for signs of wreckage.

☐ Understanding Patterns of Grief: Beyond Gender

All of these individuals are grieving a significant loss. And all are troubled by what they believe to be inappropriate responses to loss. In fact, each has effective ways to experience and adapt to his or her losses, yet they each reflect a societal understanding that the keys to experiencing grief lie in overtly expressing emotion and consciously seeking support.

This book challenges that presumption. Its basic thesis is that there are many different ways in which individuals experience, express, and adapt to grief. Affectively-oriented strategies are one way, but other strategies, building upon activity or cognition, can be equally effective.

This book describes two patterns of grieving. One is an intuitive pattern where individuals experience and express grief in an affective way. In this pattern, grieving individuals will find adaptive strategies that are oriented toward the expression of affect. But there is another pattern as well, one that we label instrumental. Here, grief is experienced physically, such as in a restlessness or cognition. Here the adaptive strategies individuals use tend to be, as the vignettes indicate, cognitive and active as well.

This instrumental pattern is typical of the way many men grieve, due to contemporary patterns of male socialization. Yet as the book emphasizes, while there is a clear relation between gender and grieving patterns, this is not seen as deterministic. Women also may exhibit an instrumental style. And many women and men represent grievers who demonstrate more intuitive patterns. Clearly, patterns are *influenced* by gender but not *determined* by it.

☐ The Bias Toward Affective Expression

While instrumental and intuitive patterns exist, are equally effective, and have complementary sets of advantages and disadvantages, instrumental styles are often viewed negatively within counseling, self-help, and grieving literature.

This reflects a general Western bias in counseling that tends to value affective expressiveness as inherently more therapeutic than cognitive or behavioral responses. Sue and Sue (1990), in the groundbreaking work, *Counseling the Culturally Different*, criticize the counseling paradigm for overemphasizing affect:

> "Emotional expressiveness is also valued, as we like individuals to be in touch with their feelings and to be able to realize their emotional reactions." (p. 36)

This bias, Sue and Sue note, can inhibit counseling with other cultural groups that do not place significance on affective disclosure.

This bias is also evident in what has been termed the "grief work" hypothesis (see Stroebe, 1997; Wortman & Silver, 1989). This hypothesis, or operating set of assumptions within the field of grief counseling, has emphasized that unless one expresses one's feelings openly, grieving cannot be successfully accomplished. For example, Vail (1982) expressed the sentiment often found in self-help literature about grief.

Of course, those who allow themselves to experience the gamut of emotions are probably the least likely to actually go crazy. It is those of us who attempt to suppress, deny, and displace grief who eventually have real problems coping with the loss. (p. 55)

In fact, there is danger in identifying grief with any affective expression. The danger is that the absence of affect is taken to be an absence of attachment. As Weiss (1998) notes:

There may indeed be people who were attached to someone whom they lost to death, who fully acknowledge that loss, and yet do not grieve. Their absence of grief is not defensive; they simply do not grieve. I cannot, myself, understand how a relationship of attachment is consistent with an absence of separation distress or interruption of that relationship, and absence of grief or loss of the relationship, but perhaps it is. There may, perhaps, be people so fully autonomous that they can experience attachments, and on loss of those attachments, experience brief distress, after which they go on as before; or there may be some other emotional constellation that permits attachment without giving loss to grief. (1998, p. 347)

But perhaps there is an answer to Weiss' honest query, one that accepts both the attachment and acknowledges the grief. The answer here would be to look beyond affective distress to other expressions of grief.

This affective bias finds its boldest expression in literature about men and grief. It is unsurprising, given the bias toward affective expressiveness that many clinicians have seen aspects of the male role placing men at a disadvantage in grieving when compared to women. Women are seen as more ready to accept help; and express emotion, both of which are viewed as essential to the process of grieving. Since men are perceived as less likely to show emotion or accept help, they are seen as having more difficulty in responding to loss. LeGrand (1986), for example, states: "This does not mean men are not grieving; it does indicate that they may not accomplish the task as successfully as women" (p. 31).

The underlying assumption is that there are limited ways that one can effectively cope with loss. Staudacher (1991) expresses this succinctly:

Simply put, there is only one way to grieve. That way is to go through the core of grief. Only by experiencing the necessary emotional effects of your loved one's death is it possible for you to eventually resolve the loss. (p. 3)

While Chapter 7 explores the relationship of gender and grieving patterns, that assumption can be questioned. On the surface, if survivors were to grieve in identical ways, one would also expect analogous expressions of affect, duplicate behavior patterns, and feelings that would be indistinguishable from one another. In fact, there are many ways to cope with loss. To assert that only one pattern is acceptable is empirically ungrounded, at variance with current theory, and clinically unhelpful—points that will be further explored in later chapters.

Beyond Gender: A Journey From Male and Masculine Grief

When this work began, there was clearly an interest in men and grief. It quickly moved beyond that. At the first description of what was called "male grieving patterns," a female colleague remarked that it had validated her own way of grieving—her pattern of adapting to loss. In fact, she had responded to her own early perinatal losses in two distinct ways. She began to do some of the basic work and research on how to best support survivors of perinatal loss. Then, once that research base was established, she became a pioneering advocate who both challenged and changed the ways hospitals dealt with such losses. Her comments were taken seriously, changing the terminology for this book to "masculine grief." (see Martin & Doka, 1996).

There was much to recommend the use of the terms "masculine grief." First, it allowed us to build a clear bridge to Jung on ideas of *animus-anima* (1968). Like Jung, we saw masculinity-femininity as a continuum that exists within a person as well as between individuals. Even our concept of grieving patterns is that they fall along a continuum. The use of these terms draws from that theoretical base.

Second, we believe that this pattern of adapting to loss is related to gender, at least in North America and many Western cultures, even if it is not determined by it. The use of the term "masculine" then reaffirms that gender relationship. It seemed foolish to pretend that gender does not play a role, since it influences so many other aspects of life.

Third, we wished to directly challenge the notion, so prevalent in the popular literature, that many men are ineffectual grievers. We asserted that "masculine" patterns of coping with grief are different but not less effective than more "conventional" or "feminine" ways of dealing with loss. Thus, there is a practical rationale for the use of the term. Since most popular literature does offer a view of the male as an ineffectual griever, we believed that only by using a gender-related term might our work be available to clinicians interested in or dealing with male or masculine grievers.

Finally, the use of masculine and feminine has great heuristic value that will, we hope, encourage continued discussion and further research.

However, we ultimately decided to eschew gender-related terms for a variety of reasons. First, they caused confusion. While we identified a pattern of grief that we believe many males use, we also sought to recognize and to validate female grievers who exhibit such a pattern. But for many the term "masculine" grief had unfortunate baggage. This was most poignantly illustrated by a conversation with such a griever after a presentation. This woman was a pioneering female rabbi, one of the first to be recognized. "All my life," she said, " I have tried to be perceived as not just one of the guys. You described my grieving pattern. Please, use a language to describe it that does not make me 'one of the guys' again."

It was confusing for other reasons as well. The distinction between "masculine" and "male" was often lost on readers who kept identifying one with another. And it made us apologize about using male examples, diverting us from a critical aspect of our work that instrumental styles are, in fact, utilized by a majority of male grievers.

Moreover, the use of gender-related terms created discomfort. To assert that "masculine" modes of coping with loss are cognitive and active seems to perpetuate stereotypes, only partly true, that view such responses as typical of male response to loss, and it implies that "feminine" responses to loss are more emotive.

In addition, the use of gender-related terms creates its own difficulties. If one end of the continuum is labeled "masculine," what is the other end, the alternate pattern, called? The use of the term "feminine" has merit since it seems like the logical complement and is faithful to the theoretical base. On the other hand, the term "conventional" has merit since it reflects current conventions on grief that have tended to view seeking support and emotional responses as both desirable and normative. In addition, it avoids further stereotyping of emotional responses as feminine. But the use of the term "conventional" also runs the risk of appearing to place negative value on the term "feminine." In short, either term has merit and complementary disadvantages.

And that raised clinical concerns. Some men who do seek support and are comfortable with emotive responses may feel threatened to hear their mode of response described as "feminine." And women who tend toward solitary, active, and cognitive responses may resent the label of "masculine."

In the end, use of the terms "instrumental" and "intuitive" seemed to carry far less baggage. While these patterns will be more fully developed in subsequent chapters, it may be helpful to offer a brief description now.

First, the very experience of grief is different. For reasons that will be described later, instrumental grievers tend to have tempered affect to a loss. While intuitive grievers are more likely to experience their grief as waves of affect, instrumental grievers are more likely to describe it in physical or cognitive terms. While intuitive grievers often need to express their feelings and seek the support of others, instrumental grievers are more likely to cognitively process or immerse themselves in activity.

Sam and Jenny shared their disappointment with each other several months after the sudden death of their seventeen-year-old son. Responding to Jenny's accusations that he failed to validate their grief, Sam stated, " I couldn't allow myself to miss (him) until I figured out what this meant to our family."

This suggests that at least some instrumental grievers attempt to evaluate their experiences cognitively rather than experience them emotionally.

When instrumental grievers do respond behaviorally to a loss, it usually involves immersion in some form of activity. Sometimes this is work, but at other times it may be intimately related to the loss. They may wish to take legal or physical action in response to the loss. For example, one male client whose young daughter died of cancer found it helpful to develop a scholarship fund in her name. Others may take active roles in the funeral. Ryan (1989), while noting concern at his wife's affective response to loss, expressed his own grief by carving his son's memorial stone. Instrumental grievers may also focus on the problems caused by the loss, actively trying to find appropriate solutions or engaging in activities related to the loss.

> When Jack's twenty-year-old daughter was killed after losing control of the car, he spent several weeks rebuilding a neighbor's fence damaged in the accident. He later described this activity as crucial to "getting me through those first two months."

In short, then, this section draws attention to the fact that grievers may experience, express, and adapt to grief differently. Cognition and activity remain two key adaptive strategies often utilized by instrumental grievers. And these strategies, like any set of adaptive strategies, may be both effective or ineffective, depending upon the particular strategy and circumstances. Subsequent chapters will explore this further.

☐ Plan of the Book

This book is organized into three major sections. The first defines terms, provides an overview of our thesis, rooting it in contemporary theories of grief, and delineates grieving patterns. The second section speculates on factors that may influence individuals' patterns of coping with loss. A final section considers implications, including a self-help section and noting therapeutic interventions likely to be effective with different types of grievers.

As stated earlier, this book arises amidst a growing challenge as to what is termed the "grief work" hypothesis (see Stroebe, 1997; Bonanno, 1997; Wortman & Silver, 1989) or the belief that, unless one expresses affect, grief is not likely to be successfully resolved. And it builds upon the work of those who have begun to describe a "male" style of relating to loss (e.g., Moss, Resch, & Moss, 1997; Moss, Rubinstein, & Moss, 1997; Golden, 1994a, 1994b, 1994c, 1996). In Golden's early work (1994a, 1994b, 1994c) he emphasized physical as well as cultural difficulties to account for gender differences in grief. In his later work, he de-emphasizes gender differences by (1996) placing more emphasis on masculine modes of healing that can be utilized by either gender (1997). This book also builds on our own earlier work on masculine grief (Doka & Martin, 1998; Doka, 1994; Martin & Doka, 1996, 1998).

Throughout this book runs a common thread—that there are many different styles of coping with loss. Each has distinct strengths and limitations. There are advantages in expressing affect and seeking support. But there are also complementary strengths in stoically continuing in the face of loss and in seeking amelioration of pain in cognitive and active approaches. In short, persons who draw from a broad range of adaptive strategies are, in fact, likely to do better. Persons with the widest range of responses, who effectively integrate all aspects of self, seem best able to respond to crisis. One can learn from both types of responses because, after all, different modes of adaptation are just that—differences, not deficiencies.

I

DEFINITION AND OVERVIEW

If you have ever wondered why you grieve differently from others you know, or why someone you love is not reacting to the same loss in the same way as you, you are not alone. Perhaps you are curious about why the majority of your clients show deep feelings about their losses, yet others seem scarcely affected. Or, maybe you are concerned about those hospice bereavement cases that don't respond to any of your offers of support, even though, given the nature of the death, your team may have "coded" them as being "at risk." This book addresses these and other issues concerning grief and loss. But first, we establish the foundation for our efforts and define terms.

Chapter 1 introduces the thesis for the rest of the book—that individuals grieve differently and that two basic patterns can be drawn from the literature and from case reports. Furthermore, neither of these two patterns is necessarily desirable over or superior to the other. The book traces the history and development of the thesis and briefly describe the instrumental and intuitive patterns of grief. The chapter concludes with an out-line of the book.

Chapter 2 revisits the many definitions and various aspects of grief, grieving, mourning, loss, and bereavement. After a review of existing models, a new way of understanding grief is introduced which is based on the creation and distribution of energy. The chapter goes on to explain how and why this energy manifests differently from person to person.

Chapter 3 reintroduces the instrumental and intuitive patterns of grief and differentiates between the two patterns by the experience of grief, the expression of grief, and primary and secondary adaptive strategies. The chapter concludes with a brief discussion of a blended pattern of grief that combines, to a greater or lesser degree, elements of both the instrumental and intuitive patterns.

The final chapter in the section, chapter 4, explores disordered variants of the patterns. It begins by differentiating maladaptive or "dissonant" patterns from initial responses to a loss and introduces several types of dissonant patterns. The section ends by considering the relationship of dissonant patterns to complicated mourning.

Is the "zeitgeist" or spirit of the times right for such an understanding of grief, as well as for the general premise of the patterns of grief? For example, it is quite possible that the enthusiastic responses to concepts such as "death as taboo" or "disenfranchised grief" would have been substantially muted during less favorable historical times. Likewise, there have been periods where a more rigid concept of grief may have prevailed. Many may find our ideas questionable, yet there is a tremendous heuristic value in proffering these novel and (some would say) risky hypotheses. You, the reader, must be the judge.

Definitions

*"Everyone seems to think I should be crying since my daughter Laura died. She had a heart attack working in her garden. **But I never cried**—not for Laura, or for my mom, or my dad when they died. The day after Laura's funeral, I finished up her work in the garden. I still sometimes drive over and work there. Everyone said it isn't important anymore. I think it is."* Tom, 62 years old.

The question that brought Tom into counseling was why he wasn't grieving. Yet, as Tom talked about the varied strategies he used after his daughter's death—working in the garden, helping Laura's husband raise their three children, sharing stories of their mom with her kids—it was clear that Tom, in fact, *was* grieving. And his ways of dealing with his daughter's loss did seem to ameliorate his pain.

Tom's question really focused on his definition of grief. He, like many, defined grief as an affective reaction to loss. In the absence of overt affect, Tom simply could not see that he was grieving in his own characteristic way.

Tom's limited definition of grief reflects a bias evident not only in the field but in the counseling profession at large—a bias that places great value on affective expressiveness (Sue & Sue, 1990). Yet the literature on grief has always emphasized that grief reactions may be manifested in a wide range of strategies.

This chapter begins by exploring grief and grieving. It then further develops the thesis that there are a variety of ways in which people adapt to grief. Each of these strategies offers distinct strengths as well as limitations as individuals cope with loss.

☐ Basic Definitions: Loss, Grief, Grieving, and Mourning

Loss

Traditionally, loss and grief are associated with death. In fact, loss is a much broader concept. At its broadest, loss refers to being deprived of or ceasing to have something that one formerly possessed or to which one was attached.

There are different types of losses. For example, "physical loss" refers to the loss of something tangible that is no longer present. Death involves a physical loss, as would a robbery or the destruction of an object. "Relational loss" refers to losing a relationship with someone to whom one has an attachment. Again, death causes the loss of a relationship, as does divorce, interpersonal breakups, or other losses such as the loss of a job or moving, where ties between individuals are consequently severed. "Symbolic loss" is intangible, involving the loss of a psychological or spiritual attachment such as the loss of one's dreams, hopes, or faith. The death of someone can also create significant symbolic loss (see Rando, 1993).

Such distinctions also help in understanding the phenomenon of "anticipatory grief." As Rando (1986) notes, anticipatory grief, which refers to the grief experienced by the patient, family, and others in a life-threatening illness, does not only entail grieving the expectation of a possible or eventual death. It includes, as well, grief over all the losses—physical, relational, or symbolic—experienced throughout the course of illness.

This discussion is also a reminder of the importance of understanding "secondary loss," or the losses that follow as a consequence of a primary loss. For example, the loss of a job may also entail a series of resultant losses—the loss of self-esteem, income, friends, or dreams. Similarly, the death of a person may engender a wide range of losses in its wake, such as the loss of other, dependent relationships (e.g., in-laws, friends), losses of income, hopes, even perhaps of faith. Rando (1993) notes the importance of such secondary losses, reminding counselors that each of these losses will need to be identified and mourned.

In addition, Rando (1993) states that loss is a constant throughout human life for every change involves at least an element of loss. For example, for each transition through the lifecycle, whether a pleasant milestone (e.g., a wedding, graduation), a loss of abilities (such as in the aging process) or relationship (including changes in relationships that occur in development—for example, the change in relationship that parents might experience as a child becomes an adolescent, etc.), brings with it the experience of losses. These losses will vary in intensity and scope as well as in the social support they engender. For example, one can expect severe reactions to the death of someone significant. However, while one may expect *some* reaction to another loss, perhaps not deemed significant, one expects that reaction to be brief and controlled. For example, it is normal to understand someone's momentary upset when his or her favorite team loses, but we also assume that such a response will be limited in scope and intensity.

This raises a critical point: social support also varies for given losses. While the loss of a family member such as a parent, child, or spouse is acknowledged by many to be significant, the loss of other persons—friends or lovers—may not be perceived by others as a significant loss. Similarly, while most physical losses are acknowledged, relational or symbolic losses may have less recognition and support. In such cases, the loss and result-ant grief, may be "disenfranchised." Disenfranchised grief refers to a situation where a loss is not openly acknowledged, socially sanctioned, or publicly shared (Doka, 1989, 1989a). In that work, Doka (1989, 1989a) emphasized types of losses (e.g., divorce, prenatal deaths, pet loss, etc.), relationships (e.g., lovers, friends, ex-spouses, etc.), grievers (e.g., the very old, very young, persons with developmental disabilities, etc.) or circum-stances of death (e.g., AIDS, suicide, etc.) that might disenfranchise grief. In summary then, loss encompasses far more than death. It is interesting to remember that Freud (1957), in his seminal essay "Mourning and Melancholia," used as his illustrative example of loss a bride abandoned at the altar. Identifying loss and thereby grief solely with death-related loss then, can obscure the many losses we do experience and grieve. And it can limit the ability of grievers or counselors to draw insights from experiences of earlier adaptations to loss.

These earlier experiences can be powerful indicators of an individual's pattern of grief. Ways of adapting to previous losses, such as a relational break-up, are evidence of an individual's basic pattern.

> From an early age, John, in a wide variety of losses, showed a more instrumental approach. As a teenager experiencing a romantic breakup, he reacted by intensify-ing his involvement in sports and other activities. This pattern persisted. When his mother died he found solace in planning the funeral and in thoughtfully clearing away her clothing and possessions. Even in his own premature death from cancer in his thirties, he rarely ventilated about his own inner feelings. Instead he concen-trated on making arrangements for the care of his young son.

For that reason, case illustrations used are of individuals experiencing a range of losses. However, most of these illustrations are death-related losses. There are three reasons for this: fiirst, it reflects the base of our experiences; second, most death-related losses involve physical as well as relational and symbolic losses (secondary losses also tend to be most in-tense in a death-related loss); finally, death is a universal experience, while other losses, such as divorce, are not.

Bereavement

Another term used to denote a state of loss is the term "bereavement." As Rando (1993) states, bereavement shares a root with the word "rob." Both refer to a state in which something has been violently taken away. Within the field of thanatology, bereavement tends to be used to refer to the basic fact or objective reality of loss, while grief refers to the person's response and reactions to the loss (see Doka, 1989). Remember, one can experience bereavement without an intense grief reaction. For example, a survivor may have little attachment or connection to the deceased, as in the following case.

> Mark was a fifteen-year-old boy who had lived with his mother, Sue and stepfather, Tom. His own biological father had separated from his mother two weeks prior to his birth. For much of his life, and all that he could remember, he lived with his stepfather, with whom he enjoyed a close relationship. His biological father, Jack, played a very limited role in his life, intermittently sending cards and gifts and visiting on rare occasions. When Jack died after a sudden heart attack, Sue called her son in to tell him his father had died. His eyes welled with tears. "Tom's dead?" he said. When his mother told him it was his "real" father, Jack, he was visually relieved. "Wow," he stated, "for a minute, I thought you meant Tom." His mother reported that he took little interest in details or in sending the flowers that bore his name. "It was much more important to me," she said. But she continued to worry that "one day the loss would hit." Almost 20 years later, she asked him as he openly wept at Tom's funeral, if he thought much about his biological dad. He seemed surprised. "He never meant much to me."

Not every such case might yield that reaction. In some cases, it is the very absence of the relationship, or the fact that any future relationship is precluded, that engenders grief. But this case does illustrate the conceptual distinction between "grief" and "bereavement" and reinforces the fact that the meaning of loss both differs among people and is a central component in understanding the grief reaction.

Grief and Grieving

Grief or grieving[1] arises as a reaction to loss. Specifically, grief can be defined as the psychic energy that results from tension created by an individual's strong desire to

---

[1] While the term "grieving" has had wide, varied, and inconsistent usage in the literature (see, for example, Corr, Nabe, & Corr, 1997; or Rando, 1993 for discussion), "grieving," in particular, has been defined, at times, as the process of adapting to loss. In this book, grief and grieving are used synonymously, referring to internal experiences and external behavior that results as a response to loss. Thus, to say an individual "experienced grief," "was

(a) maintain his or her assumptive world as it was before the loss,

(b) accommodate themselves to a newly emerging reality resulting from his or her loss,

(c) incorporate this new reality into an emerging assumptive world.

For example, a person whose spouse dies wishes to hold onto that relationship, yet knows it is not possible and is unclear on what the future may be. It is that conflict between the world that was, what it cannot be, and how it may become that creates the tensions that engender grief. This grief energy is converted into the various domains of human experience, including the physical, affective, cognitive, and spiritual. These internal experiences are often expressed outwardly in varied grief-related behaviors.

Such a definition of grief, while building upon classical perspectives (Freud, 1957; Bowlby, 1980), offers certain advantages. First, classic definitions focused on withdrawing the attachment from the deceased or lost object and reinvesting elsewhere. Current treatments of grief emphasize that many individuals maintain a connection with the lost object; however, the nature of this connection is now changed (e.g., Worden, 1991; Klass, Silverman, & Nickman, 1996). The clearest example may be found in divorce. Individuals will grieve a divorce, yet the divorce does not so much end a relationship as change it. Even in death, bereaved survivors may still find a sense of connection in such things as memories, legacies, and their spiritual beliefs.

Moreover, it was the possibility of bridging some of the differences between psychological and sociological perspectives of grief. Psychological theories of grief (see Bowlby, 1980) have stressed that the biological/psychological roots of grief lie in attachment. In this regard, mourning and grief, it is noted, seem to be exhibited by primates and other social animals. Sociological explanations tend to eschew language such as "drives" or "instincts," while emphasizing the symbolic constructions or meanings that are disrupted by the loss (see Neimeyer, 1997; Nadeau, 1998). This definition acknowledges that there is a primal aspect to grief, but notes that the nature of that primal tension is very much affected by the meaning of the loss.

Second, this definition of grief uses the term "psychic energy" to connote a dynamic force created by the emotional arousal and tension resulting from the loss. This energy needs to be expended; however, the manifestation of this energy varies in different individuals. And indeed, the theory and research on grief have stressed that grief can be exhibited

---

grieving," or "grieved" all express the similar idea that in some way that individual was reacting to or presumed to be reacting to the loss. As stated in the next section, "grief work" is used to refer to the process of adapting to loss.

physically, affectively, cognitively, and spiritually, as well as expressed in a wide range of behaviors (see Lindemann, 1944; Doka, 1989, 1989a; Rando, 1984, Worden, 1991).

Third, such a definition of grief is congruent with current theories on cognitive appraisal, stress, emotion, and emotion regulation (these will be explored further in Chapter 5). In addition, "emotion" is a word with different meanings. On one hand—particularly in the field of thanatology—emotion generally has been identified with affect or feeling (Elias, 1991). However, that is a narrow definition. A wider use of the term "emotion," evident in psychological literature, defines emotion as: biologically based adaptive reactions that involve changes in physical, affective, cognitive, spiritual, and behavioral systems in response to perceived environmental events of significance to the individuals.

Grief, then, can be perceived in this broader sense as an emotion, an attempt to make internal and external adjustments to the undesired change in one's world brought upon by the loss. Grief triggers changes in various adaptational systems—affective, physical, spiritual, and cognitive—that constitute the individual's response tendency.

Response tendencies are predispositions that operate subconsciously, allowing quick and efficient reaction to environmental challenges, threats, and opportunities. These predispositions are shaped by powerful forces, namely, cultural influences and personality styles. Individual response tendencies veer toward either an affective or intuitive grief response or a cognitive, behavioral, or instrumental response. Whether one's grief is intuitive or instrumental depends on whether the individual is more sensitive or "tuned in" to their thoughts (cognitions) or their feelings. As noted above, instrumental grief is largely a function of the individual's emphasis on cognitions.

These response tendencies have been noted throughout the literature of grief that documents a wide range of physical, affective, cognitive, spiritual reactions that manifest themselves in varied behaviors. This literature (see Lindemann, 1944; Rando, 1984; Rapheal, 1983; Worden, 1991) has documented and described reactions such as the following:

Physical Reactions

Physical reactions can include a wide range of somatic complaints and distress including:

- headaches
- muscular aches
- nausea
- tiredness and exhaustion
- menstrual irregularities

- loss of appetite
- pains
- insomnia
- tenseness
- sensitivity to noise.

Here the energy generated by the grief may be converted to physical symptomology as in the following case.

> Bob was overwhelmed when his wife died leaving him to balance his job with the demands of raising four young children. While he claimed he responded to the loss reasonably well, he complained of incessant neck and back pain. His physician could not find any evidence of physical injury, but the doctor reminded Bob of the language he had been using in describing life after Jen's death. "Everything now is on my back," he often would state.

Many individuals will experience a host of grief reactions that will include physical ones, but some, like Bob, may experience grief *primarily* as a physical reaction.

Moreover, physical complaints may allow an individual to elicit care in ways that do not seem threatening to autonomy. Interventions that use physical behavior as a way to expend energy resulting from grief are also helpful (or commonly used) in assisting individuals to deal with other forms of stress, where exercise often is prescribed to medicate stress levels. This can be seen in the following case:

> Susan, a middle school counselor, was attempting to assist students after the death of a classmate, an adolescent girl with whom most of them had had an ambivalent relationship. She was seen as sexually and behaviorally precocious. In fact, she had died in a car crash with a college student who had been under the influence of alcohol. While many girls sought out Susan the day following the death, few boys did. Susan questioned a consultant who suggested that the boys have some extra gym time and play dodge ball. She later reported that it was an intensely competitive game with many references to the driver and the crash. At the end of the game, she noted, the boys seemed much less tense.

Affective Reactions

The energy of grief is commonly manifested in affect. Individuals can experience a wide range of affective responses, including (but not limited to) the following:

- sadness
- anger
- guilt
- jealousy
- anxiety and fear

- shame
- feelings of powerlessness or hopelessness
- relief
- feelings of emancipation.

These emotional responses bear further comment as bereaved individuals may be upset at the wide range of feelings they experience in response to a loss. In fact, virtually any feeling can manifest itself following a loss. And it is not unusual that bereaved persons experience a host of affective responses, even contradictory ones, simultaneously. While a wide range of affective responses may follow a loss, it is critical to reiterate a central point. Affective responses are but one way grief may be manifested.

Cognitive Reactions

Cognitive reactions can include:

- obsessive thinking
- inability to concentrate
- fantasizing
- apathy
- dreams
- disorientation and confusion
- continued thought about the loss, rehearsing and reviewing the circumstances of the loss
- in cases of death, persons may experience a sense of the deceased's presence
- attempts to rationalize or cognitively understand the loss.

Given the effect of loss upon cognitive processes, it is not unusual that work at home, school, or in the office can be adversely affected. It is also critical to remember that cognitive responses are not necessarily attempts to deny or suppress affect. They are simply another way that grief is manifested.

Spiritual Reactions

Grief affects us spiritually as well. These reactions can include:

- searching for meaning in loss
- changes in spiritual behaviors, feelings, or beliefs.

Spirituality, broadly defined, is used here to connote the ways that people seek to understand the meaning and purpose of life. These transcendental systems of belief may center on religious tenets or other philosophical frameworks. While some losses may fit easily into one's underlying beliefs, other losses may proudly challenge those beliefs. Such was the following case:

> When Rita's mother died, she grieved the loss deeply. But her mother's long and happy life, as well as peaceful death at 91 years of age, reaffirmed her beliefs about the way that life should be. She found great comfort in her religious beliefs and rituals. Yet, when her younger brother was brutally tortured and murdered, she had a faith crisis. She could not understand why God would take her brother so young, leaving a wife and children in dire straits. Nor could she find explanation in her faith for the terror and pain he must have experienced.

In such cases, the reconstruction of meaning in the face of loss may become one of the most critical aspects of the grieving experience (Doka & Morgan, 1993; Neimeyer, 1997). For here, grieving individuals must, in the face of loss, reconstruct such issues as their own identity and the identity of the deceased, as well as their assumptions about the world. Loss, then, can create an intense spiritual crisis that challenges all of an individual's core beliefs, necessitating reevaluation, if not a reformation.

Behavioral Experiences

The different reactions that persons experience in each of these four response tendencies may be outwardly expressed as behaviors. Among observable behaviors of grief are:

- crying
- illness-related behaviors (observable symptoms, expressions of illness, etc.)
- outward expression of emotion (e.g., anger, euphoria, etc.)
- observable changes in religious/spiritual behaviors and expressions
- searching behaviors
- avoiding or seeking reminders of the loss
- obsessive activity
- activities that provide some sense or continued connection to the loss (e.g., visiting the cemetery, etc.)
- physical activities (e.g., exercise, sports, gardening, etc.)
- social withdrawal
- absentmindedness
- accidents
- changes from preloss behaviors
- social withdrawal
- increases in the use of alcohol, smoking, and other chemical use.

While behaviors are external expressions of internal reactions, care should be taken when inferring from the external to the internal. Behaviors such as crying or withdrawal, to name two, could be outward expressions of a variety of internal states such as anger, sadness, or embarrassment. The connection between the two is a clinical question.

This also reinforces that many different behaviors, such as physical activities or activities that provide a connection to the deceased may, in fact, be manifestations of grief even if that connection does not seem obvious.

> *When her younger sister died, Marla, a high school student, continued to coach her sister's soccer team. Her parents wondered how she could do that and were concerned that she was denying her grief. In fact, continuing to coach made her feel close to her sister and provided opportunities to reminisce with her sister's teammates and their parents.*

Over time many of these behaviors may diminish among bereaved individuals. As with other responses, there can be negative and positive aspects of different behaviors. For example, withdrawal can both isolate one from sources of support or give people space to effectively grieve. Crying may elicit help and restore emotional homeostasis, perhaps even correcting stress-related chemical imbalances (Worden, 1991). But crying can also generate feelings of guilt and shame and exacerbate withdrawal.

In summation, grief involves multifaceted responses to loss. The energy of grief, generated by the tension between wishes to retain the past and the reality of the present, is felt at many levels—physical, emotional, cognitive, spiritual, and expressed in a wide range of observable behaviors. In many cases these responses will be varied or blended—even in individuals who tend to have different styles of grief. This is particularly true early in the loss when the amount of energy generated tends to be high. Thus, it is not that the instrumental griever has no affect or exhibits no affectively oriented behavior; rather, it is that his or her response tendencies tend to emphasize cognition.

The Individual Experience of Grief

Not only does the *way* individuals express grief differ, the very *experience* of grief is different as well.

Many factors have been identified in the literature that frame these individual reactions. For example, Worden (1991), Rando (1984), and Sanders (1993) have noted such variables as:

- type of loss
- relationship and attachment to the lost object (e.g., in cases of death, the relationship to the deceased, issues of ambivalence, dependency, etc.)
- circumstances surrounding the loss (e.g., was it sudden or long term, preventability, timing, presence or absence of additional stressors, etc.)
- extent of and responses to prior losses

- personality of the bereaved and effectiveness in coping with loss
- social variables (e.g., age and gender, cultural beliefs and practices, social class, presence and strength of spiritual systems, external and internal support systems, etc.)
- personal variables (e.g., health, lifestyle management, etc.)

Recent research has been inconsistent in assessing the actual degree to which these factors do affect bereavement outcomes. Lund, Caserta, and Dimond (1993) found religion, gender, health status, and marital happiness relatively important predictors of adjustment in a sample of older widows and widowers. Social support was a moderate predictor. As Lund, Caserta, and Dimond (1993) note, social networks often have both positive and negative aspects (e.g., offering encouragement, placing unrealistic expectations, etc.). The most predictive factors were positive self-esteem and personal competencies in managing the tasks of daily living.

In a study of younger German widows and widowers, Stroebe and Stroebe (1993) indicated that in sudden loss a sustained belief in one's internal control seemed to buffer the stress of loss. They reasoned that persons who experience an unexpected catastrophic loss need a strong belief that they can still retain control of their life to recover from depression. On the other hand, persons with little belief in internal control may find that the loss reinforces a sense that they have little control over life, exacerbating feelings of depression and hopelessness. Other risk factors did not seem as important in Stroebe and Stroebe's (1993) study, though it is critical to remember Sanders' (1993) caution, in her review of research on factors affecting adjustment, that it is difficult to analyze the individual effects of interacting factors.

These factors emphasize that the "very meaning of loss" varies both in different circumstances and among individuals. All of these variables emphasize that a given loss means different things to different people. For example, the meaning of the loss of a child or a spouse will be very different depending on the role attributed to that person by the survivor. If one primarily lives life in the private sphere of home and family, the meaning or role of "spouse" or "parent" is likely to be more central than one who has significant roles in the public sphere of work and the larger community. This may be one reason why Schwab (1996) found that mothers and fathers not only varied in the intensity of grief but in their perception of the events. The critical point is that grief is a very individual experience. This will be further discussed in Chapter 5 in the exploration of the appraisal process.

Beyond the psychological and social variables, other factors too can frame the meaning of a loss. Certainly, for example, loss may be perceived differently in other cultures, historical periods, or social and economic circumstances. Take, for example, the interview of a ninety-year-old woman a number of years ago. She had been born prior to the turn of the 20th century in Spain. Reflecting on the death of a four-year-old son in a typhus epidemic, she remarked: "I was very lucky. I had six children, five survived to be adults." Few modern Western parents would have such an interpretation of a similar death. Yet her meaning reflects a time when there was an expectation that not all of one's children would survive to adulthood. Kastenbaum (1971) suggests that in cultures with high childhood and infant mortality, social norms and structures actually serve to limit such attachments.

Thus, to summarize, one both experiences and expresses grief differently. It is that simple statement that underlies much of this book.

Mourning and Grief Work

While grief is defined as the psychic energy generated by the loss, grief work may be defined as a process, both short- and long-term, of adapting to the loss.[2] It includes the shorter term process of "acute grief" where the griever deals with the immediate aftermath of the loss. Building on Rando (1993), immediate reactions in this period may include such things as:

(1) feelings about the loss (e.g., guilt, anger, sorrow, etc.);
(2) reactions to the effects of the loss (e.g., shock, physical symptoms, cognitive confusion and disorganization, spiritual intensity or alienation, etc.);
(3) behaviors resultant from or adaptive to the loss (e.g., acting out, crying, withdrawal).

All of these grieving reactions represent initial, albeit fragmentary, attempts to adapt to the immediate aftermath of loss.

In short, this acute period is characterized by both shock and numbing, and after they recede, by a series of intense reactions and adaptations to the newly experienced loss. Because of the intensity of this period, it should be noted that reactions and adaptations observed may not be typical of those observed later. For here, in this early period, the energy released may overwhelm the person's typical adaptive strategies leading to uncharacteristic responses. The following case illustrates this:

---

[2] In short, adaptation involves the process of continually adjusting to circumstances that have changed or are changing. Adaptation is an ongoing process. People continually have to adapt daily to minor, sometimes major environmental challenges. Significant loss creates major changes—both long- and short-term—to the environment, challenging one to employ all resources—both internal and external—as one tries to adapt to those changes in the world. Grief work is simply a specific instance of an ongoing and multifaceted process.

When Dan's dog, a companion for a decade, had to be euthanized, Dan held him and stroked him as he died. When he went to his car, he uncharacteristically cried for about 10 minutes. After that, his reactions took on more typical forms. He buried the dog, etched a memorial, stored or disposed of the dog's artifacts, and went through a variety of photographs of the animal. After that, he often thought of the dog, but he never again cried.

The role of initial responses and its relationship to patterns of grief is explored further in Chapter 4.

But beyond this period of adaptation to acute grief, which itself can last for many months or longer, there is a longer term process that involves living the rest of one's life in light of that loss. This process is often referred to as "mourning." The term "mourning" has had mixed usage within thanatology. It has been used to refer to the social customs and/or outward behaviors that manifest grief. Doka (1989b), for example, in the *Encyclopedia of Death* defined mourning as "the culturally patterned expressions or rituals that accompany loss and allow others to recognize that one has become bereaved" (p. 126). For example, attending funerals or wearing black clothes or armbands may be seen as mourning behaviors. In some ways, that is a useful distinction since it reminds us that one may grieve and not mourn or mourn without grief. Illustrations of the former include many cases of disenfranchised grief (e.g., divorce) that are devoid of rituals or other outward manifestations of loss. On the other side, many attend funerals in support of others but experience little direct grief over that particular loss. Nonetheless, by attending they are "mourning."

However useful that definition of mourning has been, Rando's (1993) work on mourning has been increasingly accepted within the field. Rando has built upon Freud's (1957) definition of "mourning" as a psychological process that occurs as individuals experiencing loss reorient their relationship to the deceased, their own sense of self, and their external world. As Rando's (1993) work describes it, this involves three distinct operations. The first involves reorienting one's relationship to the deceased and stimulates the period of acute grief as one acknowledges that current ties can no longer be maintained. A second operation involves redefining oneself and one's own identity after the loss. A third operation involves any modifications that occur as survivors seek to redefine their world and adjust to the many changes necessitated by the loss. In this definition, mourning is a long-term process that involves living the rest of one's life in the face of the loss. Persons who are unable to effectively mourn their loss may experience deterioration in physical or mental well-being or even death (Sanders, Parkes, & Weiss, 1983; Rando, 1993).

Building on this work, Rando (1993) then offers a model of mourning that identifies three different phases of grieving with six "R" mourning processes.

Avoidance Phase
1. Recognizing the loss (e.g., acknowledging and understanding the death);

Confrontation Phase
2. Reacting to the separation, (which includes experiencing the pain, expressing the psychological reactions to the loss, and identifying and mourning secondary losses);
3. Recollecting and re-experiencing the deceased and the relationship, (which includes cognitive and affective dimensions);
4. Relinquishing the old attachments to the deceased and the old assumptive world;

Accommodation Phase
5. Readjusting to move adaptively into the new world without forgetting the old;
6. Reinvesting in new relationships.

Another model is the "dual process" model offered by Stroebe and Schut (1995), who posit two sets of interrelated and dynamic processes that individuals utilize in adapting to loss. One set of processes is loss-oriented, where individuals cope with things as the new reality of loss of separation. Restoration-oriented processes refer to the processes that individuals employ as they readjust to the new demands of life now in the face of this loss. This is a critical point. "Restoration" does not mean a return to the old reality, for that no longer exists. Rather it emphasizes that individuals are challenged to develop new patterns of behavior and assumptions as they respond to loss. To Stroebe and Schut, individuals vacillate between these two complementary demands of grieving, "oscillating" as they cope with each in turn.

Worden (1991) offers another popular model of the grief work process. Instead of processes, Worden refers to four tasks that one has to accomplish as one does grief work. These tasks are:

1. to accept the reality of the loss,
2. to work through the pain of grief,
3. to adjust to an environment in which the deceased is missing,
4. to emotionally relocate the deceased and move on with life.

Since these tasks represent cognitive, affective, and behavioral adjustments to the loss, Doka (1993) has suggested the addition of a spiritual task:

5. to reconstruct faith or philosophical systems challenged by loss.

While acknowledging the different definitions of "mourning," "grief work," and even "grieving" that exist within the field, the preferred term in this text is "grief" or "grieving."

In summary, the process of grieving can be compared to a roller coaster, where bereaved individuals find themselves on an up-and-down cycle, sometimes overwhelmed by the stress of the loss. The energy generated by that tension may wax and wane as they continue to redefine life in the presence of the loss. The low points are often punctuated by varied crises that accentuate the loss. In cases of death, these can include such events as anniversaries, birthdays, holidays, or varied "settlement reactions," such as when the insurance check is received. This cycle tends to be more intense in the first two years; after that, generally the low points become less intense, are experienced less often, and do not last as long. Over time most bereaved persons experience an amelioration of their grief. This means:

1. Generally, the energy generated by tension created by the loss has abated. There tend to be few manifestations of ongoing grief. Much of grieving is now complete.
2. Persons begin to function at the level similar to, in some cases even better than, that experienced prior to the loss.
3. However, there still may be periods where they do experience smaller crises, long after the loss, that create renewed tension. For example, Doris feels a tinge of grief every time she sees her great grandson. He, like her late husband who died over 30 years ago, is the only redhead in the family.

The end result of the process does not involve a relinquishing of all ties with the loss. Instead, persons continue to retain bonds with the lost person, albeit in a different way (see, for example, Klass et al., 1996). The following case illustrates this.

> Rose and Joe were an older Italian-American couple living in New York City. Rose's great joy was her tomato garden grown with much effort in a small backyard plot. Joe would affectionately complain about the trouble and cost of the tomatoes. Rose would joke that if she died first, he could turn it into a carport.
>
> He would rejoin that the cement trucks would soon follow the hearse. Rose did die first and Joe lovingly tends "Rose's Garden."

Adaptation

Grief work is then a process of adaptation. Adaptation can be defined as how individuals adjust internally and/or externally to their loss. It involves the short-term process of adapting to the demands of grief as it is experienced and processed. However, it also includes the long-term process or ongoing work of redistributing the energy created by the loss. It requires persons to reformulate their definitions of who they are and what they lost, and redefine and reformulate their assumptive world. While the term "grieving" has had wide, varied, and inconsistent usage in the literature (see, for example, Corr et al., 1997 or Rando, 1993 for discussion), "grieving," in particular, has been defined, at times, as the process of adapting to loss. In this book, grief and grieving are used synonymously, referring to internal experiences and external behavior that result as a response to loss.

Throughout this process, individuals may use a variety of adaptive strategies as they attempt to deal with the loss. These adaptive strategies may vary and can include:

- Cognitive strategies such as redefinition and reframing, logical analysis, avoidance, or denial;
- Affective strategies such as affective regulation, ventilation, or acceptance;
- Spiritual strategies such as prayer, surrendering to a higher power, spiritual reframing, or redefinition (e.g., a test, judgment, etc.);
- Behavioral strategies such as seeking information and support, physical activity, taking action to solve subsidiary problems, acting out behaviors.

The term "adaptive strategies" comes from the work of Silverman (1986). Adaptive strategies are the learned response persons utilize to manage disequilibrating events. There are two significant aspects of this definition. The first is the affirmation that these strategies are "learned." Throughout a crisis, individuals can learn and employ new strategies. In fact, to Silverman (1986) one of the most valued aspects of widow-to-widow programs or other similar support groups is that they provide opportunities for new learning. This also reinforces the fact that adaptive strategies are dynamic. Individuals may attempt a variety of adaptive strategies, including those both in their repertoire as well as those newly learned or applied. Individuals who have both a larger repertoire of strategies to draw upon, and/or a capacity and willingness to learn and employ new strategies, are likely to be more successful in managing the crisis.

The second valued aspect of this definition is the understanding that these strategies are employed in "disequilibrating" or transitional events that challenge an individual's ability to manage. These strategies then enable the person to manage a transition and adapt to a new reality created by the loss.

Silverman's definition of adaptive strategies is similar to much of the present language that is used to describe "coping" (see Lazarus & Folkman, 1984; Moos & Schaefer, 1986). But it avoids some of the problems associated with the use of that term. First, for example, the term "coping" has been criticized for failing to make clear distinctions between reactions (such as anger or physical pain) and adaptive strategies utilized to manage that reaction (e.g., ventilating, anger, acting out, seeking information, etc.) (see Ellis, 1997). As Weisman (1979) (who does use the term "coping") notes, a clear distinction has to be made between a show of distress and behavior that copes with distress. Guilt, for example, is a form of distress. But writing a letter to the deceased or punishing oneself to expunge guilt are reactions to that distress. This critical distinction is often lost in discussion as coping. Second, "coping" has been used to describe responses to both extraordinary and everyday problems (e.g., Weisman, 1979; Lazarus & Folkman, 1984). For example, while most who use the term (see Corr) refer to extraordinary events such as dying or experiencing a significant loss, everyday usage can be clouded; people can be said to cope with crises like death or annoyances like taxes. Furthermore, the term coping has other difficulties. It has a negative connotation often perceived as merely managing, while "adapation" or "adaptive strategies" carries no such onus. "Adaptation" or "adaptive strategies" carries a different connotation. Adaptation is a process common to humans and, for that matter, other animals as they continually have to adjust to changes within their environment. Finally, "coping" suggests a time-bound process while "adapting" seems more ongoing. "Coping" has been used in confusing ways. It has been defined as strictly behavioral responses or as a range of varied responses. For those reasons, we prefer Silverman's "adaptive strategies." Clinicians, however, are wise to recognize that for each individual, words have different meanings and adaptations can suggest conforming or acceptance. Clinicians then, should always listen and reflect the words their clients use whether grieving, mourning, coping, dealing, struggling, or whatever terms describe their experiences.

A further point should be made about varied adaptive strategies. While these strategies represent attempts to manage the crisis, they may be more or less effective in any given situation. Any strategy may, in and of itself, complicate or facilitate one's response to the crisis. For example, venting one's feelings can both allow a release of tension and can simultaneously, depending on the situation or the perception of others, drive away or generate support. Some strategies of avoidance may allow one to function at work, but abusing alcohol to avoid grief can create other difficulties such as health or relational problems, thereby complicating grieving. Individuals who can utilize multiple adaptive strategies and skills may have distinct advantages both in responding to and surmounting crises. Often, exploring an individual's adaptive strategies allows people to assess the strengths and limits of their styles as well as to learn and practice alternate adaptive strategies. Chapter 4 will revisit this issue as it deals with dissonant grieving.

Conclusion: Rethinking Grief Work

One approach to understanding the grieving process has been framed by an often implicit "grief work" hypothesis. This hypothesis emphasizes that only by experiencing strong affect such as distress or depression and "working through" such feelings can a bereaved person ever expect to reach a sense of resolution about the loss.

As stated in Chapter 1, the hypothesis has been challenged (see Wortman & Silver, 1989; Bonanno, 1997). In fact, there is little research to support such a hypothesis (Wortman & Silver, 1989) and there is evidence that disassociation from negative emotion and use of alternate approaches such as positive reframing can facilitate grief adjustment (Bonanno, 1997).

Ultimately, the problem with the grief work hypothesis is that it identifies grief solely as an affective response to loss and posits one adaptive strategy as the only effective response. Such an approach ignores both the multifaceted manifestations of grief and the multiplicity of adaptive strategies bereaved individuals use as they grieve. It denies that individuals experience, express, and adapt to loss in highly individual ways.

The danger of such an approach is that in the final analysis, it disenfranchises grievers who use such cognitive and behavioral strategies. But as Corr (1998) points out, disenfranchised grief is far more inclusive a concept. Much can be disenfranchised in grief. Corr (1998) notes that when grief is identified purely as affect and one insists on a single set of responses as appropriate reaction, considerable risk is incurred.

> What is central is the recognition that human beings may and indeed are likely to respond to important losses in their lives with their whole selves, not just with some narrowly defined aspect of their humanity. Failure to describe grief in a holistic way dismisses and devalues its richness and breadth. (Corr, 1998, p. 13)

The challenge to the "grief work" hypothesis is part of a larger rethinking of the paradigms of grief. This has included such tenets as a move away from stages (Corr, 1992), an extension of the concept of grief in nondeath circumstances (Doka, 1989), a recognition of the role of continuing connections with the deceased (Klass et al., 1996), a greater appreciation of the elements of grieving beyond the affective (Attig, 1996; Neimeyer, 1997; Doka & Martin, 1998), the application of new models (Rando, 1993), and the recognition of growth even in the midst of loss (Prend, 1997). This work draws from and hopefully adds to that paradigmatic revision by positing two patterns or adaptive strategies by which individuals respond to loss—instrumental and intuitive.

3

CHAPTER

Patterns of Grief

In this chapter, the differences between the instrumental and intuitive styles or patterns of grief are discussed by contrasting them in terms of the experience of grief, the expression of grief, and the primary adaptive strategies that grievers choose to adjust to their losses. Also examined are less differentiated or blended patterns. The chapter begins by illustrating the various patterns of grief using the following case example.

It was Friday morning. After briefly discussing an upcoming fishing trip with his youngest son, making dinner plans with his wife, and teasing his teenage daughter about her date that evening, David left for the post office where he planned to mail a check to cover his younger son's fraternity dues. He never got there. A massive heart attack killed him as he waited at a traffic light. He had just turned 46.

David's family was shocked by his death, yet they each responded to the crisis in different ways. His eldest son, Josh, showed no emotion until his voice quivered and failed him as he eulogized his father at the funeral on Monday. On Tuesday, he returned to work. He remained impassive, avoiding any discussion of his father and refusing any offers of help and comfort from his girlfriend. Yet, when he was alone, powerful feelings threatened to overwhelm him. Josh dealt with this threatened loss of control by drinking himself to sleep every night. Two weeks later, he received his first DWI. Finally, after an angry outburst at his supervisor, he reluctantly agreed to see a counselor. He never kept his first appointment. Within a year of his father's death, Josh had withdrawn from everyone, including his girlfriend. He had also developed ulcerative colitis and was well on the road to alcoholism.

David's 15-year-old daughter, Sarah, was inconsolable. She returned to school several days after the funeral but found it impossible to concentrate. She had trouble sleeping and cried for hours every day. Sarah eventually found comfort in attending a bereavement support group sponsored by a local funeral home. Sarah's mother urged her to also get professional counseling, following an episode of acute anxiety. After eight months, she reported feeling much better, although she still experienced painful feelings whenever she thought about her father.

As soon as he heard of his father's death, Vincent stopped preparing for his final exams and immediately returned home. While he felt overwhelmed with feelings, he managed to limit his crying to the times he shared with his sister and his mother. Two days after the funeral, Vincent returned to school and successfully completed his exams. He later told a frat brother that he was able to do well on his exams only because he knew his father would have wanted him to "get on with living." In the months that followed, Vincent was often overwhelmed with painful memories of his father, yet he found he could remain focused on his classes if he shared difficult feelings with his closest friends.

Janice, David's wife, threw herself into making the necessary arrangements for his funeral. She wept at the funeral on Monday, but by Wednesday she was immersed in settling her late husband's estate. While Janice made several inquiries about support services for her daughter and accompanied her to the first bereavement support group meeting, she chose not to return. She found the raw emotionality of the group uncomfortable and unhelpful. She felt restless and channeled her excess energy into her garden, enjoying the time alone to reflect on her years with David. When her friends called to offer their support and companionship, Janice politely declined, stating that she preferred to be alone with her thoughts.

Although Janice felt sad and diminished by David's untimely death, she was never overwhelmed by the intensity of her feelings. Much of her grieving involved thinking about the issues and the challenges created by David's death as well as discovering the skills she needed to confront those challenges. Janice confronted (and conquered) everything from an unruly lawnmower to an overzealous insurance agent. The following fall, Janice enrolled at a local college, and two years later she was well on the way to completing dual degrees in secondary education and nutrition.

Each of these family members grieved, but their grieving took very different forms. The daughter's grief, although intense and persistent, eventually subsided. She found comfort in sharing her plight with other grievers who had similar losses. Her response to her father's death represents the pattern generally thought to be "intuitive" grief. In many respects, the wife's response is the most interesting, since it defies classification. She experienced her grief as more rooted in thinking than in feeling, and she focused her energies on solving problems presented by her husband's death. She preferred reflection and chose not to talk with others about her feelings. She discovered outlets for her grief that were apparently healthy. In this case, the wife's grief could be seen as "instrumental" grief.

While there were clearly observable differences between the wife and daughter's responses, both had similar outcomes. Conversely, the sons' public reactions appeared similar, while the outcomes were very different. Josh's response was seemingly impassive, but it eventually resulted in damage to his relationships, job, and health. His outward stoicism be-lied his inner anguish and turmoil. This might be seen as the typical "male" response to bereavement. In fact, this son's reactions represent a mal-adaptive or dissonant response. (Dissonant responses are explored fur-ther in the next chapter.)

Vincent, too, appeared outwardly unaffected by the death, yet found effective ways to express his grief through sharing feelings with just a select few and rechanneling his energy into his academic work. Unlike Josh, Vincent chose strategies that did not damage his health or relation-ships. His reactions represent a more blended pattern of grief.

☐ Patterns of Grief and Adaptive Strategies

Identified so far are two distinct major patterns of grief—intuitive and instrumental—and a third, blended pattern, combining elements of both. These patterns vary in two general ways: by the griever's internal experi-ence of his loss and the individual's outward expressions of that experi-ence. In other words, patterns (or styles) of grief differ according to the direction taken by converted, grief-generated psychic energy, as well as by the external manifestation of that energy. The modalities of internal experience that are most useful in discriminating between the patterns are the cognitive and the affective. The intuitive griever converts more of his or her energy into the affective domain and invests less into the cog-nitive. For the intuitive griever grief consists primarily of profoundly pain-ful feelings. These grievers tend to spontaneously express their painful feelings through crying and want to share their inner experiences with others. The instrumental griever, on the other hand, converts most of the instinctual energy generated by bereavement into the cognitive domain rather than the affective. Painful feelings are tempered; for the instru-mental griever, grief is more of an intellectual experience. Consequently, instrumental grievers may channel energy into activity. They may also prefer to discuss problems rather than feelings.

Thus, it is the relative degree to which the griever's thoughts and feel-ings are affected that accounts for the differences between the patterns. However, what a griever is experiencing can never be directly observed; it only can be inferred by observing how the individual expresses his or her experience. In particular, the griever's desire for social support, the need to discuss his feelings, and the intensity and scope of his activities are vary-ing ways of expressing grief and are often important in distinguishing between patterns. These expressions of grief usually (but not always) re-flect choices, both past and present, that the griever has made or is making to adapt to his losses. These choices are the griever's adaptive strategies.

Intuitive and instrumental grievers usually choose different primary adaptive strategies. Primary adaptive strategies are the principle ways grievers express their grief and assimilate and adapt to their losses over long periods. These strategies tend to differ according to the pattern of grief. Grievers use additional or secondary adaptive strategies at various times and under specific circumstances. Secondary adaptive strategies are those strategies that grievers employ to facilitate the expression of the subordinate modalities of experience. For example, intuitive grievers choose additional strategies that aid them in accomplishing tasks requiring planning, organization, and activity—all expressions more common to their instrumental counterpart. Conversely, instrumental grievers need to find ways to express their feelings about their losses, and while intuitive grievers are quite familiar with strong feelings, instrumental grievers are less so. These secondary adaptive strategies are not as familiar or accessible as primary adaptive strategies, nor are they as critical to the individual's overall adjustment to the loss.

Those with a blended style or pattern of grief are less likely to be identified with a specific primary or secondary adaptive strategy. These grievers choose strategies that are more evenly balanced, reflecting the greater symmetry between the cognitive and affective responses of the individual. The overall responses of blended grievers are more likely to correlate with what have been identified as the various phases (Parkes, 1987) or stages (Kavanaugh, 1972) of grief. For instance, early on, the griever may need to subjugate feelings in order to plan and implement funeral or other arrangements. Later, he or she may give full vent to feelings, seeking help and support in sharing. Later still, cognitive-driven action may overshadow the individual's feelings as the griever finds it necessary to return to work, assume parenting roles, etc.

But whether the pattern is primarily instrumental, intuitive or blended, the griever with the greatest number of available and useful strategies has a distinct advantage over the griever limited to just a few. This may become a special burden for blended grievers, whose experience of grief may be more diffuse than either intuitive or instrumental grievers, necessitating a greater repertoire of adaptive strategies.

In the next section of the book, the origins of the patterns of grief are explored. For now, remember the following caveats:

1. Patterns of grief exist along a continuum; that is, it is extremely rare to observe either a "pure" intuitive or a "pure" instrumental pattern of grief. Although there are key elements that are useful in discriminating between the two, these represent differences in degree, not kind. The vast majority of individual grievers experience and express their grief in ways common to both patterns but toward either end of the

continuum. Whether grievers are "intuitive" or "instrumental" or "blended" depends on whether their internal experiences are more affective than cognitive or a fairly equal portion of both. It depends also on their willingness to talk about their feelings rather than their issues, and whether they are more focused on difficulties related to their internal experiences or to solving external problems created by the loss. Since it is rare to find grievers at either extreme, the safest description for almost all would be "blended." But this denies us the usefulness of understanding that patterns are, indeed, different. Likewise, it would be foolish to arbitrarily select a point on the continuum and declare that, "beyond this point blended becomes instrumental or intuitive." Perhaps the wisest course is to understand that most grievers are "more instrumental than intuitive," or "more intuitive than instrumental," rather than as either instrumental or intuitive or blended.

2. A few grievers may respond to different losses with a different pattern of grieving, and to refer to a person as an "instrumental griever" or an "intuitive griever" or a "blended griever" can be misleading. However, most individuals are relatively consistent in their pattern of grief, whether it is primarily instrumental, intuitive, or blended, although their position on the instrumental/intuitive continuum may change through life. This may be particularly true of the griever's choice of primary and secondary adaptive strategies. In other words, a griever may be "more instrumental" in his grieving earlier in life and become "less instrumental" in grieving over time. The same holds for those whose primary pattern of grieving is intuitive. This is consistent with the theorizing of Carl Jung (1920), who believed that those aspects of ourselves that are not dominant during the first half of life tend to find more expression as we age. Jung embraced the concept of balance, believing that we achieve balance between all the different aspects of ourselves over the course of a lifetime (See Sidebar 3.1).

3. For the sake of clarity and brevity, those who consistently display elements inherent to the instrumental pattern will be referred to as "instrumental grievers"; those who follow the intuitive pattern as "intuitive grievers"; and those whose experiences and expressions are a balanced combination as "blended." The reader should continue to view the patterns along a continuum.

4. Whether a griever skillfully negotiates the challenges presented by being bereaved and moves on with living, or founders and stagnates, remaining forever compromised by his or her experience, depends on whether he or she chooses and successfully implements effective adaptive strategies. Both instrumental and intuitive grievers may choose ways of adapting to loss that are more or less complementary to their

---

Sidebar 3.1. Pattern Development From a Lifecycle Perspective

There are many questions about how and when the various patterns begin, and how they might change over the course of a lifespan. While it is suggested (Chapter 3) that most grievers remain relatively consistent in their patterns, one must acknowledge that there may be a shift towards the opposite end of the continuum with age.

One of the reasons this book has not examined how patterns begin and how they change as people age is that, at this point, one cannot confirm whether these patterns are cohort specific or not. Stated differently, it is not known if differences among patterns can be attributed to advancing age, or to the sociocultural conditions that existed during a particular historical period. For instance, people who are 85 years old at the turn of the millenium were born in 1915. They were children during the "Roaring 20s" and emerged as adults during the great depression. They also lived through, and may have served, during the Second World War. They saw the advent of the television, space travel, and the personal computer. How much did any or all of these experiences affect their patterns of grief?

A related concern is discerning whether the key ingredients for the patterns are present at birth, evolve gradually during childhood, or occur in response to when an individual experiences their first significant death? Could losing a parent in childhood, especially during critical periods of personality, gender role development, or both, determine whether one is more intuitive or instrumental in their grief? While attempting to provide some evidence to answer these and other questions (studies of temperament, gender-role socialization, cultural changes), the definitive answers have yet to be uncovered. It may take a large, well-designed longitudinal study to answer many of the questions. We will leave that to those following who are intrigued by the existence of different patterns and would like to confirm or disprove their existence.

---

natural style of grieving, and result in a more positive than negative outcome. Unfortunately, the griever who chooses and maintains a primary adaptive strategy that is incongruent with his or her inner experience does so at peril. Also, both intuitive and instrumental grievers must find additional ways to express themselves that may be unfamiliar. For instrumental grievers, this means they must find outlets that allow them to vent whatever internal levels of affect they experience. On the other hand, intuitive grievers need to discover ways to facilitate the expression of their cognitions as well as their feelings. Thus, effective adaptive strategies must accomplish two goals:

(a) They must facilitate the expression of the griever's dominant inner modality of experience (affect for the intuitive griever, cognition for the instrumental style);

(b) They should also expedite expression of the subordinate modality of experience. This means expressing feelings for the instrumental griever and cognitive-based activity for the intuitive pattern.

5. Although the blended pattern equally combines the elements of the intuitive and instrumental patterns, it should not be seen as a "goal" or "ideal" form of grief. No pattern is superior or inferior to the other. It is the individual griever's choice and implementation of effective adaptive strategies that determine how well he or she adjusts to his or her loss.

6. Described in the next section are the experiences, expressions, and choice of primary adaptive strategies that distinguish instrumental from intuitive grievers. These elements of the patterns are intended to represent the overall response of the griever. Explored in Chapter 4 is how the griever's initial reactions to loss may depart from his habitual pattern and blur the distinctions between intuitive and instrumental grievers.

☐ Intuitive Grief

Intuitive grievers experience their losses deeply. Feelings are varied and intense and loosely follow the descriptions of acute grief that have been cited so frequently in the literature (see, for example, Lindemann, 1944). Emotions vary, ranging from shock and disbelief to overwhelming sorrow and a sense of loss of self-control. The intuitive griever may experience grief as a series or waves of acutely painful feelings. Intuitive grievers often find themselves without energy and motivation. Their expressions of grief truly mirror their inner experiences. Anguish and tears are almost constant companions.

Intuitive grievers gain strength and solace from openly sharing their inner experiences with others—especially other grievers. Some intuitive grievers are very selective about their confidantes and, consequently, may not seek help from a larger group. Others seek out larger groups, especially those with similar types of losses. For intuitive grievers, a grief expressed is a grief experienced (or a burden shared is half a burden). Because openly expressing and sharing feelings is traditionally identified as a female trait, intuitive grieving is usually associated with women. Of course, this is not always the case; male intuitive grievers grieve in ways similar to female intuitive grievers.

Some intuitive grievers may seek professional counseling to have the intensity of their feelings and responses validated as being part of a normal grief process. This is especially true of the male intuitive griever, whose experiences and expressions run counter to gender role expectations. Other intuitive grievers, both male and female, look to counseling to provide new, effective adaptive strategies or to augment current strategies.

Characteristics of Intuitive Grieving

The following are summaries of the features of grief and grieving that differentiate the intuitive from the instrumental griever. Intuitive grievers differ from their instrumental counterparts in three ways. First, their *experience* of grief is different. This may represent the most significant difference between the two styles. Second, the intuitive griever *expresses* his or her grief differently. This expression usually reflects a third difference between patterns: choice of primary adaptive strategies. Before proceeding, it should be remembered that these elements are not separate entities. Rather, these features are part of a system of functioning, and interact with each other to produce the emotional response that is grief.

The Experience of Grief: Intensity of Affect over Cognitions

Intuitive grievers experience grief, above all, as feelings. As illustrated below, their descriptions of these feelings reveal vivid brief glimpses of intense inner pain, helplessness, hopelessness, and loneliness.

> *"Oh Christ, what am I going to do? I have an ache, an ache in my stomach. An emptiness, a feeling sometimes that there's no inside to me. Like this sculpture a friend of mine made before he died of a second heart attack. It's a man with no chest, that's the way he felt. I look at that, that's the way I feel. It's a state beyond aloneness. When you lose somebody, you can have a feeling of missing the person you've lost. But then you can go beyond that, to almost a personal annihilation. And I don't know that I haven't visited that second place sometimes. Where I feel that it's not that I simply lost Carol, but that I've lost . . .*
>
> *I sometimes have the feeling where is she? She's coming home, this is a bad dream. It has an unreal quality to it. Maybe the process of grief is to make reality out of what doesn't feel real. It seems like it couldn't have happened. In the mornings, it feels so strange to be . . . Often, we would have tea together. In the evening, we would have something to eat. We would talk to each other—you know—and I miss her. I miss her desperately. I mean, there's no mystique to the nuts and bolts of living alone for me. But I miss her, I miss her presence, I miss her physically, I miss her, I miss, I mean I want to, I want, when something has happened, I want to talk to her, I want to tell her something, usually something very funny, and sometimes I talk to her, but I usually start to cry when I do, very quickly."* (p. 33)

This voice of pain belonged to "George" and is an excerpt from an interview with a widower presented in the book *Widower*, by Scott Campbell and Phyllis R. Silverman (1996). Although the book focuses on gender differences and tends to be biased in favor of the ways most women grieve and against male grievers (Martin, 1998), it contains many vivid descriptions of bereavement. "George" describes most of his experiences as feelings, such as . . . "I sometimes have the *feeling* where is she?" or "Maybe the process of grief is to make reality out of what doesn't *feel* real." For George, his inner life is primarily one of feeling. Like most intuitive grievers, George responds more to internal cues, which are experienced as feelings, rather than to thoughts. In fact, for the intuitive griever, thoughts and feelings are one and the same. In this way, intuitive grievers are probably more "in touch" with their feelings than instrumental grievers.

There is a tremendous depth and intensity of feeling in George's reflection of his wife's death. An intuitive griever's feelings are dominant, powerful, and enduring. They are the primary features of grieving. In his classic children's work, *Charlotte's Web* (1952), E. B. White described Wilbur's response to hearing of Charlotte's impending death: "Hearing this, Wilbur threw himself down in an agony of pain and sorrow. Great sobs racked his body. He heaved and grunted with desolation. 'Charlotte,' he moaned. 'Charlotte! My true friend!'" (p. 165).

Intuitive grievers are also unable or unwilling to distance themselves from feelings expressed by others. These grievers cry right along with other grievers who may be crying while telling their story. In this way, intuitive grievers may experience feelings either directly or vicariously from sharing the feelings of another who is expressing his grief.

The Expression of Grief: A Grief Expressed is a Grief Experienced

The outward expression of the intuitive griever mirrors his or her inner experience. The pain of loss is often expressed through tears, and ranges from quiet weeping to sobbing to wailing. Additional features include depressed mood, confusion, anxiety, and loss of appetite, inability to concentrate, and anger and irritability.

It has been said, "Grief isn't real until it's shared with someone else." This speaker certainly had the intuitive griever in mind. So did William Shakespeare when he wrote, "Give sorrow words, the grief that does not speak knits the o'erwrought heart and bids it break" (*Macbeth*, Act IV, Scene iii). These are commonly expressed sentiments. For example, most mental health professionals subscribe, at least in part, to the "talking cure" for the treatment of grief. Likewise, bereavement support groups foster sharing one's burden of grief with others, discussing it openly and often.

Of course, these same bereavement support groups can be social outlets as well. Simply being with other people can be comforting. Thus, we are making a distinction between "social behavior," which encompasses vast numbers of activities and experiences, and "social disclosure" of one's inner experiences. It is possible to maintain privacy about feelings and still benefit from the company of others.

Intuitive grievers want and need to discuss their feelings. They often do this by "working through" their grief. Summarizing the traditionalists (Bowlby, 1980; Parkes & Weiss, 1983) position on "working through," Wortman and Silver (1989) make the following point:

> Implicit in this assumption is the notion that individuals need to focus on and "process" what has happened and that attempts to deny the implications of the loss, or block feelings or thoughts about it, will ultimately be unproductive. (p. 351)

For the intuitive griever, talking about his or her experience is tantamount to having the experience. This retelling the story and reenacting the pain is a necessary part of grieving and an integral part of the intuitive pattern of grieving. It also represents the intuitive griever's going "with" the grief experience.

Primary Adaptive Strategies: Going "With" the Experience

Going "with" the experience means centering activities on the experience of grief itself. Intuitive grievers structure their actions by responding to their feelings. The intuitive griever's need and desire to talk about his or her feelings is the most prominent example of this. Other examples include the griever's efforts to find time and space for tears, seeking help, sharing time with others who are bereaved, and offering heartfelt condolences to those grievers whose losses may be more recent. This is not to say that intuitive grievers neglect their responsibilities towards others. For instance, intuitive grievers still find enough energy to care for their families, friends, and other dependents. But this means putting their grieving on hold. Thus, intuitive grievers must supplement their primary adaptive strategy of "going with their experience" with channeling sufficient energy to accomplish meaningful and necessary goals.

Intuitive grievers expend most of their energies coming to terms with and expressing their feelings; this may mean diverting energy from normal activities. They may require more time to rechannel their energies to routine activities, such as self-care, work, volunteer activities, etc. For example, D. G. Cable (personal communication, February 13, 1998) provided the following instance illustrating how neglecting one's health is potentially dangerous and may need to be discussed with the griever.

Theresa sought a counselor's help after her husband died suddenly. As the counselor listened attentively to Theresa's story, he noticed how pale she was, how her hands trembled, and how short of breath she was. He asked several times if she had seen her physician. The woman seemed not to hear the question. Finally, as their first session came to a close, the counselor confronted Theresa with her physical condition. He stated, "Before I will see you again in counseling, you must make an appointment with and see your doctor." The woman stared at him for several seconds and then, in a sheepish tone replied, "I am a physician, and I know you are right. I just haven't cared or wanted to know about the state of my own health."

Intuitive grievers are also less likely than instrumental grievers to "problem-find," to seek out potential problems and solve them. Because so much of their energy is focused on their internal experience, intuitive grievers may appear to outwardly adjust more slowly to their losses. This is not necessarily so. Intuitive grievers are adapting to their losses by going with their feelings. The following case example illustrates how intuitive grievers find outlets for expressing their feelings.

Nathan had a secret: his twice-weekly visits to a therapist's office where, for 50 minutes, he sobbed. He needed to keep this activity from his coworkers and friends (who were primarily one and the same) in order to keep his job.

Nathan had always wanted to be a fireman and, unlike most kids, he followed his dream. He began volunteering as a "fire scout" when he was 12 years old, washing his beloved trucks and running errands around the firehouse. As soon as he turned 18 he applied and was accepted to his state's fire school. Now, at 25 years of age, he was living his dream as a professional firefighter. His only problem was that he had always been "sensitive," and "sensitivity" was not one of the attributes expected—or tolerated—by his fire chief (an ex-marine who honestly believed that tears were for "sissies"). When his mother died unexpectedly, Nathan found himself overwhelmed with feelings. Several weeks after her death, he was sobbing alone in the station locker room when the chief walked in. He ordered Nathan to "pull yourself together" and warned him that if he (the chief) was not confident that Nathan could handle a crisis that he would suspend him. Unfortunately, home was not a sanctuary either, since Nathan shared an apartment with two other firefighters.

Desperate to gain control of his feelings, Nathan sought help. After explaining his dilemma to the therapist and sobbing while talking about his mother the two made a contract that permitted Nathan as much of the session time as needed for him to simply cry. Knowing that for at least 50 minutes a week he had a safe haven for his tears gave Nathan the strength to hide his feelings from others.

Nathan's adaptive strategy was successful, since it afforded him the opportunity to grieve openly. Nathan found a way to "go with" his grief.

Secondary Adaptive Strategies: Handling Problems, Meeting Challenges

Since the majority of grief energy infuses the intuitive griever's feelings, there is less energy available to activate the cognitive and physical domains of experience. (Spirituality, both as it is experienced and practiced, is highly individual and is not a useful tool for discerning patterns.) Nonetheless, intuitive grievers do have cognitive and physical responses to loss and must find ways to express these facets of their experience.

Cognitively, intuitive grievers may experience prolonged periods of confusion, lack of concentration, disorientation, and disorganization. This often impairs their ability to work or complete complicated tasks. In fact, intuitive grievers must find ways to master their thinking in order to fulfill important roles and activities such as parenting or settling an estate.

Physically, intuitive grievers experience grief energy in any number of ways; however, two physical experiences seem to dominate. First, the griever may feel exhausted. Intense expressions of feelings like crying or venting anger can fatigue the griever, as can unusual responsibilities, such as preparing for the funeral or single parenting. Likewise, fitful sleeping and a poor diet can contribute to fatigue.

Second, intuitive grievers may be aware of physical energy manifesting as increased arousal. This is the hallmark of anxiety—an individual's awareness of a heightened sense of arousal. In turn, anxiety that remains unchecked may exacerbate the griever's fatigue. Thus, intuitive grievers should explore ways to augment their energy stores. They must also develop strategies for coping with heightened anxiety.

☐ Characteristics of Instrumental Grievers

Identified so far are three key elements associated with the instrumental griever:

(a) focus on cognition/moderated affect,
(b) a desire to master feelings along with a general reluctance to talk about feelings,
(c) problem-solving activity. As with the intuitive style, these elements function together as a system. Readers should not assume that they operate independently of each other.

Experience of Grief: Focus on Cognition/Moderated Affect

Instrumental grievers are more comfortable in dealing intellectually with their losses. Conceivably, this might indicate that grief is experienced more in the cognitive domain than in the affective domain. Perhaps instrumental grievers respond initially to thoughts explaining the circumstance of their losses, rather than to affective cues. This also suggests that instrumental grievers may perceive their losses somewhat differently than intuitive grievers. Generally, this means that the thoughts they process are less vivid and more neutral in content. Also, instrumental grievers may have a different world view—one that emboldens them with a sense of control, a belief that they can eventually master the crisis. In cognitive terms, an instrumental griever may view adaptation to his or her loss as more of a challenge than a threat (Meichenbaum, 1977). Whether he or she can rise to the challenge depends on his or her choice and effective use of adaptive strategies.

Given that the chief experience for the instrumental griever is cognitive, it should come as no surprise that many of the most initially troubling aspects of grief involve impaired cognitive activity. Confusion, disorientation, an inability to concentrate, and disorganized thought are major handicaps to the instrumental griever whose fundamental manner of interacting with the environment is through cognition.

Instrumental grievers do not experience feelings associated with grief as intensely as intuitive grievers. These grievers often report that they cannot cry and can't remember the last time they cried. In fact, some instrumental grievers don't feel as if they need to cry. Thus, instrumental grievers may appear to have a difficult time expressing feelings relative to intuitive grievers when, in fact, the feelings are simply less intense (Bohannon, 1991; Carroll & Shaefer, 1994).

This is not to suggest that instrumental grievers don't react affectively to their losses—they do. Instrumental grievers share common feelings experienced by intuitive grievers such as sadness, anxiety, loneliness, and yearning (see Worden, 1991). What is different is the strength of these feelings. For the intuitive griever, feelings are vibrant, intense "colors"; for the instrumental griever, they are pastels.

Whereas intuitive grievers confuse thoughts and feelings, instrumental grievers can differentiate between the two, separating specific thoughts from feelings. "Whenever I think about how she used to fuss at me for my choice of clothes, making fun of my color combinations, I feel sad." Being able to "think about thinking" implies that instrumental grievers may do best with adaptive strategies that stress management of thinking over the purging of feelings. However, instrumental grievers must also find appropriate outlets for their feelings. Whereas intuitive grievers are more in touch with their feelings, as the following case illustrates, instrumental grievers are more comfortable with their thoughts, though they find ways of expressing their feelings as well.

> *Leonard, a psychologist, and his wife Sheila each lost both of their parents within an eight-month period. Ironically, both mothers' deaths had been anticipated, but both fathers died unexpectedly. Sheila could not talk about any of the deaths without sobbing. When she was not crying, she sat in front of the television in a stupor.*

She could not concentrate. Three weeks after the last death (her mother's), Sheila tried to return to her job as a city engineer. That afternoon, she walked out of an important meeting after she choked up while trying to give a report. Her colleagues offered to pool their vacation and sick leave so that she could remain at home; she gratefully accepted. Four more months passed before she tried again to go back to work. This time she succeeded, although several times every day she would be forced to close her office door to weep in private. Two years later, she felt that she had recovered.

Leonard immediately went back to his busy practice. He saw patients, negotiated a new contract with a nursing home, and returned to teaching others about his hobby of photography through a community adult education program.

Leonard sought an internal explanation for his losses, stating that "I was always being reminded of the good times, memories of how important my parents were to me. Yes, I had feelings, but they were a kind of backdrop to my thoughts. It was similar to having a low-grade fever, uncomfortable, but not debilitating." He confessed that he wondered if his feelings would overtake him—that he would eventually "crash." Sheila shared his concerns and pleaded with him to share his feelings with her. He chose instead to shut himself in his den and listen to the "big band" sounds of Tommy Dorsey, his parents' favorite music, and reminisce. Leonard did not "crash." As he later explained, "I guess I simply accepted the fact that all people die, including parents."

Thinking about experiences without feeling them deeply is not easy for the intuitive griever. This contributes to the communication problems often seen between different grievers. The griever who feels intense sorrow may misconstrue the reaction of one who responds intellectually to a loss. The following example illustrates how a griever who experiences a loss as an almost total affective event may not understand a griever who reacts intellectually to the same loss.

The nightmare started with a "thump" in the middle of the night. Robin was immediately awake. Her first thought was that her six-year-old son, Stephan, had fallen out of his bed. Stephan had already missed the previous three days of school because of a bad cold. Robin then thought of her 17-year old son, Eric, who had also been home from school. Eric had been complaining of headaches for the past several weeks. His parents were not alarmed; after all, Eric had been anxiously waiting to hear whether his application to Penn State University had been accepted. Eric had always been "a worrier." Once Eric worried that he had failed his soccer teammates and his entire school when, as goalie, he had missed an opposing player's last second, winning goal. That time, too, he had stayed home from school for several days while complaining of a headache. His headache disappeared when he learned that he had been named to the All-County Soccer Team.

Hearing nothing else, Robin lay back down and promptly fell asleep. Her husband, Jack, never stirred. The next morning, after Jack had left for work, and while Stephan was taking his bath, Robin knocked on Eric's door. There was no response. Robin returned to help Stephan bathe. Ten minutes later, she knocked on Eric's door again. Again there was no response. Although she had always respected Eric's need for privacy, this time Robin decided to walk on into his room. She had decided it was time to confront him about his "malingering" of the past several days. She discovered him lying half out of bed, his face to the floor. He was not moving or breathing. Desperately, Robin turned him over and screamed at him. Then she dialed 911.

Eric was dead. Although he was not pronounced dead until he arrived at the hospital, he had apparently died sometime during the night. An autopsy revealed a ruptured aneurysm in his brain stem. Later, the doctors concluded that he had been born with the weakness in his brain.

Robin was devastated. She stopped working, and spent her days in bed staring blankly at the television. Jack tried to comfort her by suggesting that she "get busy," but to no avail. Two months after Eric's death, and after a serious attempt at suicide, Robin voluntarily entered a psychiatric hospital.

Jack returned to writing computer programs at work immediately after the funeral. Although he had always helped out around the house, Robin's condition forced him to get more directly involved in Stephan's care and the management of the household. Jack felt heartbroken by his son's death, but while he wept at the funeral, that was the end of his tears. He had always been "unemotional" and dealt with previous losses and disappointments by keeping busy. This time, he had no choice but to keep busy.

Several months later, Robin and Jack separated. With the aid of psychotherapy and medications, Robin had resumed her life but felt that she could not forgive Jack his lack of emotion following Eric's death. Jack, in responding to Robin's accusations that he had failed to validate her grief, declared, "I couldn't allow myself to miss my son until I figured out how our family was going to survive this. I mean, how could we continue to pay our bills until you got a handle on things and returned to work? By then, I had accepted the fact that God had a purpose for Eric in heaven. Anyway, how do you know what I was feeling? Believe me, I felt plenty miserable those first two months!"

Jack and Robin reunited. Two years later they separated for good. Robin never forgave Jack his apparent lack of feelings about Eric's death.

Jack and Robin failed each other. Jack did not acknowledge Robin's pain and provide appropriate measures of comfort; Robin misunderstood Jack's stoicism as a lack of feeling and caring and negated his efforts to preserve the family.

The key point is that instrumental grievers can and do experience feelings. While they may not experience them as intensely or be as directly responsive to them as intuitive grievers, they address some of these feelings by redirecting their energies and resolving the issues generated by their thoughts and feelings. As Robin and Jack demonstrated, conflicts arise when feelings are experienced and expressed in ways not seen as appropriate.

This can be true in professional as well as personal settings. For instance, after speaking to a group of hospice nurses about the differences between the intuitive and instrumental patterns of grief, one of the authors was approached by two of the nurses. They appeared visibly relieved. Apparently, they had both recently considered getting out of nursing, or at least hospice nursing. They offered the author copies of recent evaluations given by their nursing supervisor (who did not attend the training). The supervisor's negative evaluations were not based on their skills as nurses (in fact, she recognized that they both seemed more committed to their patients than many of their peers) but as she cited, ". . . for failure to actively participate in staff support group." In this weekly group their peers openly wept about losing certain patients. For this pair of nurses, there were no tears to be shed. In fact, they felt extremely uncomfortable when the other nurses cried. Apparently, neither of them had ever cried easily, nor did they feel overwhelmed when one of their patients died, yet both believed that they got "close" to their patients and were saddened at their deaths. But they were also beginning to question their effectiveness as nurses, since they did not experience the intense pain expressed by their colleagues. When questioned about their overall responses to their losses, each described ways that they acknowledged the deaths. One of them wrote poetry that they often shared with the families of their patients, while the other (unbeknownst to her peers) took a single rose to the graves of almost all of her patients. In these ways, they were able to "feel" grief. They were also able to actively decide when and how they wanted to experience their feelings.

The Expression of Grief: Mastering the Environment

Instrumental grievers are often identified by the absence of behaviors—notably crying and help seeking—rather than their actions. In a sense, the instrumental griever is most often defined by his lack of expression. Since most of their psychic energy is infused into the cognitive realm of inner experience, instrumental grievers often sit quietly, contemplatively, expressing energy through thinking and planning activities. However, some instrumental grievers do show heightened levels of arousal through restlessness, rote behaviors, pacing, impaired concentration, insomnia, and muscular tension.

Since their feelings are neither as intense nor as overwhelming as they are for their intuitive counterparts, instrumental grievers do not show a great deal of affect. This often reflects the instrumental griever's desire to master or control his or her feelings. It also points to the simple fact that it is less difficult to master feelings if the feelings are lower in intensity to begin with.

Instrumental grievers do seem to be more willing to express anger than other feelings. For the intuitive griever anger reflects an overall intensity of affect. Instrumental grievers express anger when their efforts to implement their chosen adaptive strategy are thwarted. Anger is also a way to discharge excess psychic energy. Finally, anger does not threaten the griever with as great a threat of loss of personal control. Thus, while both styles express anger, they generally do so for different reasons (See Sidebar 3.2).

Sidebar 3.2. Anger

And when He had looked round about on them with anger, being grieved for the hardness of their hearts (Mark 3:5).

The word "anger" appears 228 times in the Bible. Yet, even here, we find ambiguity when commanded, *Be ye angry, and sin not* (Ephesians 4:26). The literature on grief views anger as a normal, though not universal response (Bowlby, 1980; Shuchter & Zisook, 1993), but beyond a distortion of normal grief (Raphael, 1983) if excessive. What is anger? Are some individuals more prone to anger than others? Is there a gender connection?

Spielberger (1988) differentiates between *state anger*, a brief, acute, situational-specific response and *trait anger*, an enduring dimension of personality (though individuals with high trait anger generally experience more frequent, intense, and lengthy states of anger). Hence, though anyone may become angry, some are much more prone to do so. Applying this to patterns of grief, anger is both an emotional response as well as an adaptive strategy. While all grievers are capable of anger, some use it productively (motivation for adaptive action), while others discharge it in inappropriate and unhealthy ways (aggression, self-destructive behaviors).

Nor is anger the province of one gender. While a number of studies found that outside of anger and guilt, men had a difficult time expressing affect (Glick, Parkes, & Weisss, 1974; Goldbach, Dunn, Toedler, & Lasker, 1991; Lang & Gottlieb, 1993; Schwab, 1990), others (Sharkin, 1993, Deffenbacher, Oetting, Thwaites, Lynch, Baker, Stark, Thacker, & Eiswerth-Cox, 1996) have begun to challenge the conventional link between anger and gender. Deffenbacher et al. (1996), for instance, concluded that "men and women are angered by similar things, and to similar degrees, express themselves in similar ways, and suffer similar consequences" (p. 146).

Thus, irrespective of gender, patterns of grief may differ on the experience and expression of anger. Intuitive grievers, with their immense capacity for intense affect, would seem the more likely candidates for experiencing deep anger. Yet instrumental grievers may express anger just as frequently. Why is this so?

Anger may be an easier choice for the instrumental griever if perceived as a way to generate activity and to master the environment. Since most of their grief energy is cognitive, expressing anger becomes a useful secondary strategy to bolster solving problems and achieving goals.

However, given anger's identification with men, male intuitive grievers searching for an acceptable vehicle for expressing powerful affect are more likely to choose anger.

Instrumental grievers value maintaining control over their behaviors. Although this may be interpreted as controlling feelings, it represents a greater goal—personal control. These grievers find satisfaction in mastering their own feelings. They also seek ways to master their environment. Thus, the desire for mastery affects all facets of the instrumental griever's life. It begins with a predisposition to control one's inner experiences. This is more easily accomplished for the instrumental griever since he has a reduced capacity for experiencing intense feelings. Also, instrumental grievers develop strategies to master their situations including minimizing affective expressions, and solving problems created by their losses. Again, it is important to remember that instrumental grievers do have feelings.

Instrumental grievers are also usually uncomfortable sharing whatever feelings they have with others. This feature of instrumental grieving has been referred to as a "desire for solitude" (Martin & Doka, 1996, 1998; Doka & Martin, 1998). In their earlier work, the authors confused reluctance to self-disclose about feelings of grief with a wish to remain isolated from others. Many instrumental grievers benefit from the company of others.

> When his wife Nancy died, Rob found solace by spending time with his neighbors. Every Tuesday and Wednesday evening, Rob, along with three other neighbors, would descend on John's garage. There they would be joined by Frank, Jeff, and Susanne (who had been the only girl among six children and had always described herself as "one of the boys") and spent several hours constructing an ultralight aircraft. Occasionally, someone would ask Rob how he was handling Nancy's death. He would usually respond with "fine." A few times Rob would share his concerns about some issue involving his teenage daughter. Susanne would offer useful suggestions about parenting a teenage girl. Most of the time, the silence would be punctuated with statements like, "Hand me that torque wrench," or comments such as, "Do you think this bird will ever fly?" Rob found the time he shared with the group therapeutic. He believed that the others understood him and were responding to his needs.

The point is that Rob not only chose to be with others, but he shared his grief-related issues with them without self-disclosing his feelings of grief. Instrumental grievers distinguish between talking about problems and discussing their feelings. In fact, the instrumental griever's degree of introversion is more important when he chooses solitude over sociability than his style of grief. Earlier it was shown some intuitive grievers preferred sharing their feelings with a select few rather than a larger group. Instrumental grievers are the same. Shy, introverted instrumental grievers tend to limit their disclosure of issues related to their losses to one or two others.

Instrumental grievers may discuss grief-related issues as part of their primary adaptive strategy, yet avoid disclosing their feelings. Since many instrumental grievers are men, most hospice bereavement coordinators struggle in vain to get them to participate in hospice bereavement programs. This is especially true of bereavement support groups. Perhaps their well-intentioned concern is misplaced. In fact, Tudiver, Hilditch, Permaul, and McKendree (1992) concluded that a facilitated mutual support group had no effect (and possibly a negative impact) on widowers' recovery from conjugal losses. This aversion to seeking help from support groups is often misinterpreted as isolation, when, in fact, it is not the company of those present that the instrumental griever is avoiding; it is the nature of the discussions.

> *Willie's wife died after a long illness, and the hospice bereavement worker called weekly to invite him to groups or to ask if he wanted counseling. He attended a group once, hoping to discuss the practical concerns he had in raising his nine- and ten-year-old daughters. But every time Willie tried to talk about his children, the group leader would interrupt and ask, "What about your feelings?" Willie, quite frankly, was uncomfortable with the question. There were times (rare, to be sure) when Willie experienced painful feelings. Alone in his car he would put on a tape with "Earth Angel," their song, and he would weep. But most of the time, he was focused on holding his job and raising his children.*

Willie chose not to return to the support group because of the pressure he sensed to self-disclose about his feelings. In fact, one of the fundamental social rules about self-disclosure is the "rule of reciprocity" (our term)—if I tell you my feelings, you should tell me about your feelings. Instrumental grievers (assuming they are not introverts) are comfortable in reciprocating about issues and events but not about their innermost feelings. This hidden "rule of reciprocity" is illustrated by the following example.

> *Patricia found herself in the unenviable position of avoiding her closest friends. For years, the "Tuesday night group" had gathered at one of their homes (they rotated each week). They discussed their children, their husbands, books they had read, plans they had made. They mostly just enjoyed talking with each other. True, Patricia was a little uncomfortable whenever their talks seemed more "gossip" than discussion, but she looked forward to Tuesdays.*
>
> *Then Harold was diagnosed with a particularly virulent strain of melanoma. Four months later Patricia was a widow. After several weeks of focusing her energies on coping with a number of financial and legal issues created by Harold's death, she realized how lonely she felt and decided to resume her membership in the Tuesday night group.*
>
> *The pain of grief became topic of discussion. Patricia found herself reluctant to talk about her own feelings, yet tried to listen attentively as, in turn, each of her friends talked about their own painful feelings associated with past losses. Eventually, Patricia became very uncomfortable with the intense feelings shared by the other members of the group; she became even more uncomfortable at the not-so-subtle pressure to share her own feelings. At the conclusion of that first Tuesday meeting, one of her closest friends suggested that she should seek professional help to overcome her "denial," and to "open up and let it out."*

Confused about her reactions, Patricia did seek help and discovered, to her relief, that she was not "in denial" of her Harold's death; she was simply handling it differently. She chose not to return to the group and began seeking out and forming new friendships.

In summary, instrumental grievers do not like discussing their feelings. They may, however, be comfortable in disclosing their concerns about issues. Whether they choose to remain solitary or to socialize depends on their degree of shyness or extroversion. Hence, the instrumental griever's expression of his or her grief may, at first glance, appear to be a lack of expression. But instrumental grievers do express their grief. They may demonstrate feelings; they just don't show the depth and intensity of feelings that intuitive grievers do.

Also, like their intuitive counterparts who choose a primary strategy of centering on their grief experience, instrumental grievers express their grief through their choice of a primary adaptive strategy-active problem-solving.

Primary Adaptive Strategies: Directed Activity/Problem-solving

Since instrumental grievers convert more psychic energy into thinking rather than feeling, it is not surprising that they find expression for this energy by channeling it into activity. Becoming and remaining active are key features among the instrumental griever's adaptive strategies.

However, movement (or action) alone is usually not enough. Instrumental grievers adapt best to their losses through planned movements. These planned actions may accomplish any number of the following goals:

1. Action is a way that instrumental grievers sometimes channel excessive affective energy. However, it is important to remember that expressions of grief and adaptive strategies that are primarily driven by feelings are far more common among, and important to, intuitive grievers. Examples of using action to channel excess psychic energy include activities like running, weightlifting, martial arts, and "mindless" work like mowing grass or stacking wood. Less intense ways of displacing energy include needlepoint, knitting, sewing, gardening, painting, walking, and low-impact sports like golf or horseshoes.

After several years of treatments, remissions, and relapses, Jordan succumbed to her lymphoma. Her husband, Ken, had been at her side throughout the years of valiant struggle against the disease. After Jordan's death, Ken felt lost. He had devoted so much of his energy to caring for Jordan, he found himself experiencing moments of restlessness, or as he described it "cabin fever." Ken had always described himself as "low-key" and "not very emotional." Yet he found himself with feelings with which he had no previous experience. He could not cry, although there were times he thought he should. He tried talking to his friends about his feelings but as he described it, "I simply felt stupid talking about it. Talking didn't bring her back." The restlessness persisted. Since he did not have a job to return to (he was retired), Ken decided that he needed to do something to combat his discontent. He consulted with his minister, who suggested that he look into finding an outlet for his excess energy, perhaps a hobby.

Ken and Jordan had often camped together, especially after he had retired. Of course, Jordan's idea of camping was spending the evening quietly reading in their Winnebago while Ken's was to mingle with the other campers sharing their RV campground. As a widower, Ken found himself isolated from others. He craved human contact but wanted it to center on shared activities, not discussions about life without Jordan. He rejected the idea of camping alone since that had always been something he shared with his wife.

Eventually, his brother-in-law invited him to join a group that regularly went whitewater rafting. Ken agreed and, to his surprise, discovered that the physical challenges of rafting and the shared sense of danger and adventures with his fellow rafters left him feeling tired but content. He also recognized that he was embarking on a different path than the one he had shared with Jordan.

2. Activity is also used as a way to memorialize the deceased. Carving an urn, digging a grave, chiseling a tombstone, planting a memorial tree, and beginning a memorial fund or scholarship are just a few of the ways action becomes mourning. In particular, rituals surrounding the death may be used as outlets for emotional energy (see Chapter 9).

Mike's mother was worried about him. Although his father had died in a diving accident just three weeks earlier, Mike did not want to talk about his dad's loss. The 12-year-old boy had shown little emotion at his father's funeral and had rejected any offers of help or comfort from his mother and other family members and friends.

In fact, Mike's only expression of feeling was intense anger at his mother when she brought his father's ashes home in an expensive marble urn. That evening Mike went to his father's workshop, where he remained alone for several hours. When his mother questioned him about his activities, he maintained a sullen silence. He repeated this pattern for the next several days. Finally, Mike surprised his mother with the gift of a beautifully carved wooden urn. Together they placed his father's ashes into the urn. Afterwards, with tears on his cheeks, Mike read his favorite story that his father and he had shared, "Casey-at-the-Bat."

3. Solving problems created by or associated with the loss provides the instrumental griever with an effective outlet for action. Examples include:

(a) taking over a business left by the deceased,
(b) beginning or joining an organization promoting a cause associated with the death (e.g., MADD-Mothers Against Drunk Driving), or
(c) making restitution for damage or injury in the wake of the death.

One of the proudest moments in Ted's life was also fraught with trepidation. Ted experienced both on the day his daughter Karen received her driver's license. Karen had failed the driving portion of the driver's examination on her first and second attempts. It was Ted's gentle instruction and encouragement that gave Karen the courage to try a third time.

Two weeks later, tragedy struck. On the way home from after-school band practice, Karen lost control of her car, ran through a picket fence, and died instantly when her car struck a telephone pole. Ted was initially overwhelmed with a sense of confusion and numbness. He paced restlessly and could neither eat nor sleep. He also began blaming himself for Karen's death. Realizing that he was floundering, Ted made a conscious decision to survive his daughter's death. When his wife had died four years previously, Ted focused his energies on getting Karen and her younger brother the emotional support he believed he could not provide. He then directed his attention to the challenges of raising a 12-year-old daughter and 9-year-old son on his own.

Now Ted chose to deal with his grief by carefully rebuilding the fence destroyed in Karen's accident. After he explained his circumstances and gained the owner's permission to rebuild the fence, Ted purchased the necessary materials and began to work.

4. Activity becomes a way to restore normalcy and a sense of security in the wake of a loss. In particular, returning to work or to school, or completing a project interrupted by the loss are examples of this.

Jack was always helping somebody. When his best friend asked his help in repairing a leak in his roof Jack didn't hesitate. Tragically, Jack slipped while descending the ladder from the roof. His skull was crushed when he struck the concrete sidewalk below.

When his widowed mother, Becky, heard of his death, she felt numb with shock. Within an hour, her shock was replaced by an overwhelming sense of urgency to do something, anything. She temporarily closed the antique shop that she and Jack had run together and threw herself into making the funeral preparations. During the funeral, friends comforted her as she wept. Two days later, much to everyone's surprise, Becky reopened her shop. When friends expressed to her their concern at her quick return to work, Becky explained. "Jack was such a huge part of my life after his dad's death that I thought that I would miss him a little less if I surrounded myself with his memory. I feel as if Jack is still here."

Planned Activity as a Secondary Adaptive Strategy

Choosing an adaptive strategy that involves planned activity facilitates the expression of the instrumental griever's primary inner experience. It can afford secondary benefits as well. In addition to becoming an outlet for affective-driven energy, certain activities may also provide a way to express feelings, while maintaining mastery over them. Many instrumental grievers who have difficulty crying have discovered that certain experiences unrelated to their losses enable them to shed tears. In particular, watching certain movies seems to trigger such a release. Thus, grievers can control how their affective energy is expressed by discovering and pushing their own "buttons," or cues that are associated with tears. Shedding tears while watching a stirring moment on a television screen or in a darkened movie theatre permits instrumental grievers to experience and express their feelings, while remaining in control. Again, the reader is reminded that the ability of instrumental grievers to effectively master their feelings is largely due to their lesser capacity for intense feelings.

Additional Characteristics of Instrumental Grievers

In contrast to his or her intuitive counterpart, the instrumental griever experiences grief physically as augmented energy. This energy can take the form of restlessness or nervousness. It can heighten the griever's desire to "do something." Physical energy can also translate into arousal. However, instrumental grievers, unlike intuitive grievers, may not be consciously aware of feeling aroused. That is, they may report feeling calm when, in fact, their heart rate, respiration, and blood pressure all indicate a state of arousal. (This is discussed further in Chapter 6).

Instrumental grievers may become confused, disoriented, disorganized, and unable to concentrate. However, in contrast to the intuitive griever, these cognitive reactions are generally of a much shorter duration. This is because the instrumental griever is more adept at processing events cognitively than affectively.

Characteristics of Blended Grievers

Blended patterns have elements common to both instrumental and intuitive patterns, but with a greater emphasis on one or the other. Of course, the "pure" blended pattern would be a perfectly balanced combination of instrumental and intuitive grief. Just as pure intuitive and instrumental patterns are rare, so too is the perfect blended pattern. Since no one pattern is superior to the other, this includes the pure blended style. The reader will recall that it is the individual's choice of adaptive strategies and how these strategies fit with the various patterns that determine the eventual adjustment to the loss.

Earlier it was suggested that there are probably more blended grievers than intuitive or instrumental, with most leaning more toward the intuitive end of the spectrum. This should not suggest that blended/intuitive styles become the standard of healthy grief. It merely reflects what patterns dominate at this point in time.

Since blended grievers experience and express grief in ways characteristic of both patterns it follows that blended grievers would need a greater variety of adaptive strategies to select from. Since these grievers straddle both instrumental and intuitive experiences they may already possess a larger repertoire of strategies. Of course, the opposite might also be true: the blended griever whose experiences are widely varied and whose store-house of adaptive strategies is severely limited. Thus being a blended griever has it strengths as well as its weaknesses.

Patterns of Grief and Anticipatory Grief

The literature presupposes that being forewarned of a potential loss may affect the quality and intensity of one's grief. There remains, however, some question as to just how anticipation of a loss affects post-death grief and what terms best describe this phenomenon (see Rando, 1986).

The meaning attached to a particular loss still remains the most important variable in determining the character of the grief response, including choice of adaptive strategies, *within the bounds of a particular individual's pattern of grief.* Intuitive grievers will still grieve intuitively and instrumental grievers instrumentally whether the loss is sudden or unexpected. What will most likely differ is the general strength of their responses and how it affects their adaptive strategies.

Where sudden or unexpected deaths seem to exert their greatest influence is among blended grievers. The following example illustrates the impact of anticipatory grief (or mourning, or bereavement) on the blended pattern.

> Susan remained calm and objective while caring for her mother during her mother's long battle with ovarian cancer. Although she was distressed by her mother's apparent physical discomfort, she kept her concerns and feelings to herself. Susan experienced satisfaction in her role as caregiver and found her mother's death a godsend. Following the funeral, which she had arranged, Susan spent several months settling her mother's estate. While she missed her mother, there were only a few times she openly wept.
>
> Three years later, Susan's response to the accidental drowning of her favorite 13-year-old nephew shocked her family and friends. When she learned of his death she felt shocked and numb. She then became disoriented and struggled to keep busy caring for her three teenage children. During the nephew's funeral Susan suddenly burst into tears and rushed out of the church. She became listless and withdrawn for several weeks after the death. She finally attended her church-sponsored support group and shared how upset she was at the unfairness of the death, how much her nephew had to live for, and how much she would miss watching him mature and develop into a young man. Her mood improved and she began to feel more in control.

Susan responded to her mother's death in an instrumental way while her grief over her nephew's death reflected the intuitive pattern. What differed was her interpretation of the two losses. Her mother's death, while difficult, came at the end of a long life and released her mother from her suffering. Her nephew's death seemed unnatural and prematurely ended a promising life. Here it was her perception of the unexpected nature of the loss coupled with the death of someone so young that channeled Susan's grief more toward the affective modality and away from the cognitive. She also chose different strategies to adapt to her losses, goal-directed activity in the case of her mother and "going with" and sharing her feelings following the death of her nephew. Given Susan's wide range of experiences and expressions, we would conclude that she was a blended griever.

Summary

Intuitive and instrumental grievers are often more alike than not, yet there are important differences between them.

Intuitive Pattern:
1. Feelings are intensely experienced.
2. Expressions such as crying and lamenting mirror inner experience.
3. Successful adaptive strategies facilitate the experience and expression of feelings.
4. There are prolonged periods of confusion, inability to concentrate, disorganization, and disorientation.
5. Physical exhaustion and/or anxiety may result.

Instrumental Pattern:
1. Thinking is predominant to feeling as an experience; feelings are less intense.
2. There is general reluctance to talk about feelings.
3. Mastery of oneself and the environment are most important.
4. Problem-solving as a strategy enables mastery of feelings and control of the environment.
5. Brief periods of cognitive dysfunction are common.
6. Energy levels are enhanced, but symptoms of general arousal go unnoticed.

Again, patterns occur along a continuum. Those grievers near the center who demonstrate a blending of the two styles experience a variety of the elements of both patterns, although one is somewhat more pronounced than the other. This suggests a need for more choices among adaptive strategies than the griever whose style is more toward the extremes.

CHAPTER

Dissonant Responses

What happens when grievers consistently choose adaptive strategies that do not "fit" or complement their style of grief? Is this tantamount to "complicated mourning?" In this chapter maladaptive responses to loss as "dissonant" are identified. In some cases, these reactions may become semi-permanent ways of responding to loss and may sometimes serve as cornerstones for complicated mourning. This chapter begins by looking at the initial responses that may cloud the distinction between intuitive and instrumental grievers. Again, remember that patterns exist on a continuum, and those nearer the center are a blending of both styles.

☐ Initial Responses

It is important to remember that, with a few rare exceptions, the redirection of psychic energy from the griever's initial pattern of behavior to his or her enduring pattern of adaptation to loss occurs gradually and over time. The speed with which energy is channeled into the pattern that is customary may vary as an individual develops and matures. It may also vary from situation to situation. Thus, it may be difficult to categorize an individual griever's global response immediately after a loss as either intuitive or instrumental.

While models may vary somewhat, most of the literature identifying reactions to death-related loss presupposes an initial period of disorganization (see, for instance, Bowlby, 1980; Rando, 1993; Worden, 1991), where responses may include shock, numbness, hysteria, and confusion. These initial features are especially evident following sudden and/or traumatic losses. Taken together, these responses may represent an atypical expression of grief for a particular griever. In other words, initial responses may not be indicative of the individual's customary pattern of grieving. During this period, it may be virtually impossible to distinguish instrumental grievers from intuitive grievers or blended grievers.

Intuitive grievers may initially focus on suppressing intense, painful feelings and controlling their grief-related behavior. The following case illustrates how an individual's initial responses may reflect adaptive strategies typical of the other pattern of grieving, yet differ from his or her enduring pattern of intuitive grieving.

> *When Glen's 24-year-old daughter was killed in a boating accident he was overwhelmed by pain. His previous experience with bereavement included the losses of both of his parents, a younger brother, and a stillborn infant son. Through these encounters, Glen had learned that for him, grief was a profoundly painful, overwhelming feeling experience. Glen's eventual adjustment to his losses required that he focus and refocus on his feelings and that he share these feelings with others. Glen described himself as highly emotional and very sensitive.*
>
> *Despite experiencing crushing agony, Glen took charge, as events unfolded over the next several days. He made the initial identification of his daughter's body, arranged her funeral, and provided transportation for the scores of relatives and friends who traveled from a distance. He comforted his wife and two children and cooperated with the police investigation into his daughter's accidental death. He later identified his strategy for coping with his daughter's death as "absolutely shutting down my feelings."*
>
> *It was not until the funeral was over and the relatives and friends were ferried back to local airports that Glen, as he described it, "imploded." He became dejected, and cried incessantly. He withdrew from others and contemplated suicide. Finally, he joined the local chapter of The Compassionate Friends, a support group for bereaved parents, and began his long, torturous journey to recovery. Today, he is a local chapter president of The Compassionate Friends.*

It may take hours or even days for the person's true pattern of grieving to dominate his or her behaviors. In Glen's case, he might easily have been identified as an instrumental griever when, in fact, he had always followed the intuitive pattern for grieving.

Glen illustrates how intuitive grievers may initially choose adaptive strategies that typify an instrumental response to allow them to manage both their experiences and expressions of grief. These grievers may choose to manage their feelings by avoiding certain thoughts. Many grievers choosing this form of adapting effectively "dose" feelings by managing pain-eliciting thoughts (Shuchter & Zisook, 1993). They accomplish this by selectively displacing some conscious thoughts into their subconscious. This pain inventory remains in subconscious storage until they choose to reintroduce some or all of its contents into consciousness, re-experiencing the affective component of their grief. This usually occurs at times and places that do not interfere with the griever's self-defined goals and tasks.

Other ways that grievers may attempt to distract themselves include forcing painful thoughts from consciousness and substituting pleasant memories. In fact, it is the effective management of memories and thoughts that enables most grievers, regardless of their pattern, to eventually adapt to their altered worlds.

Generally, intuitive grievers revert to their customary pattern of grieving and choice of primary adaptive strategies—in this case, going with their intense feelings and openly expressing those feelings.

Instrumental grievers use these same strategies (dosing, distraction), but are generally less conscious of choosing them and invest less energy in maintaining them. Instrumental grievers naturally perceive and interact with the world through their cognitive systems. Readers should recall that however similar their behaviors are, intuitive grievers differ from their instrumental counterparts in the relative intensity of their feelings and in their motivation for dealing with their feelings.

Whereas intuitive grievers may express stoicism in the face of loss, instrumental grievers may show evidence of feelings such as crying. They may also show signs of cognitive impairment, becoming confused, disoriented, and disorganized. Eventually, instrumental grievers' cognitive control, their desire for mastery, and the muted intensity of their feelings lead to their adapting strategies usually identified with the instrumental style. Such was the case of Jim in the following illustration:

Jim was holding Alice's hand when she died after a long fight with lymphoma. He was surprised at his intense feelings of grief since he had been anticipating this moment for months. When the hospice nurse arrived just a few minutes later, she found Jim sobbing. He looked up at her and said, "I don't know what I should do." She replied that she would take care of everything and then began making the necessary calls. Fifteen minutes later, she was surprised when Jim walked into the kitchen and said, "Can I fix you a cup of coffee?" He made the coffee and then sat down and asked the nurse whom she had called and what arrangements had been made. As she described it later at the hospice interdisciplinary team meeting, "It was like he threw a switch that said 'Okay, I'm over that and back to my old self.'"

By the time the funeral staff arrived to remove Alice's body, Jim was fully back in charge. He insisted on carrying Alice down the three flights of stairs to the waiting vehicle. He then threw himself into whatever needed to be done. He contacted relatives, cleaned the house, and ordered food for the anticipated onslaught of relatives and friends. He arranged for the medical supplies company to pick up Alice's hospital bed. He did not cry again. He returned to work the day after the funeral. He politely refused offers of help from the hospice bereavement coordinator, although he did have lunch with the nurse, where they laughed and shared funny stories about Alice.

One year later, Jim became a hospice volunteer and arranged several fund-rais-
ing events. He chose, however, not to be involved in direct patient care.

In this case, if the hospice nurse had left before witnessing Jim's transformation, she would have assumed that Jim would be having a very rough
time of it and, even if he refused it, would probably need whatever help
could be given to him. Jim's initial choice of discharging his feelings as an
adaptive strategy would have identified him as an intuitive griever, when
in fact, he was most comfortable with resolving losses by mastering his
feelings and remaining active.

☐ Dissonant Patterns

Some grievers may be unable to alter their initial strategies; it may be
maladaptive for these grievers to persist in managing or giving into their
feelings and behaviors beyond the initial period of loss. These grievers are
not only expressing grief differently than it is experienced, they are truly
at war with themselves.

For example, male intuitive grievers are often at odds with societal norms
for gender-stereotyped behaviors. For the male intuitive griever whose
identity is determined solely by societal stereotypes, intense feelings of
grief are more than a mere inconvenience; they represent a threat to the
Self. For these grievers, their need to express their feelings and share
them with others is overshadowed by a rigid definition of manliness. In
disenfranchising their own grief, these unfortunates may contribute to
the stereotype of the poker-faced male griever. Being at odds with one's
feelings has its consequences, and those who choose this method of coping might best heed the warning implicit in an ancient Chinese proverb:
Expression of feelings leads to momentary pain and long-term relief; suppression leads to momentary relief and long-term pain.

The term "dissonant" is used to describe a persistent way of expressing
grief that is at odds with the griever's primary internal experience. The
choice of this term is consistent with the theorizing of Festinger (1957),
who defined one's awareness of a contradiction among two or more elements of the mind and the resulting discomfort as "cognitive dissonance."
In most cases, individuals are motivated to behave and think in ways that
reduce dissonance. This is why most grievers experience disharmony at
one time or another in their grieving, yet eventually achieve resolution
through expressing their experiences of grief. Unfortunately, for some,
this lack of harmony between an inner state and an outer expression
persists, resulting in dissonance.

Dissonant Response: Suppressing Feelings

Earlier it was discussed how grievers manage their expressions of grief through the "dosing" feelings. This usually involves manipulation of thoughts and memories, i.e., cognitive management. For instrumental grievers, the management of their thoughts and memories becomes a cornerstone of their adaptive strategy. Since most of the psychic energy is channeled into the cognitive rather than the affective realm, instrumental grievers do not need to re-channel as much energy from other realms of inner experience to manage their cognitions as do intuitive grievers. This allows instrumental grievers to harness more energy for activities—both planned and unplanned. Instrumental grievers commonly employ dosing and other cognitive strategies, such as repression as they adapt to their losses.

On the other hand, intuitive grievers are usually not as adept at managing their cognitions; thus, they expend more energy reining in their feelings. As seen previously by Glen's experience after his daughter's death, this can be an effective strategy if employed temporarily. Unfortunately, some grievers confuse dosing with suppression and attempt to permanently contain their strong feelings. (Here the distinction between "suppression" from "repression" is made. Repression is seen as an autonomous way of adapting to loss; suppression is seen as the ongoing conscious and deliberate act of avoiding painful feelings by pushing painful thoughts aside).

This is risky business, particularly if the grief is intuitive—that is, of primarily a feeling nature. The more intuitive the griever, the greater the danger. Thus, perpetual suppression of feelings, where the griever's expression of grief is incongruent with his or her inner experiences, becomes a way to avoid the reality of the loss as well as a way to avoid feelings. As the following case illustrates, self-deception extracts a price from the griever's mental and emotional health.

> After 12 years of loving companionship, Tim decided it was time to say goodbye to his canine best friend, Zeus. Over time, Zeus had grown increasingly feeble. For the previous several months, Tim had been forced to lift the dog's hindquarters off the ground, so that Zeus could stagger into the yard to relieve himself. Zeus became disinterested in food. Then the dreaded day arrived, when Zeus had his first accident in the house. After three consecutive days of cleaning up messes and carefully bathing Zeus, Tim and his wife reluctantly decided that the dog's quality of life did not warrant the additional time with Zeus that Tim and his wife desired.
>
> Tim carefully and deliberately arranged to take Zeus to his veterinarian the following morning. Both Tim and his wife remained at Zeus' side, stroking him, and talking to him as the vet administered the drug. As Zeus drew his last breath, Tim

began sobbing. He cried uncontrollably, unwilling to leave his companion behind. It was not until he was seated behind the steering wheel that he forcibly regained his composure. The rest of that day and into the evening, Tim distracted himself from thinking about Zeus. He removed the food and water bowls and stored the collars and leads.

During the next several weeks, Tim ejected memories of the events at the vet's office, replacing those images with images of Zeus as a young dog, frolicking on the beach. He also increased his daily consumption of alcohol from his customary two beers to a six-pack and began avoiding his friends. Unfortunately, Tim never allowed himself to review Zeus' last months and moments. He denied himself the opportunity of realizing that he had given his old friend the greatest gift he could— release from his suffering.

Two months later at his insistence, Tim and his wife began visiting kennels, and after several months of careful researching, searching, and planning, they introduced a new puppy into their home. However, Tim could not bring himself to accept the new puppy. He would not help choose a name, avoided spending time alone with the dog, and declined to participate in any of the normal grooming and care activities that had cemented his bond to Zeus.

Eventually, Tim's wife confronted him with his lack of interest in the puppy, and the resulting conflict stressed the marriage. When the puppy died from an accidental poisoning, Tim was initially relieved, but then experienced intense feelings of guilt and began withdrawing from others. He drank himself to sleep every night. At his wife's prodding, Tim sought counseling for his depression. In reviewing his previous losses (father, high school best friend), Tim recognized that he had always allowed himself the luxury of his feelings and had sought the support of friends and family during times of emotional crisis. Eventually, Tim began to understand how concerned he was that his friends and coworkers would find his intense grief over a dog "silly." He also gained insight into his habitual ways of maintaining the approval of others at the expense of his own feelings. Confronting his unresolved grief over Zeus and expressing his deep feelings over the loss finally bore fruit and led to Tim's consequent recovery.

In Tim's case, one can trace the redirection of his affective energy to a cognitive strategy (avoiding all reminders of the loss, suppressing feelings) as he began removing all of Zeus' possessions. Although choosing suppression as an adaptive strategy may have been wise initially (enabling Tim to drive home), it soon disenfranchised him from his true experience of grief, which remained primarily affective. As Tim suppressed more and more affective energy, he estranged himself from his grief and established the enduring pattern of avoidance and suppression for adapting to his loss—in this case, Tim's grief became dissonant.

Intuitive grievers adapt to their losses by actively experiencing and expressing their feelings. Complicated grief responses may result if the intuitive griever's initial adaptive strategies, which temporarily enabled them to control their feelings and behaviors, persist.

Instrumental grievers, too, must find ways to express the grief energy experienced as feelings. They are often at a disadvantage since their strengths usually do not include being comfortable with an uninhibited expression of feelings. Whatever the limits of an individual's capacity to experience vivid feelings, that person will become increasingly uncomfortable as the ceiling of that boundary is approached. This fact reinforces the notion that the experiences and expressions of grief exist on a continuum.

This may severely limit the choices of secondary adaptive strategies. For instance, if the only way an instrumental griever has learned to express feelings is through anger, he or she will most likely find himself or herself in difficulty with his or her environment. Stated differently, what is initially a time-limited pattern of grieving may become an ongoing dissonant response to a specific loss.

What could motivate a griever to ignore his or her disharmonious behavior? Are certain people predisposed to use suppression as a response to bereavement? The answer may lie in exploring the concept of "impression management" (Goffman, 1959).

Preexisting Pattern: Image Management

Comparing Tim's responses to Glen's (see above) reveals that the key difference between the brief and benign nature of Glen's efforts to suppress his feelings and Tim's ongoing, deleterious attempts to accomplish the same, is that of motive. Whereas Glen temporarily suspended his feelings to handle the immediate aftermath of his wife's death, Tim was concerned with how others would view his grief over a dog. Tim was responding in his habitual way of needing to control the impression that he presented to the world.

Thus, rather than temporarily suspend their customary pattern of grieving in order to accomplish necessary tasks, some grievers may be motivated by a desire to preserve their self-image, especially the image they display to the public. These "image managers" carefully screen their behavior for content that corresponds with the image the person believes is needed at the time. Despite primarily experiencing grief as painful feelings, these grievers cope by suppressing and disguising their feelings.

The concept of image management is consonant with the research on impression management, which is defined as ". . . attempts to control images that are projected in real or imagined social situations" (Schlenker, 1980, p. 6). While most people are motivated by the twin needs of getting along with others and thinking well of themselves, some people carry this to extremes. Individuals who consistently try to control others' reactions to them are identified as "high self-monitors" (Snyder, 1974).

Whereas "low self-monitors" maintain consistency in their behavior from one audience to another, high self-monitors modify their behavior to please their current audience. As one might expect, high self-monitors care more about social norms and conformity. Thus, image managers are grievers who are high self-monitors and whose outward reactions to their losses are motivated by their desire to control how others think of and respond to them.

This may be particularly true of the male intuitive griever, who may tailor his behaviors to match gender role stereotypes that he believes will match the expectations of his immediate audience. For example, the male image manager might hide his sorrow and grief from those he believes would judge the open expression of these feelings as weak or effeminate. He might also suppress his feelings in order to maintain his own self-defined image to himself. This is an example of extreme self-deception.

Women, too, can be image managers. In fact, if the motive is to portray oneself in control of a situation, gender matters less than the need to be seen a certain way. Recall that image managers carefully screen and guard against any behaviors that they believe may give another a "bad" impression of them. Bereavement presents a formidable challenge to high self-monitors.

Suppressing powerful feelings requires constant vigilance and conscious control of all publicly observed actions—a taxing task at best! Some grievers expend huge amounts of energy in an effort to preserve their highly prized public image. Public expressions of grief are carefully tailored to the situation and are often counter to how the griever actually feels. If stoicism and self-control are deemed appropriate at the time, the griever becomes a true member of the "stiff upper lip" crowd.

This is not to suggest that image managers are the only grievers influenced by their immediate environment. Even the most extreme intuitive or instrumental grievers sometimes base their actions on the people around them at the time. The difference is in whether one is primarily motivated by a consistent desire for approval from others or driven by a need to respond effectively to specific environmental responsibilities. While some grievers may initially respond in ways not consistent with their patterns, most eventually reestablish harmony between their behaviors and their internal representations of themselves. Image managers are social chameleons; their public personas are transitory and their grief behaviors are responsive to whatever role they are playing for others.

While image managers may use some of the same strategies for managing affective expression (dosing, distraction) as other grievers, they differ in two ways. First, image managers are motivated to protect their self-images, while the others manage feelings in order to accomplish specific tasks (childcare, work environment). Second, image managers tend to continue to suppress their feelings even when others are not present, attempting to stem the tide of affective energy that needs expression. In other words, the image manager eventually seeks to hide his or her true feelings from his or her potentially most dangerous critic—himself or herself.

Since image managers depend on others to define appropriate behaviors for them, they are not grounded by a secure sense of identity. Consequently, they often experience anxiety that they carefully hide from others. When death takes a loved one, it often robs them of a primary source of self-definition. This often exacerbates their anxiety and generates intense feelings of pain and loneliness.

Unfortunately, image managers have learned only to channel energy into maintaining their public persona. With most of their efforts focused on their projected selves, they are often ineffective problem-solvers. They have little reserve energy with which to assimilate and adapt to their changed worlds.

When an image manager finds that specific situations, people, and places threaten his or her control over feelings, he or she will avoid them. This is not the same as *temporarily* shielding oneself from painful feelings. Many grievers—both intuitive and instrumental—employ avoidance as a temporary solution and are usually motivated by a need to accomplish a specific task. However, the image manager evades certain things to avoid damaging the image he or she is trying to project to others. In some cases, these may be people who previously played a central role in the griever's life. Unfortunately, some image managers not only lose the support and comfort that others may provide, but also terminate lifelong and important relationships.

Similarly, some image managers avoid feeling-eliciting situations by remaining alone. They do not choose solitude as a way of harnessing energy to problem-solve or engage in mourning-related activities; rather, they shun situations that threaten their control over their feelings of anxiety, anguish, and anger. Again, they are not consciously choosing to redirect their feelings into adjusting to their changed circumstances; they are hiding those impulses, which might overwhelm them and tarnish the image they want to project.

One strategy image managers select to control their public expression of grief is to outwardly deny the importance of the loss. Unfortunately, this public denial may extend to a private denial of the significance of the loss—a true act of self-deception. Although using self-deception occasionally may have a role in maintaining one's self-image, it is a risky mechanism to employ, especially for the individual motivated by a desire for social approval. For example, pretending that the death of one's parent is not significant because "they were old and sick" can result in a denigration of the relationship one had with the parent. Because the image manager already has a weakened sense of Self, redefining a relationship to enable him or her to control their public expressions of grief may deepen the estrangement from his or her true feelings about the deceased.

Another way of suppressing feelings is to anesthetize them. For most people this means using mood-altering substances. Again, there is a difference between image management and the initial numbness that is characteristic of an uncomplicated grief response. Although there are a variety of both prescription and nonprescription drugs that can generate the quiescence associated with a more desirable feeling state, the most popular choice—alcohol—is also the easiest to obtain (see Sidebar 4.1).

Why are most image managers—especially male grievers—found toward the intuitive end of the continuum? Why are there not more instrumental image managers?

1. There are more intuitive grievers and blended-intuitive grievers in the population to begin with.
2. Managing one's expression of feelings and projecting a sense of control remain consistent with the male role.
3. Over time, intuitive grievers may lose support for their public expressions of grief. As others tire of comforting them, they may be forced into an image management role.

In summary, most image managers experience their losses in the affective domain, but because of their habitual need to seek approval of others they are burdened immensely by their grief as they struggle to hide their true feelings. This differs from another dissonant response in which grievers may not actively attempt to alter their expression of grief, but may experience intense guilt because they believe that their inner experience and outer expression should be different from what they are.

Dissonant Response: Penitence

Whereas image managers are usually intuitive grievers who hide their feelings from others by censoring their expressions of grief, "penitents" are often instrumental grievers who condemn themselves for not having feelings to hide! The two responses are outwardly similar except that in the first, grievers experience anxiety at the potential failure to cover up their feelings, while in the latter grievers experience intense guilt because they cannot pretend to have feelings that they believe they should have. They also differ in that image managers are simply continuing a habitual way of handling general stress, while bereavement may precipitate the inner crisis of the penitent.

Sidebar 4.1. Alcohol: Balm or Bane

While intense debate has often centered on using psychoactive medications to treat normal bereavement (see Rando, 1993) there is generally a consensus that alcohol is the most frequently chosen agent for self-medication, especially among men (Hughes & Fleming, 1991; Parkes & Weiss, 1983; Stroebe & Stroebe, 1993). What remains clouded is the question of when, outside of the disease of alcoholism, is imbibing either help or hindrance to the griever?

For the past 5,000 years humankind has been participating in a largely uncontrolled natural experiment of the relationship between alcohol and health, with few conclusions reached. Partly, this is due to ambiguous counsel from normally unimpeachable sources. For instance, as Noah stepped from the Ark God bid him to plant vineyards, and Proverbs (31:6,7) reads:

> Give strong drink unto him that is ready to perish,
> and wine unto those that be of heavy hearts.
> Let him drink, and forget his poverty,
> and remember his misery no more.

Of course there is admonition to the contrary:

> For he shall be great in the sight of the Lord,
> and shall drink neither wine nor strong drink,
> and he shall be filled with the Holy Ghost,
> even from his mother's womb. Luke (1:15)

Likewise, advice about using alcoholic products from the American Medical Association (AMA) is equally ambivalent. For instance, the AMA warns that drinking can cause a whole series of health problems including heart disease, certain types of cancers, liver disease, and of course, alcoholism. At the same time, a recent issue of JAMA (January 6, 1999) included a finding that moderate consumption of alcohol actually reduces the risk of stroke and heart disease. (This effect is not limited to red wine as previously thought). However, there is little debate that habitually consuming too much alcohol is not a good thing.

In our own work we have found that people who already drink alcohol tend to increase their intake following the death of a loved one. This behavior does not seem to be related to any particular pattern. Different grievers may use alcohol in different ways. For example, intuitive grievers may use alcohol to anesthetize grieving, while to instrumental grievers drinking might be an activity. To dissonant grievers, alcohol may view the release of pent-up emotion. For the vast majority of grievers, however, alcohol consumption returns to preloss levels within a year of the death. While we would not recommend beginning or increasing drinking, we are not clear about whether alcohol interferes with grieving or simply makes it more bearable. Stay tuned.

Unfortunately, some penitents attempt to conjure up such feelings by using various substances, such as alcohol. Here, alcohol is employed in an attempt to elicit feelings versus being used to numb or suppress feelings. Other penitents share concerns that are common to image managers and may avoid or withdraw from people. The difference, of course, is that penitents fear that others will discover that they have no feelings to express! This may be especially true of the female instrumental griever, as seen in the following case.

Anyone who knew Shirley described her as "low key." She was also very bright, finishing at the top of her graduating class from Georgia Tech. She began her career as a chemical engineer for a Japanese firm. Within six years she had been promoted several times and became a senior vice president of her company. She then met Marshall.

She and Marshall were opposites: he was moody, passionate, and excitable; she was stable, cerebral, and controlled. In fact, when she calmly accepted his proposal for marriage, he became upset that she wasn't more "excited."

After three years of marriage, Shirley finally gave into Marshall's pleas for a baby. Although she was happy being pregnant, Shirley couldn't begin to match Marshall's euphoria. His recently widowed mother was equally excited, believing that her first grandchild would give her a reason to go on living.

Tragedy struck when the baby's umbilical cord wrapped around its throat. It was born dead.

As one could expect, Marshall and his mother were devastated, weeping constantly. Shirley was hurt and disappointed by her loss, but reasoned that she and Marshall could have another child. Marshall and his mother were aghast at her lack of reaction. Even many of her coworkers, especially the women, suggested to Shirley that she seek help for her repressed grief. Her mother-in-law refused to speak to her. When Marshall threatened to leave her, she began to wonder and feel guilt at her own lack of feeling. She found that being with others exacerbated her guilt so she began avoiding people. She also discovered that after two large glasses of wine, she would become depressed and begin to cry. Soon, two glasses of wine became three, and then four. Although he at first encouraged her drinking since it enabled her to "feel," Marshall became alarmed as her drinking increased. She was also confronted at her office with her frequent lapses in judgment. Eventually, Marshall, along with her employer, convinced her to enter an alcohol rehabilitation center. Fortunately, one of her therapists recognized her as an instrumental griever and was able to validate Martha's tempered feelings as normal for her. Two years later, she and Marshall had another baby and the family is still intact. Sadly, the mother-in-law withdrew from her son and her new grandson as she had from Shirley.

Although she had never experienced intense feelings, it was not until her baby's death and the responses from her family and friends that she became "penitent."

Male instrumental grievers are also vulnerable to excessive self-criticism as highlighted by the following.

As his wife, Helen, lay dying, Peter grew increasingly alarmed at his own lack of feelings about her impending death. He began experiencing a profound sense of guilt. Peter's guilt deepened, when Helen herself accused him of not loving her. She, too, could not understand how he could calmly sit by her bed as she wrestled with her anxieties about dying and her grief at having to say goodbye. As he searched his soul, Peter realized that he had never felt that deeply about either of his parents' deaths. Consequently, he began to drink more heavily, as he later described it "to feel something." The alcohol relaxed him but did not generate any feelings other than additional guilt about his drinking. Peter asked for, and received a referral to a counselor from the hospice providing services to Helen and him.

Peter shared his sense of guilt with the counselor. Rather then focus on how Peter felt, the counselor asked Peter to describe what he was doing for Helen. As it turned out, he was doing practically everything! Peter cooked Helen's meals, changed and washed her linens, managed her medications, and cleaned her room. He provided personal care as well, including washing Helen's hair, ferrying her to the bathroom, and when there were accidents (and there were many) wiping and washing her bottom.

Peter's sigh of relief was clearly audible when, with the counselor's assistance, he finally realized that he was expressing his love and concern by "solving problems" rather than by expressing feelings.

What is so remarkable about Peter's case is how blind he was to the significance of his caring actions toward Helen. Peter did not have or share deep feelings, yet he tenderly performed tasks that most others would find repugnant.

Identifying Dissonance

When does a response become dissonant? Without knowing the individual's history and patterns of behavior it is difficult to identify dissonance. Often, grievers themselves will recognize the clash between their feelings and their behaviors.

In general, the twin compasses of movement and direction may serve as beacons of adaptation. For example, some grievers become "stuck" in their grief. Examples include image managers who do not find appropriate ways of discharging affective energy and penitents who become mired in guilt. And while the path from acknowledging a loss to a final reconciliation is rarely direct, there is an overall progression. Often, others may notice improvement before the grievers themselves. In short, a recovery that becomes stalled for an extended period, or a pronounced regression that cannot be attributed to the usual causes (anniversary dates, specific events, additional losses, and the like), may signal a dissonant response. In particular, any behaviors that interfere with the overall health and functioning of the individual should be suspect and viewed as possible indicators of a dissonant response (see Sidebar 4.2).

To summarize, image managers act in ways to suppress or avoid their true feelings, while penitents experience guilt because they don't have feelings they believe that they should. Both of these responses represent immature or maladaptive strategies and, if persistent, are dissonant ways of responding to losses. It is important to explore a griever's motivation for responding in a dissonant fashion. While image managers and penitents are motivated by the fear of damaging their public and private self-images, other dissonant responses may represent attempts to avoid accepting the reality that a loss has occurred. This presents an interesting question: When does a dissonant response become complicated mourning?

☐ Complicated Mourning

Therese Rando's remarkable text, *Treatment of Complicated Mourning*, remains the standard for the field. Rando (1993) defined complicated mourning as ". . . some compromise, distortion, or failure of one or more of the six 'R' processes of mourning" (p. 149). Rando's "R" processes is looked at

---

Sidebar 4.2. Grief and Health Promotion

Stroebe and Stroebe's (1993) longitudinal research has found that men may be more at risk for health difficulties during the course of bereavement. That research looked at gender rather than grieving patterns. It is difficult to determine, therefore, what patterns may truly incur more of a health risk. Nevertheless, Carverhill's (1997) suggestion that therapists promote health with male grievers is sound advice, regardless of the individual's grief pattern. Both Worden (1991) and Rando (1993) have theorized that conversion reactions, where grief manifests itself in another way such as illness, often occur when other responses are deemed unsuitable and blocked. Dissonant patterns, particularly since affect is suppressed, may be especially vulnerable to health problems.

But the very experience of grief threatens health. Grief and the inherent change accompanying loss generate enormous stress. Eating and nutritional patterns as well as exercise regimens and adherence to medical treatments may suffer. Counselors are wise to assess changes in health, alterations in daily routines, and to suggest to clients the prudence of a health examination with a physician who both knows the patient's medical history as well as their current status, and who is aware of the health risks inherent in bereavement.

in Chapter Two. Rando further explicates complicated mourning as hinging on the mourner's ". . . attempts to do two things: (a) deny, repress, or avoid aspects of the loss, its pain, and the full realization of its implications for the mourner, and (b) hold on to and avoid relinquishing the lost loved one" (p. 149). While every dissonant response does not lead to complicated mourning syndrome, many do. In this respect, dissonant responses may be precursors to complicated mourning.

A dissonant response represents the griever's failure to effectively discharge grief energy over time. Since it requires energy to restrain energy, dissonant responses may delay or inhibit the griever from resolving his or her losses. This is especially true of the image manager who consciously suppresses and avoids deep loss-related feelings.

Dissonant responses meet Rando's requirement of avoiding aspects of the loss, particularly the pain. These responses may also represent a failure on the griever's part to complete Worden's (1991) second task of experiencing the pain. Recall, however, that complicated mourning must involve the griever's refusal to let go of the lost love. Not all dissonant grievers are motivated by their desire to cling to the deceased. As seen previously, some image managers are motivated to protect only their public personas. While this may rob them of the opportunity for comfort and support, it is not necessarily a way of clinging to the deceased or avoiding the reality of the death. Penitents, too, may experience self-doubt and self-condemnation at their perceived lack of feeling but not deny the reality of their loss.

Other dissonant grievers may suppress their thoughts and feelings to avoid acknowledging the reality and finality of the loss. For instance, image managers may continue their deceptions even absent of an audience. And some grievers use penitence as a way to generate discomfort, viewing their pain as the only link they may have to the deceased. These grievers fit the definition of complicated mourning.

☐ Summary

Since it is natural for an organism to return to a state of homeostasis, grieving becomes an adaptive response that attempts to adjust to the external and internal changes wrought by a loss. Unfortunately, these adaptive strategies do not guarantee success (see Sidebar 4.3). By choosing a strategy that permits an unfettered expression of grief congruent with the inner experiences of loss, the griever can promote healing and recovery. Likewise, persistent incongruity between the individual's inner experiences and his outward expressions of grief often inhibit recovery and increases the griever's vulnerability to complicated forms of mourning. However, choosing an adaptive strategy congruent with inner experience does not necessarily guarantee success; even effective strategies fail if the individual does not possess the necessary skills to implement them.

Sidebar 4.3. Grieving and Violence

In some cultures or even subcultures, the grieving rules may allow or even encourage violence as an adaptive strategy. For example, in certain cultures or subcultures, there may be norms that allow "blood feuds" or encourage revenge slayings. Here, the death of someone by violence necessitates taking another's life. That person might be the suspected perpetrator of the initial act, a member of their family or group, or perhaps any bystander.

Barrett (1997), too, notes the relationship of homicide violence as an expression of grief in subcultures of urban adolescent males. He emphasizes that in such subcultures, violence becomes a rite of mourning when the violent death of a friend or family member occurs. In this culture, the retaliatory violence has the same role as other mourning rituals, that is, it reasserts control, expresses respect for the deceased, reaffirms the loyalty of the group, and allows the ventilation of feelings such as anger.

Parkes (1996a), in his research on violence in Rwanda, speculates that such violence may arise when affect is repressed as is the case in Rwandan society. However, both anecdotal evidence as well as Barrett's (1997) research suggest the answer may be more culturally complex. In an essay, the rapper Ice T (1995) describes the violence evident in his community of South Central Los Angeles:

When you see these drive-bys and kids are hitting five or six people on the street, they are retaliating for the murder of one of their boys. I've seen crying men enter cars and when the doors shut, they go out and murder (p. 180).

Perhaps in cultures where violence is an accepted form of expression, it can serve instrumental or intuitive grievers equally well. For those with an intuitive pattern it allows ventilation of affect. For instrumental grievers, it offers action as a way to reassert a sense of control. Even dissonant grievers can find a culturally acceptable way, consistent with the male role, to ventilate at least one acceptable feeling—anger. In fact, one can speculate that violence, for that reason, is a likely response of grievers with dissonant patterns. Their affect can be channeled to anger and discharged through violence. The answer to violence as an expression of grief may lie less in changing the individual's way of adapting to loss, and more in constraining and ultimately changing cultural norms that allow or encourage violence.

PATHWAYS
TO THE PATTERNS

Why are some people more instrumental than intuitive in their grief, while others are the opposite? Why isn't everyone a true blended griever, that is, being equally instrumental and intuitive in his or her grief? In the next section, several potential answers to these questions are offered. In Chapter 5, an outline is given for a theoretical basis for the differences between patterns of grief based on the distribution and final expression of grief-created psychic energy. In Chapter 6, the role played by the individual griever's personality in shaping his or her pattern of grief is explored. Chapters 6 and 7 deal with the investigation of related concepts of culture and sex-role socialization and how they shape patterns of grief.

While personality, culture, and gender-role socialization are assigned to separate chapters, there is a true interactive nature of the shaping agents. Personality is strongly influenced by culture, which in turn is influenced by personality. Individuals are active participants in shaping cultural norms, including gender role expectations.

Given that the majority of instrumental grievers are men, and that women are generally more intuitive, the role that gender, as a cultural factor, plays in influencing behavior is highlighted. While acknowledging that gender is an important element in determining patterns of grief, readers are encouraged to remember that there are other equally important elements, namely, personality and culture.

There are other potential explanations for patterns of grief that are not considered. For instance, some might suggest that the instrumental pattern has survival value.

In sum, there are many different, but interactive pathways, leading to a particular pattern of grief. Yet one should never forget the primary premise of this book: Different patterns are just that—different, not deficient.

Theoretical Basis
for Patterns of Grief

In this chapter a theoretical basis is constructed that accounts for many of the differences between instrumental and intuitive grief. The chapter begins by revisiting grief as a concept and identifying a model of emotion. Then, a comprehensive model of grief is constructed and the chapter goes on to elaborate on the function and development of the structures and mechanisms responsible for differences among grievers. Finally, the agents that shape the development and influence the individual's unique pattern of responding to loss are introduced.

☐ Grief as Emotional Energy

In Chapter 2, grief was defined as a multifaceted and individual response to loss. In short, grief is energy—an emotional reaction to loss. In order to lay a theoretical foundation for patterns of grief, it becomes necessary to revisit and expand on the definition.

Although the word "emotion" is often used as a synonym for the word "feelings," the modern definition of the term "emotion" is far more comprehensive, with "feelings" being just one component of emotion. For this book's purposes, emotions are defined as biologically based, adaptive reactions involving changes in the physical, affective, cognitive, spiritual, and behavioral systems in response to perceived environmental events of significance to the individual.

Grief, then, is emotion, an instinctual attempt to make internal and external adjustments to an unwanted change in one's world—the death of someone significant to the griever. Grief involves both inner experience and outward expression. Building the foundation begins by looking more closely at emotion and adopting the general model of emotions proposed by Gross and Munoz (1995).

The model in Figure 5.1 incorporates both a component as well as a process view of emotions. The component perspective of emotion includes a biologically based adaptation program for survival and a conglomeration of response programs (spanning all of the adaptive systems or modalities) referred to as response tendencies. These various programs represent learned predispositions, which usually operate at a subconscious level and enhance the chances of an individual's survival by being readily available and quickly activated.

Whereas the adaptational program is genetically and biologically determined, response tendencies result from previous and ongoing interactions with the environment. From birth, the person's response tendencies are molded by powerful, often imperceptible influences. As will be shown, two of the most influential forces are the individual's culture (both societal and familial and their influence on gender-role development) and personality.

Two processes are active in emotions. Appraisal is the cognitive-based, semiconscious process, which activates the adaptational program and continues to shape the eventual response. The second process is modifica-

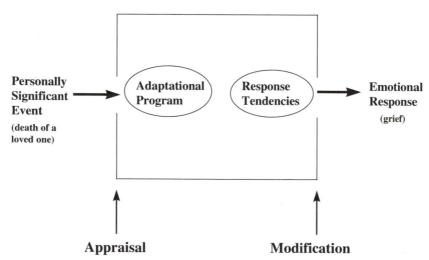

FIGURE 5.1. General model of emotion (Gross & Munoz, 1995).

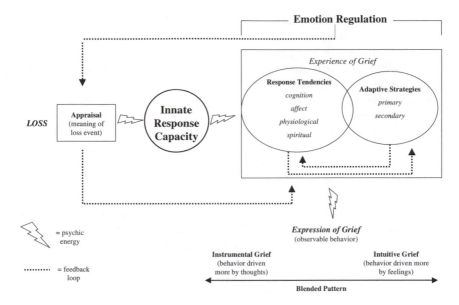

FIGURE 5.2. Comprehensive model of grief.

tion, a conscious effort on the part of the individual to determine the final emotional outcome.

Whether one is more intuitive than instrumental in his or her grief depends on a variety of factors related to emotion. Thus far, as seen in Figure 5.1, emotion has been reduced to its fundamentals—two components and two processes. How do these various components interact to produce either the instrumental or intuitive style of grief? Using the aforementioned model as a starting point, a comprehensive model of grief will be offered.

Figure 5.2 presents a comprehensive model for understanding instrumental and intuitive grief. In the first phase of the model, an individual appraises an event involving a loss as negative.[1] The appraisal process is essentially the way the individual gives meaning to an event, in this case, a loss. This initiates a preprogrammed biological response—the arousal of psychic energy—that varies in capacity from person to person.

This instinctual arousal of energy triggers changes in various adaptive systems—affective, cognitive, physical, and spiritual—that constitute the individual's response tendency. Response tendencies are predispositions, operating subconsciously and allowing people to quickly and efficiently

---

[1]A loss could be appraised as positive—an end to extreme suffering—in which case the grief reaction would be modulated as well.

react to environmental threats, challenges, and opportunities. These predispositions are shaped by the powerful forces of culture and personality and are mediated by the process of emotion regulation.

Emotion regulation mediates the griever's adaptive strategies as well as response tendencies. Adaptive strategies represent the conscious, effortful aspect of emotion regulation and are the griever's attempt to manage both his internal experience of grief and the outer expression of that grief. Whether one is more cognitive or affective in his or her response tendencies and his adaptive strategies determine whether his or her is more instrumental or intuitive in nature.

The proposed comprehensive model is not closed. In other words, actions that happen later in the process can produce a change in the appraisal process, resulting in different arousal levels of psychic energy, different response tendencies, different adaptive strategies, different expressions of grief, and so on. In particular, the griever's choice of adaptive strategies produces changes in behavior that may influence the griever's immediate internal or external environment, thus generating a new appraisal of an altered situation. In fact, it is the constant alteration of the griever's perception of his or her plight that continually generates energy, eventually resulting in an accommodation to the loss. Additionally, previous adaptive strategies modify response tendencies that in turn, influence the selection of current and future adaptive strategies.

Gross and Munoz (see above) identified modification as a process involving a conscious effort on the part of the individual to shape his final emotional response. While this is useful, we have chosen the term "emotion regulation." Emotion regulation is emerging as an important concept in the general study of human behavior and has both automatic (subconscious) and conscious properties. Furthermore, it plays a pivotal role in mediating between shaping agents and response tendencies.

Thus, patterns of grief are a function of two variables: the individual's innate response capacity and emotion regulation, with emotion regulation governing response tendencies and adaptive strategies and, through feedback generated by the chosen adaptive strategy, indirectly influencing the appraisal process or

$$\text{Grief (Instru/Intui)} = f \text{ (appraisal, innate response capacity, emotion regulation), where emotion regulation} = \text{response tendencies} + \text{adaptive strategies/ appraisal.}$$

The following chapters examine the agents that shape the individual's pattern of grief, but begin with the processes of appraisal and emotion regulation and the structure of response tendencies.

☐ The Appraisal Process

The appraisal process is the starting point since it involves cognition, and cognition is crucial to differentiating instrumental from intuitive grief. What is cognition? What roles does cognition play in how people live and what people do?

Definition of Cognition

"Cognition," as used here, refers to conscious and subconscious mental activities that involve thinking, remembering, evaluating, and planning.

Cognitive activity is vital to the instrumental griever; it connects his or her feelings and motivations and serves to differentiate the instrumental style of grieving from the intuitive grief pattern. Understanding the dominant role played by cognition in grief is tantamount to understanding the instrumental grief response. Searching to further clarify the relationship of cognition to emotions and thus grief (instrumental grief in particular) leads directly to the field of stress research and the role of cognitive appraisals in emotions.

Cognitive-Appraisal Stress Theory

Relating stress to grief is not a revolutionary idea; grief is the response to the stress of bereavement. One theory that has dominated the field of stress research since the 1980s is the cognitive-appraisal stress theory.

In the cognitive-appraisal theory, stress is seen as a threat to the individual's well-being and as a source of undesired emotions (Lazarus, 1966, 1991; Lazarus, Averill, & Opton, 1970; Lazarus & Folkman, 1984). The quality and intensity of emotion result from ongoing attempts to understand and make judgments regarding what the individual's senses are reporting about what is happening between that person and the environment. Negative emotions arise when the individual perceives a phenomenon as a danger or a threat to his or her sense of well-being or, in some cases, to his or her very survival!

The person then considers options for responding to these dangers or threats and eventually chooses a course of action. This chain of cognitive events is cognitive appraisal. The stress inherent in the death of a significant other triggers the cognitive appraisal process, which is fundamental to the instrumental grief response. Cognitive appraisal processes determine how, and how well, the individual copes.

Just as cognition is both necessary and sufficient for emotions, emotions affect cognition (Lazarus, 1991). After the initial appraisal is made and emotion arises, secondary and subsequent appraisals can engender thoughts that are emotional. In a "kindling" sense, once aroused, emotions produce feedback that affects subsequent thoughts, which produce additional emotions, which produce new feedback, and so on. Apparently, the personal meaning one gives to an event (and its attendant responses) is a function of both thinking and feeling. Whether one is more tuned in to his or her thoughts or his or her feelings determines whether he is an instrumental or conventional griever. Now return to the model of grief and explore the nature and development of response tendencies.

☐ Response Tendencies

As noted in Figure 5.2, the individual's response tendency is initiated by a chain of events beginning with the appraisal of an event as a loss, which, in turn, triggers the arousal of psychic energy (adaptational program). This energy is channeled into the various inner modalities constituting the response system—cognitive, physiological, affective, and spiritual. Chapter 2 explored how these modalities found expression in various reactions to loss. Do not infer that there is a one-to-one correspondence between the inner experience of these modalities and their final expression seen in observable behavior. As will be shown, much of the outward expression of grief depends on the griever's chosen adaptive strategies.

While response tendencies represent habitual responses to loss, they remain somewhat plastic, that is, modifiable. How do response tendencies develop? Can individuals actively shape their response tendencies by modifying and modulating their experience as well as their expression of grief? Is there any one process, beyond the appraisal process, that is responsible for both the experience as well as the final expressions of grief? These questions are best answered by examining the concept of "emotion regulation" (Izard, 1991; Thompson, 1994; Gross & Munoz, 1995).

☐ Emotion Regulation

Even the earliest studies of the link between thoughts and feelings demonstrated that some people could modulate their emotions at will. In one instance, prior to seeing a movie of people suffering personal injury while working with machine tools, subjects were instructed to either be more involved with events on the screen or to detach themselves from the emotional impact of the scenes (Koriat, Melkman, Averill, & Lazarus,

1977). The results indicated that participants could either, by using cognitive strategies, become more emotionally enmeshed in an event or achieve emotional detachment. Stated differently, these subjects managed their emotions by regulating them.

Additional researchers concluded that infants (Rothbart, 1991) and children (Saarni, 1989) developed strategies and skills for managing their emotional experiences and expressions. This process of modifying emotions is called emotion regulation. Thompson (1994, p. 27) formally defined emotional regulation as, "the extrinsic and intrinsic processes responsible for monitoring, evaluating, and modifying emotional reactions, especially their intensive and temporal features, to accomplish one's goals." What is not clear is exactly what is being regulated.[2] Is emotion regulation primarily concerned with the management of expressions of emotion or the underlying arousal processes leading to those expressions—or both?

The answer to this question lies at the heart of understanding grief as well as implementing effective interventions with grievers.[3] At present, researchers do not know whether emotion regulation is primarily the management of expressions of emotion or the underlying arousal processes leading to those expressions.

Functional Aspects of Emotion Regulation: Adaptive Strategies

It is important to understand that emotion regulation is a process that helps people achieve their goals (Campos, Campos, & Barrett, 1989; Fox, 1989). Emotion regulation is not just a way of suppressing emotions, but a vehicle for expressing them as well. The reader should distinguish between emotion control, which implies restraint of emotions, and emotion regulation, which refers to the attunement of emotional experience

---

[2]Remember that the use of the term "emotion" reflects the modalities of the individual's response tendency. Affect (feelings) is just one component of emotion. The other components are cognition, physicality, and spirituality.

[3]Some colleagues have expressed misgivings about the potential outcomes for instrumental grievers. This concern involves the question of whether instrumental grievers are better at hiding from their own feeling or are simply better than intuitive grievers at hiding their feelings from others. If so, does this lead to successfully resolving and adapting to one's losses? Kagan (1994), points out that the major problem in studying emotion regulation is to separate the intensity of the emotion from the effectiveness of the regulatory effort. Thus, a suggestion would be to reframe any questions about the prophylactic effects of instrumental grief in the following way: Are instrumental grievers better at regulating their feelings about their losses or are their feelings simply less intense to begin with, or both?

to everyday events and the achievement of goals (Davis, 1983). Emotion regulation has been defined in terms of how one uses emotions to achieve one's goals. Other writers have added that it is the individual's goals that determine the nature, type of, and persistence of emotion regulation (Walden & Smith, 1997).

Thus, emotion regulation involves both subconscious and conscious processes that govern the experience and expression of grief. Emotion regulation reflects the individual's inherent arousal capacities and influences the development of his or her response tendency. Along with the appraisal process, emotion regulation also modifies the griever's ongoing experience and expression of emotional (or psychic) energy. Ultimately, how the individual adapts to loss is largely a function of how he or she distributes emotional (or psychic) energy. He or she does so by selecting adaptive strategies.

The term "adaptive strategies" describes the conscious regulatory efforts of the individual. How the griever regulates the psychic energy created by his or her loss reflects what objectives are important to him or her at the time. This has important implications for counselors and therapists working with the bereaved, since the efficacy of the regulatory efforts must be evaluated with respect to the griever's individual pursuits. Furthermore, the professional should keep in mind that these pursuits may change as a function of place, person, or time. These regulatory efforts will be revealed in the adaptive strategies the individual chooses.

Hence, a griever modifies or adjusts the final expression of his or her grief through choosing adaptive strategies. This process acts in concert with the individual's response tendencies to produce the grief response. Response tendencies represent the subconscious, automatic responses to bereavement and are mediated by the appraisal process and subconscious aspects of emotion regulation. Adaptive strategies are the conscious, effortful acts on the part of the griever to manage his or her experience as well as how he expresses his or her grief. Yet the reader should remember that adaptive strategies, once learned, influence response tendencies (see Figure 5.2).

Figure 5.3 shows how the processes of emotion regulation, both subconscious and conscious, govern the experience and expression of psychic or grief energy. Emotion regulation operates subconsciously in shaping and modifying response tendencies, while it represents a conscious process in influencing the griever's choice of adaptive strategies, which in turn influence future subconscious processes.

Primary adaptive strategies are those that represent the griever's dominant mode of regulating emotional energy, while secondary adaptive strategies may be employed to supplement or temporarily replace primary strategies. Primary adaptive strategies provide important clues to differentiating instrumental from intuitive grievers.

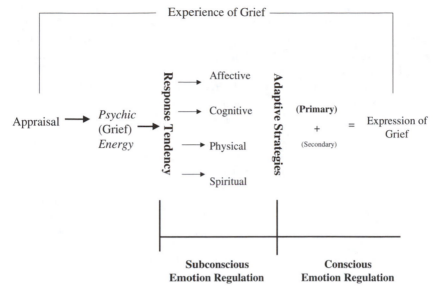

Figure 5.3. Emotion regulation of grief.

☐ Adaptive Strategies and Patterns of Grieving

The basic style of the griever is reflected in his or her choice of primary adaptive strategies. Intuitive grievers usually choose primary adaptive strategies that permit an unfettered, uninhibited experience of the affective component of grief. These strategies represent a means to an end. They may also choose secondary strategies that allow them to manage the other modalities of emotional experience—cognitive, physical, and spiritual.

On the other hand, instrumental grievers select primary adaptive strategies that help them distribute cognitive psychic energy into planned activity. They often choose secondary adaptive strategies to manage the intensity and duration of their feelings, cope with physical responses, and deal with spiritual issues such as facing the challenges to their belief systems posed by the death of a loved one.

Thus, individuals play a decisive role in selecting how they experience and express their emotions. Grievers may begin to regulate their responses either before (proactively) or after (reactively)[4] the response begins. A proactive regulatory effort might involve the adaptive strategy of avoid-

---

[4]Other authors have used different terms, e.g., antecedent-focused, response-focused (see Gross & Munoz, 1995).

ing situations that have led to unpleasant emotions in the past or choosing an environment incompatible with the unpleasant emotion. The sought after environment could be physical (choosing to be with friends in order to distract oneself from feelings of loneliness) or mental (engaging in thought control, meditation, positive imagery). Grievers often choose "dosing" methods of mental control. Proactive regulation itself can give rise to new appraisals, different levels of arousal, different response tendencies, and so on. The following case illustrates proactive emotion regulation.

> *Matt had just turned 27 when his fiancée, Susan, died suddenly after experiencing a lethal allergic reaction to a snake-bite. He sought counseling after receiving an invitation from Susan's parents to spend her birthday with them. Although Matt had always enjoyed a good relationship with Susan's parents, he felt anxious and ambivalent about the invitation. From previous experience, Matt had discovered that being with Susan's family stirred up painful memories. After a recent visit (at her parents' request), Matt was overwhelmed with feelings of despair and hopelessness. By contrast, "hanging with my single friends" had proven both relaxing and fun for him. After an intense discussion with his minister about his conflicted feelings, he decided to write a letter to his fiancée's parents, explaining his feelings and asking them to forgive him if he avoided contacting them for the foreseeable future. Susan's parents responded immediately to Matt's letter with one of their own. Their letter lay unopened for several days, until Matt chose to risk the feelings he knew that reading the letter would ignite. To his relief, Susan's parents expressed their own ambivalence about being around Matt and encouraged him to "get on with" his life.*

Whereas anticipation of a negative event or response stimulates proactive attempts to avoid painful emotions, reactive emotion regulation begins late in the cycle of emotion response. Reactive regulation means modulating or modifying already existing thoughts and feelings so that the outcome response is altered. Hiding one's true feelings or maintaining strict control over impulses or behaviors is an example of reactive regulation. The following case illustrates a reactive emotion regulation.

> *After surviving several years beyond his life expectancy, Margi's younger brother, Michael, died from complications arising from cystic fibrosis. He was 41 years old. Michael and Margi had been extremely close growing up. After their parents died and following Margi's divorce, they grew even closer and made sure they spoke with each other almost every day. Margi shared her brother's last days with him, temporarily closing her busy law practice to remain at his bedside. She was overwhelmed with intense feelings at Michael's funeral and, as she described it, "I spent about four days in a haze." Despite her intense grief, Margi knew she needed to return to her legal practice if she wanted to remain competitive in the local economy, which had a surfeit of attorneys. "I knew I needed a plan to get my feelings under control if I was to be able to concentrate at all, so I set up a schedule for grieving: I could only think about Michael for an hour every evening. Believe you me, I spent that hour being miserable!" (Question: "How did you keep your mind away from thoughts*

of your brother?") "Oh, I've always been able to distract myself from thinking things I didn't want to. Remember, I had lots of practice during his fight with CF. I just know how to turn my thoughts on and off."

Of course, as discussed in Chapter 4, grievers can choose adaptive strategies that do not lead, ultimately, to a healthy resolution of their loss. Hence, adaptive strategies can subdue (or enhance) the intensity of feelings, strengthen (or defeat) action plans, and retard (or speed) recovery.

In summary, instrumental grief is a response tendency that is driven primarily by thoughts rather than by feelings, while the response tendency of an intuitive griever reflects the preponderance of psychic energy that is experienced as feelings. Both patterns of grief response can be modified or modulated according to environmental demands and individual needs by choosing adaptive strategies and employing them either proactively or reactively. Emotion regulation is at the heart of grieving. The next section will look briefly at the development of emotion regulation and introduce the change agents shaping this development.

☐ Development of Emotion Regulation

How do emotions develop? How does emotion regulation emerge in the developing child? What role does biology play? What is the role of personality in shaping emotion regulation? Is the family a purveyor of emotion regulation? How important are gender differences in emotion regulation?

In exploring the object of emotion regulation, Thompson (1994) concluded that emotion regulation targets the various neurological processes governing emotional arousal. Congenital differences in central nervous system reactivity may represent differences in how and to what infants attend. As the infant develops, his or her attention processes become more complex than the earlier, simple strategies, such as shifting vision from an undesirable stimulus to one more desirable in order to avoid negative feeling states.

Older children use more internal strategies for emotion regulation. For example, a child might discover that thinking about the coming summer vacation becomes an antidote to worrying about tomorrow's exam. Children also regulate, to an extent, their access to support systems, when they become aroused by a noxious event. They choose whether to seek support and from whom they will seek it. Of course, the way in which parents or others respond to cries for help from the child who experiences unpleasant, painful feelings either reinforces or fails to reward future help-seeking behaviors. As emotion regulation becomes more complex and sophisticated, it is shaped more by environmental factors. Gender role socialization, the family, and cultural influences assume a larger role in determining the development of emotion regulation as they interact with individual biological predispositions and the child's emerging personality (see Sidebar 5.1).

Summary

(1) Grief is an emotion. Feelings are just one of the adaptational aspects of emotions. The other modalities of adaptation are the cognitive, the spiritual, and the physical.

Sidebar 5.1. Instrumental grief as a mature pattern

Among the many questions that arise about the patterns is, "Isn't instrumental grief simply the same pattern displayed by young children, that is, isn't this pattern an example of the griever who hasn't matured enough or become strong enough to handle difficult feelings for extended periods of time?" The question is a good one, since it is widely accepted that children have a "short sadness span" (Wolfenstein, 1966) and often grieve intermittently.

The answer is "no." In this case, the questioner may be confusing the experience of grief with the expression of grief. Instrumental grief is a pattern, marked by tempered affect and heightened cognitive activity, not a series of discrete experiences ("now I'll have feelings, now I won't, now I will . . . "), although most grievers sometimes choose to modulate and dose their feelings. Efforts of this sort are mature, sophisticated strategies for dealing with uncomfortable levels of affect and are used by intuitive and blended grievers as well as instrumental grievers.

Actually, this concern about immature responses calls into question interpretations of children's reactions to loss. Children often act out their internal experiences symbolically through play. Since traditional views of grief tend to overemphasize the importance of affect, these behaviors have been seen as the child's way to avoid or minimize painful feelings. It is equally likely that these responses are ways that children express physical, cognitive, and even spiritual energy created by their losses. Also, doing things like watching television or random play are interpreted as the child's attempts to escape uncomfortable feelings. While this may be so, could not a child experience grief without expressing it? And how are we to know if one bereaved child's minimal responses represent an attempt to avoid feelings or are indicative of that particular child's smaller capacity for feelings of any type, or of his or her inclination to process the world cognitively rather than affectively? Could this child's behaviors be part of an overall emerging pattern of responding to loss—an instrumental pattern?

(2) A comprehensive model of grief and patterns of grieving includes an initial appraisal, which creates psychic energy. This energy is distributed among various adaptational systems according to the griever's response tendencies. Response tendencies are subconscious predispositions that are mediated by the process of emotion regulation and shaped by culture and personality.

(3) The appraisal process initiates the grief response by attaching meaning to the event as a significant personal loss. This is accomplished through cognitive activity. Appraisal is also strongly influenced by the process of emotion regulation.

(4) The mechanism primarily responsible for shaping and modifying both internal and external aspects of response tendencies is emotion regulation. Emotion regulation also plays a conscious role in determining which adaptive strategies are chosen by the griever and how these strategies are implemented.

CHAPTER 6

Personality as a Shaper of Patterns

Why are some people instrumental in their grieving while others are intuitive? The search for answers begins by exploring the role that personality may play in shaping patterns of grief. While there are many constructs of personality, our investigation is concerned with the three that best relate to grief: type theory, trait theory, and heredity (see introduction to this section). We begin by defining personality. Next, the instrumental and intuitive patterns of grief are related to the personality type theory of Carl Jung. Then, the influence of one particular personality trait, repressive coping, is examined as a shaper of grieving patterns. Finally, the role played by biology and heredity in shaping personality and, thus, patterns of grief is evaluated.

☐ Personality Defined

Every person has his or her own implicit definition of personality. From early childhood, many people have already developed a schema for classifying and predicting the behavior of others "He's not very handsome but he does have a nice personality." In addition, many people still link personality with charisma and view it as a quality that outstanding athletes, popular entertainers, and (occasionally) politicians have in abundance, while others must make do with less. Even psychologists usually

87

cannot agree on a single, global definition of personality; however, most definitions of personality emphasize three major characteristics.

First, personality reflects what is unique about each of us. Whatever psychological qualities are seen as making up the individual, they set him apart from other individuals or groups, and they describe that person or that "type" of person as someone different from other types of persons.

Second, these qualities differentiating individuals are relatively consistent over long periods of time and across varying situations. In fact, much of the understanding people have of others is based on an assumption that their behavior will remain fairly stable in most circumstances.

Third, an individual's personal qualities link the person to the social and physical world and reflect the individual's pattern of adaptation to the environment.

Thus, simply put, personality is the sum of the individual's distinguishing personal qualities that remain relatively consistent over time and across situations, and serves as the person's instrument of adaptation. Personality, along with the influential role exercised by culture and gender role socialization, determines the degree to which one is more of an instrumental or an intuitive griever.

☐ Ways of Looking at Personality

Jung's Typologies

Carl Jung published *Psychological Types* in 1920, a book which was the culmination of more than 20 years of effort in exploring the nature and problems of individual differences. While Jung's typologies are often viewed as overly simplistic, a closer look reveals the richly variegated patterns that highlight individual (and group) differences. Although a comprehensive treatment of Jung's theory of typologies is beyond the scope and aim of this book, a brief summary is in order (see Sidebar 6.1).

Jung's personality typology has become so popular that many people do not realize he made any other contributions! His typology consists of four functions and two attitudes which begins with the attitudes, broad and general ways that people process life and respond to living. Jung makes the distinction between introversion and extroversion, with introverts being those who prefer their internal world of thoughts, fantasies, feelings, and dreams and extroverts favoring the external world of things and people. Introverts act primarily to understand what they perceive, while extroverts seek to express and communicate their experiences.

Jung suggested that each person has preferred modes of dealing with the inner and outer world—ways they are comfortable with and good at.

Sidebar 6.1. The Myers–Briggs Type Indicator

The Myers–Briggs Type Indicator (MBTI) is a widely used and well-known tool for identifying an individual's psychological make up. It was developed in the U.S. early in the 20th century during a period when Carl Jung's theory of personality types was receiving growing interest. The MBTI is based on Jungian theory of psychological development and evaluates people's preferences with regard to **I**ntroversion and **E**xtroversion, **S**ensing or **I**ntuitive preference, logical (**T**hinking), or values-based (**F**eeling) preference in decision-making. It also analyzes an individual's preference for making decisions (**J**udging) or taking in information (**P**erceiving). These latter functions are additions to Jung's theory. Thus, each person receives a four-letter code, which indicates that individual's preferences, **E** or **I**, **S** or **N**, **T** or **F**, and **J** or **P**. There are 16 different possible combinations.

The Myers–Briggs is one of the most popular, and most studied, tests of personality available. According to the MBTI what type you are says quite a bit about you—your career preferences, your likes and dislikes, which of the other types would make good mates, and so on. For example, if you happen to be an **INTP** (introverted thinking with intuiting), you are most likely a bookworm, a philosophy major (or "wanna-be"), and absent-minded. On the other hand, if you are an **ESTP** (extroverted sensing with thinking) you probably could double for "James Bond," since, while charming and suave, you can be ruthless and crave action.

While many people are wildly enthusiastic about the MBTI (from license plates to T-shirts and coffee mugs) the test itself, although inherently fair and nonjudgmental about the types, suffers from the same fatal flaws of most subjective measures of self. For instance, "How do I respond to questions concerning me when I'm not sure whether they describe me at the moment, the past, or my wished-for future?" Additionally, "How much of the time must I feel, act, think this way in order to select it from my other ways of feeling, acting, and thinking?" Also, the Myers–Briggs moves well beyond the theoretical underpinnings of Jung's theory of types with its addition of a judging and perceiving function. Finally, the MBTI meets with considerable resistance among scientists studying personality. For example, two highly respected personality researchers (McCrae & Costa, 1989) found the Myers–Briggs failed to measure distinct types, but did measure four independent dimensions of personality. They concluded that either Jung's theory of types was wrong or the MBTI fails as a measure of the theory.

These are the functions of personality, thinking, feeling, sensing, and intuiting. These are the alternative ways that individuals absorb or experience situations.

While the functions are the key to determining the individual's general pattern of grief, the attitudes play a pivotal role in the griever's choice of adaptive strategies. For instance, an introvert who is primarily an intuitive griever will restrict the number of others to whom he or she expresses his or her experiences of grief, while his or her instrumental counterpart will choose more solitary ways of mastering his or her feelings and expressing his or her experiences through activity. Likewise, an intuitive griever, who is an extrovert, will seek out large numbers of individuals or groups to process his or her feelings, while an extroverted instrumental griever will want to share activities that enable him or her to solve problems and master feelings.

Jung's four functions of personality operate in pairs of opposites, with one pair dominating, while its associate pair serves an auxiliary function. Sensing and intuiting are one pair of contrasting functions, and are the ways people encounter situations directly without regard to responding to them. In a sense, sensing and intuiting function as portals to experience, without filtering or refining incoming data. The sensing function focuses on details, while the intuiting function gathers impressions.

The second pair of functions, thinking and feeling, are regarded as being one step beyond the initial awareness of an experience. These functions actively process environmental information. They, too, are opposites.

When Jung used the word "type" to describe an individual's personality, he meant that one of the functions tends to be used more frequently in a given situation. Thus, combining the four functions results in the following types (with the dominant function listed first):

Thinking/sensing
Feeling/sensing
Thinking/intuiting
Feeling/intuiting
Sensing/thinking
Sensing/feeling
Intuiting/thinking
Intuiting/feeling.

Hence, whether one is primarily a thinker or a feeler determines the nature of his or her experiences and influences his or her expressions of those experiences. Also, the pairings of functions also influence experience and expression. Complementary pairings would include:

Thinking/sensing
Feeling/intuiting
Sensing/thinking
Intuiting/feeling.

These complementary combinations of functions enhance the degree to which one is an intuitive or instrumental griever. While the thinking/

feeling or feeling/thinking functions influence the pattern of grieving, the other pair of functions plays an important role in the initial awareness of loss. A griever, who has sensing as either his or her dominant or associative function, is more likely to focus on the details of the event, while the intuiting type gets a general impression of the loss.

For example, a griever, whose primary function is thinking and subordinate function is sensing (or the reverse), is more likely to experience and express grief near the extreme of the instrumental pattern since, as a thinker, he or she cognitively processes the details of the loss presented by his or her sensing function. This griever is less likely to rely exclusively on cognition as he or she processes the loss, since the initial awareness is grounded more in an impression than in detail.

On the other hand, a griever with feeling as the dominant function, complemented by intuiting (or vice versa), will digest the loss mostly as an affective experience, since his or her initial awareness of the loss is based on an impression instead of centering on details. However, while sensing and intuiting influence patterns of grief, it is important for the reader to view thinking and feeling as the functions most important in determining the individual's pattern of grief (see Figure 6.1).

In Figure 6.1 the eight Jungian types are arranged along the patterns of grief continuum. Grievers whose dominant function is either thinking or feeling are found near the extremes of the instrumental and intuitive pattern of grief, respectively. Blended grievers have either sensing or intuiting (with thinking or feeling serving as associative functions) as their dominant functions and are found more towards the middle of the continuum. These grievers still follow one of the patterns, but their reactions—experiences, expressions, and primary adaptive strategies—do not as easily identify them as either instrumental or intuitive grievers. But pairing the associative function of thinking with sensing will intensify those elements of the blended pattern of an instrumental nature. The

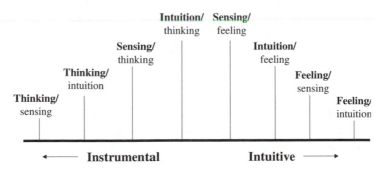

FIGURE 6.1. Patterns by Jungian Type.

same is true if the pairing is intuiting/feeling rather than intuiting/thinking.

Thinking Versus Feeling: Instrumental and Intuitive Grief

While the way in which one takes in his or her losses may affect the initial awareness of the loss, it is *where* the event is processed—either in the thinking or the feeling system—which determines how it is experienced. Hence, the feeling and thinking functions (along with additional personality, biological, and cultural factors) dictate to what degree one is an instrumental or intuitive griever.

This does not mean that instrumental grievers do not have a feeling function, nor that intuitive grievers do not think. For the instrumental griever, feelings are underdeveloped and relatively unconscious. A griever whose superior function is feeling has an underdeveloped thinking function, and his or her use of logical analysis to process losses is largely unconscious. The existence of thinking as a subordinate function to feeling, or feeling as the subordinate function to thinking, has important implications for the griever's choice among adaptive strategies.

It is important to stress the significance of intuitive grievers' discovering outlets for cognitive-driven action, while instrumental grievers must find ways of discharging affective energy. Thus, intuitive grievers who have a number of adaptive strategies for expressing both feeling and action (and have the skills or abilities to implement them) will usually fare better than those whose selections are limited. Likewise, instrumental grievers who have choices among various vehicles for expressing feelings will adapt sooner and better than those whose tools for expressing feelings are confined to one or none.

Which requires more energy—thinking intensely about something or feeling it deeply? While there is plenty of evidence that expressions of feelings like crying, wailing, or raging burn more calories than sitting contemplatively, it is debatable which internal experience requires more fuel. However, grievers who have feeling as their primary function may initially channel more psychic energy into expressing their grief than do their instrumental counterparts. Strong feelings need to either be expressed or suppressed; both processes require a large amount of energy. Thus, the intuitive griever who chooses wisely among adaptive strategies discharges enough energy into venting his or her feelings to restore a balance between the experience of grief and its expression.

For the instrumental griever, the situation is very different. The energy channeled into thinking (rather than feeling) allows mastery of feelings and finds expression in planned activities. Thus, the instrumental griever who expresses grief by carving an elaborate urn for his father's ashes, or who chisels a stone for his son's memorial, is channeling thinking into action. Likewise, the father who rebuilds a fence as a way to grieve his daughter's accidental death, or a widow who assumes the reins of her husband's business, is dispersing grief energy. The homeostasis between creating and expending energy is regained and balance is restored.

The extroverted instrumental griever may also choose to expend energy by affiliating with others, especially in shared activities, while his or her introverted counterpart may select solitary activities, such as running, writing, or lifting weights. In many cases, these grievers redirect their energies into their work. This explains why instrumental grievers tend to return to their jobs and their previous levels of performance sooner than intuitive grievers.

To summarize, instrumental grievers have thinking as their superior function, while intuitive grievers have feeling as their superior function. Those grievers for whom either sensing or intuiting is their dominant function are a blending of both patterns. The complementary pairings of thinking with sensing and feeling with intuiting influences how ardently one is either an instrumental or an intuitive griever.

Repressive Coping as a Personality Construct Related to Patterns of Grief

While efforts continue to reconcile traits with types, a trait is defined as "a relatively stable aspect of mind that predisposes one to behave in a certain way." In this way, traits become part of the person rather than part of the environment. One such trait or predisposition is repressive coping. Those possessing this trait are classified as "repressors." Repressors report less anxiety, depression, conflicts, illness, pain, and stress than nonrepressors. Ironically, repressors show higher levels of physiological reactivity to stressful laboratory procedures (Weinberger, Schwartz, & Davidson, 1979; Bonanno & Singer, 1990). While some studies report a possible correlation between repression and immune system suppression (Schwartz, 1990) and cancer (Jensen, 1987), Bonanno and Singer have questioned whether this is so. In fact, Paulhus and Reid (1991) suggested that repression is positively associated with adjustment.

How might the trait of repressive coping relate to patterns of grief? One such association involves the discharge of grief (psychic) energy as physical energy. Since the physical represents one of the fundamentals of human experience, what happens to the physical energy generated by loss? In the intuitive griever, it manifests as affect-related behavior such as crying. It is also experienced as an energy reduction such as fatigue. In addition, it increases arousal (such as anxiety) that is consciously experienced.

For an instrumental griever, grief discharged as physical energy augments the levels of energy already available for physical activity (Plante & Schwartz, 1990). It also may increase physiological arousal that is not consciously experienced as arousal. The latter is a classic example of repressive coping. Bonanno, Keltner, Holen, and Horowitz (1995) believe that repressive coping may be an autonomous adaptive strategy that is effective in adjusting to bereavement.

The researchers in the Bonanno study investigated how grievers adapted to losing a spouse during midlife. Their purpose was to challenge the widely held assumption that emotional avoidance is a maladaptive response to loss (Bowlby, 1980; Deutsch, 1937; Doyle, 1980; Raphael, 1983). They viewed emotional avoidance as a maladaptive response when it resulted in either delayed grief (overt symptoms of grief that eventually surface), prolonged grief (the mourning process is extended), or delayed somatic symptoms (grief that eventually manifests as physical problems). The researchers characterized repressive coping as a discrepancy between a participant's subjective feelings of grief and increased cardiovascular activity.

After their results were tabulated, Bonanno et al. (1995) found no support for the standard hypothesis that avoiding or minimizing feelings associated with grief is maladaptive at either 6 or 14 months after the loss. As the authors noted, this is consistent with Shuchter and Zisook's (1993) findings that a griever's ability to regulate or "dose" the amount of feeling he or she can bear is beneficial. It also verifies the work of Kaminer and Lavie (1993), which found that those holocaust survivors who were able to avoid thinking about and remembering their experiences were the best adjusted. Thus, the Bonanno group concluded that ". . . the findings were consistent with the competing hypothesis that emotional avoidance during bereavement may serve adaptive functions" (p. 983). They added the following cautionary note: "If the conclusions suggested by the present data are correct, and avoiding unpleasant emotions during bereavement is in fact not such a bad thing, then a number of important implications for clinical interventions are apparent" (p. 986).

Consequently, while remembering that personality traits are found along a continuum, the degree to which one is a repressor influences whether one is an intuitive or instrumental griever, with instrumental grievers possessing a high degree of repression. From a theoretical perspective, this can be interpreted in one of two ways: Elevated levels of repression either reflect learned response tendencies or indicate a higher threshold for stimulation (see Chapter 5).

Accordingly, in addition to Jungian-type theory, the personality trait of repressive coping may be an important variable in any discussion about the role played by personality in shaping a particular pattern of grief.

The Biology of Patterns of Grief: Temperament, Personality, and Affect Intensity

The final look at personality is from the perspective of heredity and biology (see Sidebar, 6.2). Beginning with the work of Thomas and Chess (1977), child development specialists identified constitutionally based differences in emotional reactivity among infants. These broad, general patterns of individual differences in the intensity and duration of expressions of arousal and emotionality are defined as "temperament" (Campos, Campos, & Barrett, 1989). One of the original nine temperament characteristics was the intensity of emotional response and was defined as "the energy level of response, irrespective of its quality or direction" (Thomas & Chess, 1985, p. 219). Since differences in emotional reactivity strongly affect the kinds of experiences children have, these differences become the cornerstones of personality development. Personality evolves as the

---

Sidebar 6.2. Sociobiology

Thanks to testosterone, males are larger and more muscular. Bolstered by data that consistently link aggression to males, sociobiologists might argue that our male forebears were naturally selected to defend hearth and family. For these ancestors, emotionality may have inhibited survival. For example, when the community was under attack, men who could ignore their dismay at the deaths of comrades could focus on repelling the invaders. Afterwards, the task of rebuilding could begin only if shock and grief could be laid aside. Likewise, the case could be made that conforming to society's rules, especially those involving conflicts and disputes, could be accomplished only if males curtailed their aggressiveness, perhaps through controlling, even suppressing emotions.

While such arguments are interesting and may be compelling, they are also highly controversial and are not supported by available data. Biology plays a multidimensional role in shaping patterns of grief: genetic factors, *by way of temperament*, interact with culture and are important in determining personality; while gender interacts strongly with both personality and culture in producing behavior. Differences in temperament are an established fact, while the link between historical social conditions and human genetics is still considered speculative.

individual's unique biology elicits responses from the environment—the interaction between "nature" and "nurture."

Affect Intensity

One dimension of temperament receiving recent attention is affect intensity, which is defined as "stable individual differences in the strength with which individuals experience their emotions" (Larsen & Diener, 1987, p. 2). Larsen and Diener have summarized the following assumptions about affect intensity:

1. Affect intensity is unrelated to whether individuals feel negative versus positive affect more frequently but is, instead, related to how deeply they feel them.
2. "What goes up must come down," or affect intensity "generalizes across specific emotions such that, for example, individuals who experience their positive emotions more strongly will, over time, experience their negative emotions more strongly as well" (p. 2).
3. Affect intensity is not only the subjective experience of strong feelings, but is the physiological and cognitive responses as well, including increased heart rate, arousal, ability to concentrate, and ability to control thoughts and actions.
4. Individuals who experience high affect intensity tend to view others as having emotional responses that are strong and difficult to control.
5. Women score generally higher than men do on measures of affect intensity.
6. Affect intensity decreases with age.

Thus, a difference in one's capacity to experience feelings is an element of personality that appears to be biologically influenced. However, the role exercised by the individual's environment, particularly culture and gender role socialization experiences, is pivotal in determining the final expression of this trait.

To summarize the implications of differences in affect intensity on patterns of grief:

First, affect intensity does not determine whether a griever feels. It *does* influence how deeply he may feel.

Second, the observation that intuitive grievers show a greater range of feeling responses in general—from despair to euphoria and everything in between—reflects differences in affect intensity. Instrumental grievers seem more "even-keeled" but less "colorful" than intuitive grievers.

Third, the level of affect intensity seems inversely related to the griever's ability to concentrate, make decisions, plan, and control his thoughts and feelings, all variables defining the instrumental pattern of grief. Intuitive grievers are not as adept as instrumental grievers in mastering their thoughts and feelings.

Fourth, misinterpretations of behavior and misunderstandings of intent between grievers may result from differences in affect intensity. In particular, intuitive grievers may interpret the muted display of feelings so characteristic of instrumental grievers as "covered-up" or, worse, as indicating a casual dismissal of the lost relationship by the griever. Instrumental grievers may view the lavish (to them) display of affect common to intuitive grievers as evidence of irrationality, or poor self-control. In either case, individuals with opposite patterns may not be able to understand and support each other if they fail to recognize the inherent strengths of their respective responses.

Finally, differences in affect intensity found between men and women highlight both basic biological differences and sex role socialization experiences. It reinforces our belief that the extremes of either pattern are influenced heavily by gender.

☐ Summary

In this chapter personality was defined and three aspects of personality that may influence styles of grieving were examined. Jung's type theory, the trait of repressive coping and temperament-based affect intensity, all are constructs of personality development and function that may act either individually or in concert to produce the intuitive and instrumental styles of grief. The following are characteristics of the patterns:

Intuitive Pattern
1. The most pronounced example is the feeling/intuiting type, with intuiting/feeling more towards the center of the continuum.
2. Less use of repressive coping as a defense.
3. High levels of affect intensity.

Instrumental Pattern
1. Most pronounced among thinking/sensing types; less so with a sensing/thinking combination.
2. High degree of repressive coping.
3. Low levels of affect intensity.

Blended Pattern
1. Either sensing or intuiting (with thinking or feeling serving as associative functions) is the dominant function.
2. Moderate amount of repressive coping.
3. Moderate levels of affect intensity.

7 CHAPTER

The Role of Gender

☐ Introduction

There is a sculpture entitled "Dark Elegy" commemorating the destruction by a terrorist bomb of Pan Am Flight 103 over Lockerbie, Scotland. The sculpture attempts to depict the agonizing grief of the 33 mothers who lost children on that flight.

In many ways, that memorial also illustrates the paradox of male grievers. On one hand, they are expected to be strong; their grief is largely, as in the sculpture, silent and formless. On the other hand, they are castigated for not demonstratively showing their grief, a fact touched upon in the introductory chapter.

Throughout earlier chapters, it has been argued that there are, along a continuum, two patterns of grieving—one labeled intuitive, the other instrumental. These patterns differ in the experience, expression, and adaptation to grief.

In the last chapter, several factors that contribute to the reasons that different individuals exhibit these different patterns were explored. Clearly, gender role socialization is another of these factors.

Men and women, because of their socialization into sex roles, are likely to exhibit different grieving patterns. Men are more likely to be found on the instrumental end of the continuum, while women are more likely to exhibit an intuitive style. Yet gender role socialization is but *one* factor that influences a pattern of grief. This leads to a critical affirmation that *while patterns of grieving are certainly influenced by gender, they are not deter-*

mined by gender. Put simply, a counselor, caregiver, or any reader would be well advised not to assume without assessment that any given male is instrumental or any female intuitive. In fact, one can find male intuitive grievers, female instrumental grievers, and dissonant grievers of any sex. However, because of the constraints placed on the male role, males who experience grief in a strongly intuitive way may be limited in their expression and adaptation to a greater extent than females. While dissonant grievers can be either intuitive or instrumental, they are more likely to be those who, because of constraints, cannot freely express feelings.

☐ Gender and Grief: Lessons from Research

Therapists' Perspective

The fact that men and women exhibit differences in the ways they grieve has long been noted by both clinicians and researchers. Stillon and McDowell (1997), for example, surveyed a random sample of counselors and educators who were certified by the major professional organization within the field—The Association for Death Education and Counseling. Their sample of both male and female counselors and educators agreed that there were significant differences between men and women grievers. Men were viewed as less likely to exhibit strong emotions and more likely to evoke distractions such as work, sex, play, or alcohol. Men were also seen as more likely to respond cognitively, or when affect was experienced, to show anger. Women, on the other hand, were seen as more expressive and willing to seek out the support of others. Their grief tended to be experienced on a deep, affective level. These counselors also expressed a belief that men needed less time to grieve.

This sample of counselors and educators noted that these reactions often correlated with social expectations based upon gender roles. Most noted were the expectations of friends and acquaintances that males would be strong and get over it quickly. Counselors also perceived that women received more social support for the expression of grief. Ironically, these counselors also noted that while women were more likely to be offered comfort, their grief made them more of a social risk. Conversely, men were seen as harder to comfort but more likely to function acceptably in social situations. In other words, counselors felt that the type of support offered men and women differed. Women could expect emotional support, but lessened opportunities for normal social activity and contact. Men, because they were seen as less likely to be "emotional," were more likely to be invited to resume their normal social contacts.

Nevertheless, while counselors saw clear differences in men's and women's expressions and experiences of grief, they did not see clear differences in outcome, that is, that women or men did inherently better with their grief. Instead, they perceived that each of these grieving styles ran different risks. For men, it was believed that this failure to grieve predisposed them to the risk of more complicated grief reaction, while women were seen as more vulnerable to depression and chronic mourning. The opinions of these experts were far different from those often expressed in the self-help literature (Staudacher, 1991; Wolfelt, 1990).

Research Perspectives

The perspective of these counselors and therapists, explicitly or implicitly, is grounded in much research that clearly does describe differences in the ways that men and women grieve. This research has shown that these differences exist in a wide variety of losses, including that of a spouse, parent, or child.

Spousal Loss

Much of the research has shown that the experience of grief differs for both widows and widowers. Naturally they faced distinct problems. For example, many of the widows reported financial problems (Gilbar & Dagar, 1995) and greater emotional dependence on the husband (Gilbar & Dagar, 1995). Men were more likely to talk about the loss as a "dismemberment," while women tended to use words such as "abandonment" (Glick et al., 1974).

Widowers also tended to stress the need to be realistic about the loss (Glick et al., 1974) and to show a narrower range of affect than widows (Glick et al., 1974; Campbell & Silverman, 1996). While women tended to seek emotional support, men found solace in exercise, religion, work, poetry, or in some more destructive patterns such as alcohol (Campbell & Silverman, 1996; Silverman, 1997). Men were more reluctant to reach out to others (Brabent, Forsyth, Craig, & Meloncon, 1992), but they were more likely to return to work, date, and remarry (Campbell & Silverman, 1996).

Loss of a Child

Many of these same differences were found in the loss of a child. Studies have shown that mothers tended to experience a more intense level of grief or distress than fathers (Carroll & Shaefer, 1994; DeVries, Dalla, Lana, & Falek, 1994; Schwab, 1990, 1996; Conway & Feeney, 1997). Similar patterns were observed in perinatal loss (Boch Hughes & Page-Lieberman, 1989; Goldbach et al., 1991; Kavanaugh, 1997). In Kavanaugh's (1997) study, mothers expressed a greater need to talk about the loss than fathers. And both Boch Hughes and Page-Lieberman (1989), as well as Conway and Feeney (1997), speculated on the greater level of attachment that mothers invested in the child.

Strategies for dealing with the loss also differed. Mothers were more likely to seek outside support and ventilate feelings (Kavanaugh, 1997; Conway & Feeney, 1997). Fathers were less likely to express affect (Carroll & Shaefer, 1994) and felt a need to continue to provide for and protect their families (DeVries et al., 1994). Conway and Feeney (1997) found that women were inclined to use strategies that were more emotion-focused and support-seeking. And they noted that seeking support from others may not always be effective since the quality of support offered may vary (see also Morgan, 1989). Men tended to use more problem-focused strategies. Men also controlled affective expression and intellectualized grief (Lang & Gottlieb, 1993). Where they did show affect, it was generally in anger or aggression (Lang & Gottlieb, 1993).

Unsurprisingly, these differences were evident as well in the loss of an adult child or grandchild. Goodman, Black, and Rubinstein (1996), in their sample of older men who had lost an adult child, found that most of their sample tended to intellectualize the loss. Diversion in work and humor also served as strategies. The authors suggested that some of the attributes of men—often negatively viewed by clinicians—such as individualism and self-sufficiency seem to facilitate their grieving. Fry (1997), too, found differences in grandparents who had lost a child. Grandfathers tended to offer practical assistance, while grandmothers were more likely to focus on spiritual tasks, such as helping their adult children find meaning in their loss or lives. Grandmothers also sought more affective outlets while grandfathers found outlets in active ways.

Naturally, these differences in the experience, expression, and adaptation to grief can affect marital relationships. For example, a number of studies have considered the effect of the death of a child on sexual relationships and marital intimacy. While range of sexual expression varied extensively, many bereaved parents indicated that there was a breakdown or decline in sexual relationships (Peppers & Knapp, 1980; Rosenblatt, 1997; Gottlieb, Lang, & Amsei, 1986). Some of the reasons for this breakdown included a lack of energy or interest, as well as depression in the aftermath of the loss. But there were other reasons as well. For many, the very act of intercourse was problematic—it meant inappropriate pleasure, evoked memories of the deceased child, or created anxiety over the prospect of a new child. In other cases, sexual intimacy was welcomed for the emotional comfort it offered, for the affirmation of life it provided, or for the creation of a new child. These meanings were not necessarily shared with the partner in the relationship. One partner may seek intimacy for support while the other partner sees it as inappropriate. Gottlieb et al. 1996), for example, found that men sought to express intimacy through sexual intercourse with their wives, but their wives did not necessarily interpret that as a need for emotional release and support.

This illustrates the larger problem. Without effective communication and information about the ways that individuals grieve, relationships can suffer. Men may experience concern and helplessness in dealing with their wives' grief. Women may feel a similar sense of bewilderment and help-lessness as they seek to understand their husbands' grief or lack of overt affect. More dangerously, they can interpret their mate's response as a lack of love for the child.

Counselors and other caregivers can assist this process by helping couples explore the differences and similarities in their responses, and they can help couples understand that these differences are based on a wide variety of factors. Such differences do not denote that one loved the deceased any more or less. In this exploration, all aspects of the relationships, including sexual expression and the meanings attached to it, as well as other modes of communication, need to be considered. Counselors should also counter the destructive myths that the death of a child greatly increases the risk of divorce, almost making it inevitable. This commonly held assumption is not based upon evidence (Schwab, 1997). While a child's death certainly may strain a marital relationship, divorce seems more related to prior difficulties. In such cases, the death of a child may simply remove a motivation or energy for working on resolution or staying together. In fact, one of the advantages of counseling is that it can facilitate communication and understanding that actually may strengthen the relationship.

Parental Loss

While most studies of children's reactions to the loss of a parent do not focus upon gender, Worden (1996) did find that girls, regardless of age, exhibited more anxiety and somatic symptoms than boys. Girls also seemed to idealize the deceased parent more and indicated an increased sensitivity to changes in the family following a parent's death. Boys were more likely to self-report their conduct as worse, suggesting that some of their grief was manifested in acting out behaviors. The treatment of grievers also differed by gender of the child. Boys were more frequently admonished to be strong, while girls were more able to share feelings with other family members.

Such differences were also found in adult children who had experienced the loss of a father. Two studies (Moss et al., 1997; Moss et al.,

1997) found middle-aged sons experienced less grief and fewer somatic symptoms. Sons' expressions of grief tended to be active, cognitive, and private.

Gay Men and Lesbians

Comparatively, little research has been done on the grieving patterns of gay men or lesbians. Some research has noted that because of societal constraints, significant losses of gay men and lesbians are often disenfranchised, limiting social support for gay grievers (see, for example, Doka, 1987, 1989; Kelly, 1977; Kimmell, 1978; Murphy & Perry, 1988).

Research *has* been done in the context of AIDS-related losses. These studies are problematic in that losses tend to be multiple, stigmatized, and developmentally unexpected. In addition, surviving partners may themselves be HIV-infected. These studies did find high degrees of stress, including depression, anxiety, and guilt (Martin & Dean, 1993a, 1993b; Martin, 1988; Viny, Henry, Walker, & Crokes, 1992; Cherney & Verhey, 1996). They also did find increased use of sedatives as well as alcohol and recreational drugs (Cherney & Verhey, 1996; Martin & Dean, 1993a; Martin, 1988).

Clearly, there is a need for studies of the patterns of grieving among gay and lesbian populations. While one would not necessarily expect that proportions of instrumental, intuitive, or dissonant grievers would differ among homosexual or heterosexual men and women, further research would be useful both to assist homosexual grievers and to understand the varied factors that influence the assumption of a given pattern.

Summary

These results hardly should be surprising. The very nature of relationships, that is, the meaning a relationship has to a person and the complementary roles that persons share within relationships, differs by gender. As the research indicated, time, energy, and meaning invested in relationships can very well be different for a mother or wife than for a father or husband. Silverman (1988), for example, found that widowhood in women created a crisis of identity, since they were more invested in the spousal relationship than men. It should be recognized, however, that Silverman's sample was of a content that was unlikely to have an independent career. The role of wife was at the core of their identity. Both Schwab (1996) and Bohannon (1990), for example, found lower levels of grief in fathers who had experienced the death of a child as compared to their wives. Similarly, the loss of a parent seemed to have more effect on middle-aged daughters than sons, reflecting in part, the authors believed, less of an emotional attachment to the relationship (Moss et al., 1997; Moss et al., 1997). This certainly reflects traditional gender roles that see women as more invested in familial relationships.

In addition, every society has norms that proscribe not only behavior but feelings as well. Hochschild (1979) notes that these "feeling rules" dictate what feelings ought to be expressed in each situation. Naturally, these feeling rules can differ by gender. Since a subset of these "feeling rules" relates to expressions of grieving, it is understandable that research has revealed some gender differences in patterns of grief. For example, a number of studies have found that, apart from anger and guilt, men had a difficult time expressing affect (Glick et al., 1974; Goldbach et al., 1991; Lang & Gottlieb, 1993; Schwab, 1990). Conventional views of the effect of gender on the experience and expression of anger have recently been challenged (Sharkin, 1993). Deffenbacher et al. (1996) concluded that "men and women are angered by similar things and to similar degrees, express themselves in similar ways, and suffer similar consequences" (p. 146). Similarly, studies support the fact that women's grief is expressed more intensely and affectively (Bohannon, 1991; Carroll & Shaefer, 1994; Douglas, 1990).

Moreover, these feeling rules extend to the sympathy one expects (Clark, 1987). As Clark (1987) notes, sympathy is guided not only by circumstances but by other elements of one's biography, such as gender. This serves to create Cook's (1988) double bind. Grieving males are given little support, but they are expected to support others.

These differences in experience and expression of grief are well-documented in the literature that has surveyed gender differences. These differences have been found over a wide array of losses.

Researchers have also shown that men and women choose different strategies for adapting. For instance, men used self-help groups less often than women (Osterweiss, Solomon, & Green, 1984). Rando (1986) suggested one possible reason for this reluctance to attend support groups. Following the loss of a child, men saw themselves as needing to be providers, protectors, and problem-solvers, making it difficult for them to accept and receive help. In addition, other studies have found men to be more private, intellectual, and introspective in their grief (Cook, 1988; Hogan & Balk, 1990; Lang & Gottlieb, 1993; Moss et al., 1997). And Bonanno's (1997) work suggests that such strategies may be as effective, if not more effective, than emotional expression and ventilation.

Men also appear to choose activity as a way of adapting to unpleasant feelings. For example, Glick et al. (1974) reported that widowers in their study expressed a concern with being "realistic" (i.e., focusing on solving the immediate problems of loss). They also reported that men were more likely to experience social recovery earlier, often quickly returning to work.

Returning to work may be a useful coping strategy, since it allows persons to become distracted from their grief (Osterweiss et al., 1984).

There may be other differences in adaptive strategies as well. Cook (1988) noted a number of cognitive strategies used by the men in her study, such as diversion and reflection. Employing activity and cognitive strategies to adapt to loss can be very effective. Powers and Wampold (1994) emphasized the critical role that cognitive and behavioral responses have in successfully adapting to loss.

Such differences have long been recognized in folkwisdom and custom. The Russian "Old Believer's" burial custom, in which men make the caskets and tell stories while women weep and wail, is echoed in many cultures.

Other methods of adaptations to loss may not be as effective. Studies of gay men responding to the loss of lovers and friends in the AIDS epidemic reaffirm the observations of some counselors (Staudacher, 1991) that males may be more inclined to use substances such as drugs or alcohol to mitigate the grieving process. These studies have shown that common patterns among gay men included both the use of sedatives and recreational drugs (Martin, 1988; Martin & Dean, 1993a). An investigation of men on skid row revealed that many of them had turned to alcohol following the deaths of their wives (Hughes & Fleming, 1991).

It is important to recognize that many of the gender differences cited thus far may be mitigated by the type of loss or other variables, such as social class. Furthermore, there is most likely an interaction between gender differences in bereavement and age. Differences seem less apparent in older cohorts. For example, Feinson (1986) found that any gender differences in her study seemed to disappear when social and demographic variables were factored. Another study, exploring the reactions of older persons to spousal loss, found gender was unrelated to measures of adjustment and depression (Futterman, Gallagher, Thompson, Lovett, & Gilewski, 1990). In fact, the majority of studies reporting differences involved younger samples. This is not surprising, given the general agreement that both sexes, as they age, move toward androgyny (Chiriboga & Thurnher, 1976; Huyck, 1990; Neugarten & Gutmann, 1968).

☐ Accounting for the Difference: Gender Role Socialization as a Shaping Agent

What accounts then for these differences in patterns of grief? As we said repeatedly, there is no one factor but certainly research has shown that what we label an instrumental pattern of grief is more typical of men than women.

Most likely, these differences are due, in large part, to gender-role socialization. However, prior to exploring how socialization in a gender role influences the adaptation of a grieving pattern, it is critical to acknowledge two points.

First, even within a culture, gender roles are not static. The content of a role is always dynamic, changing over time. What constitutes acceptable male or female behavior changes from one cohort or generation to another. For example, Rotundo (1993) historically reviews American definitions of the male role and notes both continuities and changes in male identity over the past 200 years. In studying the 20th century male culture, Rotundo describes how mastery of one's emotions and enthusiasm was seen as a key developmental issue that separated boys from men. Boys could not control their enthusiasm; men had to teach and model self-restraint. Among both men and boys, emotional mastery and stiff-lipped courage were seen as virtues.

However, early in the 19th century, men often shared intimate, caring relationships with other men. Since men were expected to invest much time in public and social affairs, relationships between men were perceived as natural and productive. This began to change later in that century for three reasons. With industrialization, the work role becomes more fundamental to one's identity. There were limited opportunities to bond with other men outside of work. Second, the concurrent rise of individualism also isolated men from their peers. As men became older, established in their work and marriage, there was little time for sharing feelings and thoughts with other men. Congregating with other males began to be considered a mark of the boy, not the man. Finally, homophobia reared its unlovely head. Since homosexuals had been labeled as "unmanly," it was difficult to acknowledge feelings for other men that would allow one to build supportive connections with one another. By the 20th century, contemporary visions of the male role had taken root, emphasizing the male as a rugged individual.

Recently, these conceptions of maleness have been challenged. Bly (1990), for example, offers a poetic vision of what the male role can be. Drawing from ancient myths, he envisions a male role that encompasses a vigorous sense of masculinity with an ability to be emotionally rooted. Ironically, Bly sees the male as first having to acknowledge significant griefs caused by lost fathers, dreams, and morality. Similarly, Keen (1991) also sees men forging an identity out of a struggle with grief and guilt, burdened by the demand of work and performance. To Keen, the essence of men is that they are spiritual warriors attempting to create meaning in their lives. Their quest is to fashion a new sense of male identity that allows for both emotionality and communality in some yet undefined but distinctly male way. Should the fledgling male movement succeed in redefining masculinity, it may likely change patterns of grieving as well.

Second, as mentioned previously, there are differences within gender role socialization even within a culture at any given time. For example, many of the more androgynous perspectives on socializing children into gender roles are not universally shared among each social class or ethnic group within American society. While many middle-class families may socialize both boys and girls to more diffusely defined gender roles—allowing more opportunities for individual preferences in toys, play, sports, or other activities and respecting, even encouraging sensitivity in boys—other cultural groupings, especially in lower socioeconomic groups or among varied cultural groups, may emphasize more traditional definitions of the male and female role.

Even within the larger culture, messages about appropriate roles may be both subtle and ambiguous. For example, even in groups that emphasize more androgynous rather than rigid role definitions, it is still more acceptable for girls to emulate boys' behaviors than visa versa. Just compare the connotations of the words "tomboy" and "sissy."

In addition, gender role socialization is evident throughout the culture—in cartoons, advertisements, and, of course, throughout the media. Often these messages are subliminal—the token tomboy who plays on a team of boys. A "Cathy" cartoon illustrates that subtlety: Cathy, a liberated single woman is seen buying a toy for a friend's child. She is annoyed by a saleswoman's inquiry on gender and asks for a "unisex" toy. The saleswoman suggests dinosaurs, and as Cathy wryly comments that we have to go into our prehistory to find such a toy, the saleswoman returns with two dinosaurs—one with a make-up kit, the other with weapons.

While gender role socialization, then, is neither uniform nor static, it does have broad effects. Two are most evident.

Gender Role Socialization Frames the Experience of Grief

Earlier in this chapter, the fact that in any given society gender role rules influence the ways each gender relates to varied social roles was explored, affecting the meaning they give to different attachments. For example, Silverman (1986), in her studies on widows, points out that for many males the role of husband is critical. Yet, Silverman reminds us that, it is not tied to his identity as strongly as that of a wife is to a woman.

Similarly, Thompson (1995) argues that men are socialized to live their lives in the "public sphere," balancing work, familial, and other community roles, while many women traditionally live life in a more private sphere, centering on family.

The implication of both of these ideas is that women may be more invested in family roles. Thus, when a loss occurs it has multiple impact.

A woman may lose a more central role, more critical to her identity than that of a man. In addition, there may be less opportunity for diversion in other roles or for reinvesting in such roles.

Naturally, this point should not be overstressed. Individuals' investments in roles, and the meanings that these relationships have, are affected by a number of variables, of which gender is only one. And certainly the definition of men's and women's roles, especially as they relate to work and family, continue to change.

The Influence of Gender Role on the Socialization of Emotion

In Chapter 5, the role of the family as a shaping agent was emphasized. This means that families socialize children into the need and ways to regulate emotions. Naturally, a family's definition of gender roles can very much affect this socialization of emotion.

Whereas one family may foster sexual stereotypes ("big boys don't cry"), another may pattern the open expression of feelings, regardless of gender. In some families, children are taught to disclose their innermost thoughts, seek solace in community, and value their feelings as the guide to behavior. In other families, stoicism, self-reliance, solitude, and an emphasis on rationality might be modeled. Despite changing attitudes and standards many adults continue to have traditional and stereotyped conceptions of sex roles and behave accordingly.

Gender roles are usually acquired during a child's preschool years. That is, the child adopts socially defined behaviors and attitudes associated with being a male or a female. For example, even boys and girls as young as three years old show differences in the ways they handle everyday pain. At that young age, girls are more likely to show distress and seek out adult comfort than boys (Fearon, McGrath, & Achat, 1996). Beginning with the games of childhood, boys and girls develop different (although complementary) social skills. While girls are learning to interact one-on-one or in small groups, to work cooperatively, and to have empathy for others, boys are learning to compete with one another. They practice leading, following, and working with others on a "team" toward some common goal—usually defeating another "team" (Lever, 1978)!

Experience and childrearing practices retain their eminence in shaping sex roles and emotional behaviors. In particular, the father plays a critical role in sex-role development during the preschool years. The father's degree of masculinity seems to promote traditional sex roles not only in sons, but in daughters as well (Hetherington, Cox, & Cox, 1978). That the father's masculinity (and not necessarily mother's femininity) is associated with a girl's sex-role development suggests that girls acquire sex roles through a process of reciprocal role learning (Lamb & Urberg, 1978). In other words, girls learn how to behave as females by complementing their father's masculinity—the more traditionally masculine dad is, the more traditionally feminine his daughter will be. Interestingly, the opposite is not true for boys. That is, boys tend to identify with and imitate their fathers' behavior, and those boys whose mothers are very feminine do not necessarily behave in a more masculine way.

As adults, males are attracted to sports that emphasize a competitive role. Their friendships usually center on shared activities. Men, as well as boys, view their relationships with others, particularly males, in terms of hierarchy (Gilligan, 1982).

Often, there is a tendency among males to de-emphasize emotionality, especially the more tender emotions (e.g., crying, nurturing). Socialization into the male role means learning to control one's emotions. As a result, men tend to learn active and problem-focused solutions of coping with stress. In addition, they tend to value self-reliance. Solving one's problems and facing one's difficulties alone have long been defined as hallmarks of manhood (Gray, 1992).

Women's experiences are somewhat different. From an early age, girls at play tend to be more cooperative and to have consideration and empathy for others (Lever, 1976). They are also taught to share confidences and draw support from one another. Emotional expressiveness is not repressed; in fact, females tend to learn more emotion-focused ways of coping (Barnett, Biener, & Baruch, 1987). Nothing in the female role eschews the support or nurturance of others. To the contrary, the ability to offer and accept such nurturance is a critical mark of the woman's role. As a consequence, because females are socialized to be more attuned to emotions, they may learn to pay more attention to their own emotional states as well as others' emotional states.

Yet Not Deterministic

Yet this should not be perceived in a deterministic way. Socialization experiences differ from individual to individual. And other factors such as personality, culture, or other experiences can affect the grieving pattern that an individual adopts.

For example, in certain cultures, the expression of affect is supported strongly for both men and women, while in others affect is discouraged for both. In the former culture one would likely find more intuitive grievers among both genders, while in the latter instrumental patterns may be more evident.

Patterns of grief are shaped by all of the powerful cultural forces of socialization, with the immediate family playing a most important part. Sons of instrumental grievers will, themselves, most likely model their fathers, while their sisters, based on the principle of reciprocal role learning, adopt the more intuitive response to bereavement. In families where the father is an intuitive griever, the sons will likely follow suit, while daughters learn to grieve in instrumental fashion.

There may be other factors, too, in the socialization experience. For example, comparable socialization experiences can lead certain women to grieve in a more instrumental way. Perhaps, women who are raised with strongly competitive values or given early caregiving responsibilities such as raising younger siblings may develop a more instrumental pattern for coping with loss. And boys growing up in families where affective expression is encouraged, even modeled, especially by their fathers, can show a more intuitive pattern.

Since gender role socialization is but one factor in an array of influences that delineate a grieving pattern, any combination of factors can influence whether a male or female moves toward the intuitive or instrumental end of the continuum. Thus, certain socialization experiences, cultures, or even personality traits can lead to a woman's becoming an instrumental griever or a man's becoming more intuitive in pattern.

This may help explain dissonant grieving patterns as well. Given the dominant images of the male role, males who do experience grief in a more intuitive way may feel constrained to express their grief or adapt to it in such a fashion that they will not be perceived as less manly or feel they are not fulfilling their own gender role expectations to care for others. It is in dissonant grievers that such gender role expectations truly can be said to contain and to constrain the expression of grief.

☐ Conclusion

It is critical, however, not to overstate the effect of gender role socialization on the grieving process. This is especially true in light of the fact that gender differences are often overexaggerated. Maccoby and Jacklin's (1974) landmark review of more than 2,000 studies found only a few characteristics in which girls and boys differed significantly. Highly touted cognitive differences between the sexes—girls' superior verbal ability, boys' better spatial and mathematical aptitudes—do not appear until near puberty and are very small indeed. Personality differences are few also. Girls generally cooperate more with their parents and their peers and show greater concern for and identification with others' feelings. Yet some girls love rough play and are very competitive and impassive, while some boys hate roughhousing and are very sensitive to the feelings of others. But even by age 5, boys and girls still show an equal interest in babies and a willingness to help care for infants (Berman, 1984).

Thus, we must be careful not to overemphasize differences between the genders. Those differences that do exist are statistically small and convincing for large groups of men and women but are not as valid for individuals. For gender, even though a significant factor influencing the patterns by which men and women grieve, is but one factor. Stated differently, gender *influences* patterns of grief, but gender does not *determine* patterns of grief.

CHAPTER

8

Culture as a Shaping Agent

The previous chapter considered some of the reasons why gender influences grieving patterns. A key factor or concern was the effects of gender role socialization. This naturally brings into focus the role of culture, since cultural expectations frame gender roles, that is, in every culture there are different expectations about how men and women will both feel and behave.

Gender role norms are but one way that a culture influences grief and the patterns by which grief is experienced and expressed. Culture affects other aspects of the grieving process as well. At a very fundamental level, culture influences the process of attachment. Cultural norms define kinship and regulate social relationships. Culturally based experiences even frame expectations for survival, affecting investment and attachments. Kastenbaum (1971), for example, hypothesizes that in cultures with high rates of child mortality, parental attachment, even social valuation of children, may be limited until the child reaches puberty and the seeming likelihood of survival. Culture also defines appropriate expressions of grief, ritual practices, and subsequent mourning behavior.

This chapter explores the impact of culture on grief. It begins by first defining culture and then traces its many influences on grief and the grieving process. For culture, too, is a major shaping agent, influencing the ways men and women grieve.

☐ The Nature of Culture

Culture is best defined as a way of life. It encompasses both material and nonmaterial aspects of life. Material aspects of a culture refer to all the visible artifacts—clothes, food, technology—all the items used within the culture. While the material aspects of a culture are most visible, it is the nonmaterial aspects that are most critical. These refer to beliefs, norms, and values—the ways of thinking, believing, behaving, and relating that truly define the culture. Berger and Luckman (1966), for example, state that even reality is socially constructed. By that, they mean that culture determines the ways one organizes the world. For example, in cultures such as the U.S., kinship is determined bilineally. In other cultures it may be patrilineal or matrilineal. In a patrilineal society, for instance, the sister of one's mother may not be defined as kin. But all aspects of reality are culturally determined from the ways one understands diseases to how one views the transcendental. And each culture will define its reality differently.

Cultures can be analyzed in several ways. One can distinguish between cultural universals, aspects of the culture that are widely shared; cultural alternates, or choices within a culture; and cultural specialties, or aspects of a culture that are shared by a more limited group. In complex cultures, while there may be some cultural universals, there are often large arrays of specialties and alternates. For example, in the U.S. culture generally, rules of defining kinship, laws, and certain values such as a shared belief in the worth of education are illustrations of cultural universals. The wide range of transportation options or foods are examples of cultural alternates. In fact, some foods that still exist primarily within an ethnic group might be best defined as specialties. One illustration might be that 30 years ago Mexican foods were primarily shared only within that ethnic group or within the Southwest region. Now it has become a widely accepted alternative, readily available in malls, restaurants, and supermarkets. Other examples of specialties would be professional jargon, skills, or beliefs shared only by a small group.

One might also distinguish subcultures or cocultures, which are groups within the larger culture that share many of the universals but have their own mix of cultural alternates and specialties. While one may often think of ethnic groups as cocultures or subcultures, cultures can also be delineated by other common factors such as class, age, religion, or shared behaviors and lifestyles. An illustration of the latter would be the presence in many urban areas of a robust gay subculture.

Persons enter a culture in two ways. Some may assimilate into a culture, gradually learning its ways. But most commonly, one is born into a culture. As one is socialized by agents of socialization such as families or schools, one is also socialized into a way of life that becomes the only reality one knows. The danger, of course, is the possibility that the way of life can become *the* way of life. Such ethnocentrism may be expressed as a perplexity that other cultures may do things differently or even a belief that one's own culture is superior, that other ways of viewing or organizing reality are foolish or wrong.

But cultures are not static. Early theorists of social and cultural change tended to view these patterns in sweeping, evolutionary ways. For example, both Hegel (1990) and Marx (1993) saw cultural change as the inevitable result of conflicts arising from contrasting ideas or interests. Sorokin (1937–1941) viewed cultural change more as an everlasting pendulum, swinging over centuries from sensate cultures that emphasized sense experience as an ultimate reality to those ideational cultures that see ideas or beliefs as the core of reality. The pendulum shifts because as a culture follows the inevitable path from one pole to the other, it encompasses less of reality. Sorokin might wonder whether the current revival of interest in spirituality may be the death throes of a sensate culture now reaching a crisis point prior to beginning a cultural shift.

However, whether or not these grand theories do account for cultural change, other factors generally have a significant role in changing culture. And as culture changes, the experiences and expressions of grief and death are modified as well.

Industrialization, for instance, has had a significant role in changing the experience of death and grief by changing the very demographics of death. No longer were women and children the most vulnerable populations; now the aged were. This may, as will be explored, influence the experience of attachment and grief. Industrialization affected attachment in other ways as well; it often separated men from the home; child-rearing, once shared, now became more the province of women; boys no longer worked side by side with their fathers, learning both a trade as well as how to be a man.

Other changes in attachment patterns were evident as well. The communal or civic ties, necessary in an agrarian economy, lessened. Families and individuals now shared stronger ties within the family but looser ties outside. In short, persons had attachments but within a small group. Bureaucratization and professionalization removed the care of the dying and the dead from the home to professional caregivers. Death became removed from the everyday experience. Increasing cultural diversity throughout the Western world meant that meanings accorded to death were no longer universally shared.

Such changes tend to breed reactions. The death studies movement has in many ways attempted to "deprofessionalize" death. Hospice, for example, has encouraged families to allow the dying to die at home rather than in institutions. The rise of the self-help movement has attempted to recreate a sense of community among persons who struggle with common issues.

The men's movement has sought to redefine masculinity; yet there is a paradox. These very movements have created new sets of professionals and new norms about ways that individuals should act, die, and grieve.

Thus, culture frames the experience of grief—from who survives, to patterns of attachments, to the norms for expressing grief and mourning. Yet these patterns are not static. They, too, shift as individuals within a culture face new experiences, new ideas or technologies, or new problems.

☐ Cultures and Grief: Attachment

Implied throughout the earlier section is the notion that cultural experiences and norms affect the experience of grief. This occurs on a very basic level as cultures frame the very nature of attachment. It does this in a number of ways.

First, as stated earlier, it defines patterns of kinship and relationship. Societies may also vary in their definition of critical familial roles. For example, in many Christian religions, when a child is baptized (often near birth), the child's parents may choose godparents or sponsors who promise to take a role in assisting the child in fulfilling his religious obligations and supporting the child in his or her faith journey. In many cultures, it is simply an honorary role that has little but ritual significance. But in other cultures, such as many Latino or traditional Italian cultures, the godparents are expected to play a significant role in the child's development, especially should a child be separated from a parent. A proverb expresses these expectations as well: "Life is so tough that a child needs two sets of parents." The point is that in such a society, these extra familial attachments can become exceedingly strong.

Similarly, in many subgroups there may exist other ties that bespeak a strong sense of attachment even in the absence of formal kinship. For instance, in some cultures men may be allowed or even expected to have mistresses. In the U.S., among gay subcultures, the relationship of lovers or life partners is acknowledged. In short, every culture defines significant relationships, both within and outside kinship lines. These relationships help regulate patterns of attachment and, therefore, influence grief.

Second, not only does a culture define relationships, its norms define the quality and nature of relationships. This occurs on many levels. As mentioned earlier, culture has expectations about survival that may frame attachments. For example, Rosenblatt (1993) notes that many lower income Brazilian mothers see the death of a child as inevitable. Attachments become limited then, until a child shows promise of a long-term survival.

Beyond expectations of survival, culture influences attachment in other ways. Cultural norms define the very meaning of relationships. In some cultures, a wife may be defined as little more than chattel or property, here her role being to serve her husband. But in other societies, the norms of relationship may be more companionate. In such times, the death of a spouse has greater meaning, since one has not only experienced the loss of whatever functional role the spouse provided but the loss of a friend and lover as well. Each culture, then, defines the content of roles, affecting the meaning that persons experience within the loss.

In addition to the meaning of the relationship, cultural norms influence attachment in other, more subtle, ways. For example, cultural norms define the amount of investment one places in varied attachments, therefore influencing the experience of grief. Parkes (1996b) provides a useful illustration; in traditional Malaysian society, children are reared within a communal setting. Children who are raised in this long-house culture will be reared by many "mothers" or parental figures. The loss of a parent then, Parkes suggests, is less traumatic than in a society in which a child is raised by a single set of parents. Parkes' illustration reminds us of the variety of cultural contexts that influence attachment. For example, in many Western cultures, life is organized around narrowly defined families or small intimate networks. This means that many persons are connected to a small network to which they forge strong attachments. In other cultures, the organization of social life is more communal. Here, individuals have a larger number of attachments but these attachments seem less intense. Blauner (1968) notes that such forms of organization are very functional in societies where the death rate is high and unpredictable.

Thompson's (1995) work also explores the ways that culture influences attachment. Thompson emphasized that varied cultural norms divide life into tasks completed within the private sphere of the family from those done in the public sphere of the larger society. According to Thompson, traditional gender roles in Western societies meant that many men lived life in the public sphere, while most women experienced life more in the private sphere. This meant that, while family losses affected men, they had outlets and roles outside of the family. The experience, though, for women was different. The loss of a family member such as a child struck at the center of their world, created a far different meaning for the loss. Thompson's observations are supported by the work of Silverman (1981, 1986), who found significant differences in the meaning of widowhood among older men and women. To men, the loss of a spouse meant the end of a significant role. But to women, the loss of a spouse and the assumption of the role of widow meant the end of the significant role of "wife," causing a total reassessment of identity not often seen in men.

Naturally, as described earlier, cultures do change, and changing work patterns as well as reformulation of gender roles will lead to constant redefinitions of the meaning of a particular loss. Different generations, too, have distinct experiences that shape a particular cohort, giving rise to new ways of relating to mates, children, and other relationships, changing patterns of attachment as well as norms of expression (e.g., Rotundo, 1993).

Nonetheless, the basic point still can be made that cultures define the nature of the attachments, influencing, then, the very experience of grief.

☐ Culture and the Expression of Grief

Cultural norms not only influence the experience of grief but the expression of grief as well. Hochschild (1979) states that every society has "feeling rules" that govern the expression of emotions. Just as norms regulate behavior, feeling rules attempt to regulate the experience and expression of emotion.

A subset of these feeling rules may be caused by grieving rules (Doka, 1989). Such rules define who one may grieve, what one may grieve, and how one's grief is expressed. Grief experienced outside of the parameters of these feeling rules can be said to be disenfranchised.

These feeling rules determine not only what losses one can grieve, but how an individual grieves. Cultures naturally differ in the ways grief is expected to be expressed. In some cultures, intense affective displays are normative, even considered an expression of respect. But in other cultures, such emotional expression is avoided. For example, in Bali grief is muted because emotional agitation it is believed will impede the journey of the deceased, and prayers for the deceased will not be heard unless they are spoken calmly (Rosenblatt, 1993). In other cultures, feelings are rarely expressed. For example, some cultures are known to be resistant to emotive expression. A common midwestern joke tells of the taciturn Scandinavian farmer who loved his wife so much that he almost told her. Other cultures may even express grief in violent or angry ways (Rosenblatt, 1993) or mandate other modes of expression. Rosenblatt (1997) cites for illustration one Pacific atoll. In that culture there is the Ifaluk concept of *lalomwieu*, which involves a grief response that encompasses sadness, loneliness, and obsessive thinking of the deceased. As Rosenblatt summarizes "What emotions are felt, how they are expressed, and how they are understood are matters of culture" (p. 35).

Naturally, culture will influence the patterns of an individual's grief. In affectivity expressive cultures, intuitive patterns will be more common. In those that emphasize affective restraint, persons are more likely to be socialized into more instrumental patterns.

However, it is critical to remember that cultural influences are but one shaping agent. It is likely that other factors are equally important shapers of an individual's grieving pattern. Therefore, it is not unusual that any given individual's experience of grief will be at variance with culturally approved patterns of expression or adaptation. In such cases, dissonant varieties may be prevalent. And in such cases, individuals may pay a price as they experience this discord between their experience of grief and allowable expression. For example, Parkes (1996a) suggested that one result of affective control in Rwanda has been the outbursts of genocidal violence. Similarly, Parkes viewed the cognitive suppression among the Navajos, where the deceased's name is never mentioned again as leading to depression.

It also should be recognized that in many cultures, especially those that are diverse and complex, the grieving rules themselves might mirror that complexity and diversity. For example, in countries like the U.S., with many large cultural subgroups, individuals may be exposed to a range of grieving rules—some that allow affect and others that discourage it. Feelings rules, then, can be varied, even within a society, and change over time. Biddle and Walter (1998) note that among the grieving rules in England are two predominant patterns. Private grief is, they claim, the traditional perspective. Here the feeling rules require that people grieve in private, giving subtle hints that their grief is, in fact, deeply felt but that they are maintaining a stoical appearance in order to spare others. Others, in turn, are expected to admire the stoicism, especially since it comes at such a cost. The other pattern, called "expressive grief," Biddle and Walter identify as a more recent transplant from the U.S. Here, open emotional expression is valued.

In some cases, too, the grieving rules may change throughout the course of grief. For example, in the U.S. emotional expression is encouraged early in the grieving period but not later. The result is that it is the instrumental griever who may experience disenfranchisement early in the loss, while the intuitive griever feels disenfranchised later in the loss when affective responses are less valued and accepted. This is evident in workplace policies. Most employers accord a period of time off for bereavement leave, generally 3–5 days. After this period of affective catharsis, employees are expected to quickly return to prior work patterns, compartmentalizing their grief. As time goes on, affective expression is less supported.

Persons who fail to follow grieving norms face community sanctions. For example, in one famous Australian case, a mother claimed a dingo, or wild dog, attacked and dragged off her sleeping baby. The mother's absence of strong affect caused suspicion among police. She was later charged with and convicted of the child's murder; later, her conviction was overturned. The case still generates strong controversy in Australia and debates over the mother's actual guilt. The point of this case is simply that her failure to grieve in a prescribed manner was considered strong evidence of guilt. Similarly, someone who after the initial period continues to express affect may experience the withdrawal of support and criticism, especially at work, over the ways that person is grieving.

Grieving rules vary, too, within a society. They may vary by ethnicity as different subcultures may have their own distinct ways that persons express grief (Kalish & Reynolds, 1981). Naturally, as groups become more assimilated, these norms may lose their distinctiveness. One client, for illustration, who was hispanic, spoke of his discomfort at the older generation who wailed at the casket of his grandmother. He was insightful enough to acknowledge that his older relatives were, in all probability, equally appalled by the absence of wailing in the younger generation.

Grieving rules vary not only by ethnicity but also by other factors such as age, gender, or class. The issue of gender has already been considered in an earlier chapter. But Rosenblatt, Walsh, and Jackson's (1976) research demonstrated that in many cultures grieving rules clearly varied by gender. In a study of 60 societies, they found that while close to 50% (32) demonstrated no differences between genders in crying in grief, the remainder (28) did allow more affective expressions in women.

Differences may also result from development and social class. Generally, societies permit the very young, and sometimes, the very old, greater freedom in expression. As Rotundo (1993) notes, one mark of adulthood is the ability to conform to normative standards. Class, too, can create distinctions. In certain social classes, anger, even violence, is considered more acceptable. Biddle and Walter (1998), for example, describe the upper class English feeling rules that emphasize that the well-bred person gives no indication of inner emotion.

Cultures differ not only in feeling rules but also in other ways as well, such as rituals in and norms on appropriate adaptive and mourning behaviors. Every culture has their own distinct rituals by which death is acknowledged. In some cultures, these rituals may continue for a time after the loss, marking periods of mourning. For example, with Judaism, there are a series of rituals that take place both at points within a year after the loss, as well as at other occasions. Other cultures may have rituals that recognize little beyond the disposition of the dead. Rituals, too, may differ even within a society by factors such as gender. In Madagascar, for illustration, there are two huts for rituals or grieving: a "male house," where men meet to organize rituals for laying the body and a "house of tears," where women come together to wail and cry.

Mourning behaviors vary too. In some cultures, persons may mark mourning by wearing certain clothes for a period of time, perhaps even for life. It may be appropriate or inappropriate to speak of the deceased or to use the name again. In each society, rules and norms govern adaptation.

Naturally, individuals are socialized to these norms through a variety of socialization agents such as family, religious, and educational institutions. Nadeau's (1998) work reminds us that family often becomes the key agent in socializing individuals to the appropriate ways that grief may be experienced and expressed. It is families that employ cultural meanings as they attempt to make sense of loss and grief. And it is in the family that the experience, expression, and adaptation to grief is validated.

☐ Conclusion

This chapter emphasizes that one of the critical shaping agents in determining grieving patterns is provided by cultures. While individuals within a culture will vary, cultural norms will strongly influence both the experience of grief, as well as the patterns by which individuals express and adapt to grief. These standards may influence grieving in a number of ways. They make one pattern more dominant in a given culture, or they influence the fact that certain genders or classes or other groupings may be more inclined toward one pattern than another. But because culture is one shaping agent, individuals may experience that their experience and expression of grief is at variance from cultural expectations. This may result in possible negative outcomes. For here, the experience or expression of grief may be disenfranchised, limiting social support and complicating grief.

IMPLICATIONS AND INTERVENTIONS

Since counseling does have an affective bias, instrumental grievers may be reluctant to use counseling services or may find them unhelpful. This is unfortunate because counseling may be extremely helpful in assisting any grievers to surmount a crises, particularly those who have limited support (Parkes, 1980). But, if counselors are to assist instrumental grievers effectively, they will have to examine their own biases, approaches, and interventions.

This section explores the counseling process, reviewing the ways that this process can work best with grieving individuals on each pole of the intuitive–instrumental continuum. Many of the interventive or self-help strategies commonly employed to assist grieving persons can work well with all types of grievers—perhaps for different reasons. The key is to assess, utilize, and validate each grieving individual's unique strengths.

The message of this section then underlies the thesis of the book: It is not the style of grieving that is the problem—it is only a problem when counselors fail to recognize and to adapt their approaches to that style.

9

CHAPTER

Adaptive Strategies: Implications for Counselors

Ever since the death of their child, Marie and Russ have gone to a counselor. While Marie continues to go, Russ stopped after three sessions. He believed that he was consistently "ganged up on" at these sessions. Whenever he started a conversation with "I think,"—"or some other such word the counselor would say—"I am much more interested in what you feel." After a while, Russ ceased to say much, and then stopped going entirely.

Russ's experience is shared by many instrumental grievers. They often find grief counseling, with its strong bias toward affective ventilation, of limited value. In fact, many instrumental grievers may even perceive it as threatening, for their own approaches, strengths, and strategies are discounted. Also, interventive strategies may be designed that rather than building on their strengths, ignore them and concentrate instead on addressing what is perceived as their glaring weakness—the lack of strong affect.

This chapter's goal is to explore adaptive strategies. Since the intuitive pattern is widely recognized within the counseling community as "normal," the focus is on adaptive strategies useful to instrumental grievers. It is hoped that counselors may find it useful to understand the repertoire of strategies different grievers will use. This can empower counselors as they validate and explore the strategies of grievers who do seek help. In addition, it can assist counselors as they aid other persons, such as family members, in assessing and understanding the strategies that other grievers may employ. This is critical because as stated earlier, differences in

patterns can cause conflict. Since many counselors themselves may neither validate nor understand a pattern differing from their own, they actually may exacerbate such conflicts by discounting cognitive and behavioral approaches, or become impatient with affective expression. Many of
these strategies may also serve as useful bridges, offering intervention
opportunities for dissonant grievers that allow them to find safe and compatible ways to express the grief that they do experience.

At a conference where the then termed "masculine grief" was presented,
one therapist noted during the question and answer period, "If I understand your thoughts well enough, no one is going to get rich treating
masculine grievers (instrumental)." His observation had, in fact, great va-
lidity. Instrumental grievers are unlikely to appear in therapeutic or self-
help groups, nor are they often apt to present themselves for individual
counseling. In fact, when they do present themselves for counseling in
either one individual or group context, the counselor may suspect that
they may not be true instrumental grievers but rather dissonant grievers
(see Sidebar 9.1).

As described in an earlier chapter, dissonant grievers tend to have inconsistent patterns in the way they experience and express their grief.
Here it is the confines of social roles, expectations or situational circumstances that may compel them to utilize ways of expressing and adapting
to their losses that are at variance with their experience. In one case, for
example, a 35-year-old woman was devastated by the loss of her husband, yet she felt she needed to be strong in order to provide for and
protect her children. Outwardly, she seemed like a classic instrumental
griever—stoic and rarely showing emotion. Her adaptive strategies were
those of an instrumental griever as well. She talked of her loss freely
without great emotion and devoted great energy to making her deceased
husband's business a success. But she carried substantial pain, and almost
every night quietly cried herself to sleep.

Randy's reaction to the loss of his adult daughter's death was similar.
He was a 52-year-old construction supervisor at the time of the death. At
home, he felt he needed to support and protect his wife. At work, he did
not feel it was safe or appropriate to express his great depth of feeling.
Instead, he cried in his car each day as he commuted to work.

In both cases counseling provided support and an outlet to express and
ventilate affect. In addition, it allowed them to explore alternative strategies for expressing their grief. The cautionary note, then, is to carefully
assess the reasons why a seemingly instrumental griever seeks counseling.

This does not mean to imply true instrumental grievers will never seek
professional assistance. In fact, they often do for three reasons. First, they
may simply seek validation. Since much of the self-help literature and
popular wisdom about grieving emphasizes affective ventilation, many

---

Sidebar 9.1. Counseling Dissonant Grievers

Counseling can be extremely effective for dissonant grievers. Dissonant grievers, as described earlier, are those who experience grief one way, but because of constraints fail to find compatible ways to express and adapt to their loss. Most are intuitive grievers, but perhaps due to gender role socialization, cultural constraints, or situational circumstances, hide and refrain from expressing their grief. Counseling is useful, as are self-help groups, since it provides a safe place where there is permission to express one's grief.

In counseling dissonant grievers, counselors should first assess whether the griever is truly dissonant. As stated, some instrumental grievers may be concerned that they seemingly lack affect or the ability to emote. Such grievers need exploration of the ways they do experience, express, and adapt to loss as well as validation of their pattern.

Once a counselor is confident that a griever is truly dissonant, the counselor can assist the client in analyzing constraints to their expression and adaptation of the client's experience of grief. Counselors can also assist clients in finding safe places such as self-help groups or using interventive techniques that might allow the client to find compatible ways to express and adapt to his or her loss.

Steven provides an illustration case: raised in an emotionally restricted family, Steven learned to hide his affect. When his mother died, he was troubled that he never told her he loved her. In counseling, he was helped to recognize his depth of feeling and appreciate the many ways he clearly, nonverbally showed his love. The counseling session became a safe and comfortable place for him to probe and ventilate his feelings. He became aware of the ways he used "doing" to avoid confronting his feelings. He also learned that he had missed the comfort of others, crying, for example, only when alone in his car. He was able to identify other safe places where he could feel free to grieve. In a final session, with his voice quivering, he read to an empty chair, a letter he had written his deceased mother, expressing his deep and strong feelings for her.

Counseling with dissonant grievers allows them to acknowledge their experiences, consider the factors that have blocked their expression of those feelings, and identifying effective adaptive strategies for dealing with their feelings.

---

instrumental grievers may assume the lack of strong affect is problematic. The following case is illustrative.

Marty was very close to his father; they even worked together. Throughout his father's illness, Marty took pride in the fact that he was a responsible and very present son. Often he would stay with his father at night, providing respite to his mother. During these nights, he would reminisce with his father, sharing with him his grateful memories of growing up with his dad. After his father's death, he still watches over his mother and keeps the house in good repair. He loves to share funny stories about his father with his own children. He describes feeling "a sense of peace and presence when he does such active sharing." "At times," Marty notes, "I really feel my father is proud of how I'm helping Mom." But knowing his closeness to his dad, his wife is concerned that unless he cries he will have an "emotional blowout" later on. "She just feels I haven't grieved."

Marty's case is typical of instrumental grievers who simply need reassurance and validation that they, in fact, are grieving, albeit in a different way.

Marty's case also points out a second issue that can lead instrumental grievers to counseling. When styles of grief are different within a family, family members can experience considerable conflict and stress. Instrumental and intuitive grievers may have such different ways of experiencing, expressing, and adapting to their loss that it can complicate the other's grief.

Sidebar 9.2. Family Counseling and Grieving Patterns

Different grieving patterns can cause conflict within family systems. Persons with a more intuitive grieving pattern may be concerned that family members who are more instrumental in pattern may be repressing grief or question whether the lack of affect means a lack of commitment or love for the deceased. The instrumental griever may be concerned by the intuitive griever's constant need to express feelings and worry about his or her ability to cope. Both types of grievers may feel frustrated that their pattern of adapting to loss are questioned and feel frustrated in each person's ability to help one another.

For these reasons, family counseling can be very helpful for family systems where different grieving patterns are evident. There are a number of goals for such counseling. First, it is helpful for counselors to affirm the existence of different patterns and explore the different patterns of each family member, offering insight as to the reason such patterns developed.

Second, family members can explore the ways that they can utilize these differences as complimentary strengths. For example, when one of their children died in a car crash, Wally and Carol responded in very different ways. Wally placed many of his energies in following the court case, and, subsequently, in a group that sought to change laws about drinking and driving. Carol needed to speak about the loss. In counseling both were able to affirm the value of each other's approach.

Finally, family members can assess realistically what support they can reasonably expect from others in the family system, and they can explore alternate sources of support as well.

When Ted and Lisa's son died two years ago, Lisa found it helpful to join The Compassionate Friends. While Ted joined to support her, he did not feel that the organization met the same needs for him as it did for his wife. But Lisa was frustrated with Ted's inability and unwillingness to express affect and did not understand his need to channel his energies in administrating a scholarship fund in his son's memory.

Here, different grieving styles clearly have affected the relationship. A goal of counseling in this case is to assist each party in understanding how the other party experiences, expresses, and adapts to loss. Such recognition can lead to an acknowledgment that these differences do not mean that one party loved the deceased less or was less affected by the loss. And it can lead to a discussion of the ways family members can best support each other. In Ted and Lisa's case, Ted learned he could best support Lisa by listening to her and by allowing her opportunities to ventilate feelings. And Lisa learned to accept that support without insisting that Ted also share his feelings. She could acknowledge that her grief needed overt support while Ted needed his space respected.

A third reason for counseling is that instrumental grievers may need to explore their strategies, assessing their strengths and limitations. Not all strategies that instrumental grievers use are effective—no more than they are for intuitive grievers. For example, some strategies like substance abuse merely compound problems. Other strategies, such as problem-solving approaches, can, at times, very useful but at other times lead to early and at times inappropriate attempts at premature replacement. For example, Tom both was lonely and unable to care for himself when his wife died. He accepted a hospice bereavement worker's suggestion that he join a grief group. His goal, however, was to come to the group "to find a woman like my (*deceased*) wife" that he could marry. Here, an attempt at problem solving could push him into a marriage that simply seeks to replace. And other strategies, such as humor, can work in certain situations while in other cases they may alienate support and isolate grievers. All grieving individuals can benefit from assessing their approaches to grief—the strengths as well as the limitations of those approaches.

Intuitive grievers, on the other hand, often find value in group or individual counseling. Their affective responses are generally validated within the counseling framework, and counseling provides an outlet to express their strongly held feelings.

☐ Counseling: Approaches to Different Patterns

There are a variety of different models for grief counseling. Two of the most well known include Worden (1991) and Rando (1993). Both works share certain commonalties that, in fact, represent key approaches to grief counseling. Both differ somewhat in their language of the grieving or, in Rando's terminology, the mourning process. Worden (1991) prefers to speak of four major tasks of grief while Rando (1993) identifies six underlying processes of mourning (see Chapter 2). But both affirm a similar approach to grief counseling, which includes three overlapping phases in the counseling process.

1. *Opening Phase*: In this beginning phase counselors seek to develop trust, rapport, set the counseling contract, and understand the clients history as a way to assess the effects of the loss and the clients goals and motivation in seeking assistance.
2. *Intermediate Phase*: The major work of counseling is done in this phase. While different models may use distinct language in describing this process, it essentially involves identifying what is complicating grief and assisting bereaved individuals in finding ways to ameliorate it. So, for example, Worden (1991) would advise counselors to assess what tasks grieving individuals are finding difficult and assist them in identifying ways to complete those tasks successfully. Rando's (1993) approach would recommend assessing what factors complicate the resolution of key mourning processes, again looking toward therapeutic intervention to assist clients in successfully engaging those processes.
3. *Final Phase*: This phase involves the difficult process of terminating the counseling relationship. The client and counselor review the progress that has been made, as well as identifying continuing issues that need attention, noting factors or relationships that can continue to both facilitate or complicate the grieving process. They also explore reactions that occur as the counseling relationship nears termination and set ground rules for any further contact.

This chapter assumes basic familiarity with both the process of grief counseling and with current models. It does attempt, however, to stress and expand upon three central themes:

1. Assessment should always include an assessment of grief patterns, since these patterns are likely to affect motivation in seeking counseling, as well as the adaptive strategies grieving individuals are apt to find helpful.
2. In working with clients, counselors can be most helpful when they validate and utilize clients' strengths in adapting to their loss.
3. Counselors need to be intentional in their intervention, utilizing interventions that build upon existing strengths and adaptive strategies. These themes bear further exploration.

Assessing Patterns

One of the first tasks for counselors, then, is to assess both the patterns of grief and the motivation for seeking counseling. One of the best ways of assessing a pattern is to listen to the language that grieving individuals use in describing their grief (see Sidebar 9.3). Critical incident stress de-

---

Sidebar 9.3. Tools for Assessing Individual Patterns

Counselors should routinely collect information about a bereaved client's previous and current experiences, thoughts, and behaviors. Assessment tools can aid therapists with a tangible measure of their clients' progress as well. Finally, some assessment tools, after thorough and rigorous standardization and norming procedures, may be useful in empirical research.

There are two commonly used methods for clinically assessing clients. The first is to have clients complete a paper-and-pencil inventory or questionnaire. While subjective in nature, inventories and questionnaires often render a quick and concrete measure. Two paper-and-pencil inventories have dominated the bereavement arena. The first, the Texas Revised Inventory of Grief (TRIG) (Faschingbauer, Zisook, & DeVaul, 1987) is composed of 21 items and provides information about the individual's behaviors in the immediate aftermath of the death, as well as how they are presently coping with their grief. A second widely used measure of grief is the Grief Experience Inventory (Sanders, Mauger, & Strong, 1985). The GEI consists of 135 items and 9 subscales and has become the tool of choice of serious researchers. While both instruments are very useful, they both have limitations and neither was originally developed to determine an individual's pattern of grief. (For an excellent review of measurement issues in bereavement see Hansson, Carpenter, & Fairchild, 1993).

The structured interview equips counselors with an alternative to the paper-and-pencil inventories. Many counselors create their own structured interviews, frequently based on their own theoretical perspectives of grief. For a thorough and comprehensive structured interview see Rando's Grief and Mourning Status Interview and Inventory (GAMSII) (1993). Based on the six "R" processes of mourning, Rando's interview elicits basic demographic background, current mental status, history of previous losses, and information about the client's current experiences, behaviors, and thoughts about his or her loss.

The inventory provided (see Appendix A and B) is specifically designed to provide the therapist with a general assessment of a client's pattern of grief. In no way should the Grief Pattern Inventory be a substitute for a thorough and thoughtful interview such as Rando's, nor is it designed to identify complicated forms of mourning.

briefing offers a cogent suggestion. By asking questions such as "How did you respond?" or "How did you react?" rather than "How did you feel?" counselors do three things. First, they allow clients to choose their domain for describing reactions. An intuitive griever may respond with comments such as "I felt terrible" or "I became anxious and depressed," which affirm the strong affective tone. Instrumental grievers are more likely to describe responses in more cognitive ("I couldn't believe it" or "I thought . . ."), physical or behavioral terms ("I felt sick," "I became restless," or "I just wanted to run away"). Remember, too, that it is critical to review reactions since the loss, as initial reactions alone may not be enough to assess grieving patterns.

Second, the use of terms such as "reaction" or "response" not only allows grievers to express grief in their own language, it also conveys a sense of validation. It offers the message that counselors are open to the range of domains that persons may experience or express grief. Conversely, to ask the question "How did you feel?" implies that only the affective response is worthy of examination.

Beyond listening to the clients' language in describing grief, it is always useful to examine past experiences or loss, since initial reactions may not necessarily be predictive of long-term patterns. In such a loss review, it is critical to remember that counselors should assess clients' responses to a variety of losses, encouraging the client to move beyond any earlier deaths in the family to the wide range of losses people experience. This exploration will not only illuminate patterns; it will also provide opportunities to explore the strengths and limitations of a particular pattern.

This review helps in other ways too. It offers a way to recall resources, both external and internal, that have been useful in the past, and it reaffirms to clients that they have survived earlier losses, offering hope that they can survive this one as well.

☐ Acknowledging and Affirming Strengths

In an insightful Pogo cartoon about pollution, Pogo stands in a rubbish-filled field and announces, "We have met the enemy and it is us." That can also be the case with grief, when grieving individuals or those who seek to help them fail to acknowledge and affirm their initial strengths. Reynolds (1993), for example, says that even our language can be victimizing or empowering. He prefers the use of the term "survivor" rather than "bereaved," since the former is much more positive and affirming. Instrumental grievers, because they often pride themselves on their ability to adapt to crisis and have a strong sense of self-reliance, may be particularly sensitive to offers of help and assistance.

The counseling contract, then, has to be carefully tendered. Instrumental grievers may need to be positively motivated to accept counseling. Often appeals to assist others can be helpful. For example, Janet, a young widow with an instrumental grieving pattern, found counseling helpful as she dealt with the grief of her three adolescent children. Counseling gave her an opportunity to discuss problems. Her counselor continually reinforced the value of their work together as a way to assist her children. In other cases, instrumental grievers may see value of another voice, as in "we can work more effectively together than I can alone." But counselors themselves need to be clear on whose needs are being met—the individual's, the family's, or inappropriately, the counselor's own need to be helpful. Intuitive grievers will often be clearer on their goals in counseling and more open and motivated in the process. Nevertheless, it is useful for counselors to review at the onset what any client seeks to achieve.

At the very least this will assist the process. And in some ways, the question of goals can clarify the grieving process. For example, it is not uncommon for grieving individuals to list "closure" as a goal. This can be a good time to emphasize that grief does not mean the closure of a relationship but its continuation in another form. Often the client's ambivalence about terminating that lost relationship can prove a barrier to the counseling process. Thus, for grievers of any pattern, it is always helpful to clarify goals and motivation.

All clients, too, will benefit from an exploration and affirmation of their own adaptive strategies. But this is especially true for instrumental grievers. Instrumental grievers will also benefit by affirming how the adaptive strategies they tried to employ—often cognitive and active—can be effective in dealing with loss. The recognition that these strategies are simply different, not necessarily deficient, is a critical acknowledgment for grieving individuals and those who seek to assist them. Far too often the value of these strategies is not validated. Elmer's (1994) admonition is typical: "The problem for grief counselors is to convince a man that his feelings are valid, that grief is basically good, and that asking for help is not a sign of weakness."

The danger of such comments is threefold. First, if confuses grief with feelings, ignoring the many ways grief is manifested. Second, while acknowledging the value of certain adaptive strategies—ventilation of feelings and seeking support—such a statement ignores and seemingly discredits other strategies. Third, and perhaps most critically, it sets an inappropriate helping context, for only in a context where strengths are acknowledged and respected is it possible to explore the ways these strategies can be employed, to review any limitations, and to consider alternative approaches (see Sidebar 9.4).

Sidebar 9.4. The Counselor as Griever

Counselors need to assess their own grieving pattern. While counselors may have an affective bias (see Sue & Sue, 1990) in their approach to clients, this does not mean that they are necessarily intuitive in pattern. Anecdotal evidence points to a significant number of persons who have entered the field of thanatology as a result of, perhaps even as a way of dealing with, their own losses. This pattern would be typical of instrumental grievers who often turn toward active and cognitive responses as a way to adapt to loss.

This suggests that if this were the case, issues of countertransference may loom large. Given the culture of counseling, one way that it might be evident is that it may reinforce a tendency to press clients to share affect, essentially allowing clients to emote for both.

Beyond the issue of countertransference, analysis of a counselor's own pattern may lead to an enriched sense of the many strategies individuals use to adapt loss and it can facilitate self-care.

Studies of individuals who are working with the dying and bereaved emphasize the critical importance of effective self-care. Vachon (1987) found that helpers who were able to avoid "compassion fatigue" (see Figley, 1996) or burnout were the ones who were able to find suitable activities for respite. In addition, these helpers were able to validate their own grief, utilizing strategies such as rituals to mark their losses. They also understood the limit as well as potential inherent in their roles as caregivers and counselors. They also possessed a spiritual perspective, which allowed them to confront and accept the existential unfairness of life.

And finally, they also created for themselves effective support networks, finding support and opportunities both within and outside of their work organization. These studies suggest two things. First, counselors and caregivers should become aware of their own grief patterns and embrace those strategies best suited for their particular pattern. Second, it reminds organizations of the value of stressing and supporting multiple self-care activities other than the traditional biweekly support group.

☐ The Value of Cognitive and Active Adaptive Strategies

In Chapter 2, a key point was emphasized—that many current models of the grieving process stress that a variety of adaptive strategies may be useful to grievers. For example, Corr (1992) in a review of task models, notes that one of the strengths of such approaches is acknowledgment of individuality. Such approaches, as well as process models (Rando 1993; Stroebe, 1997) affirm that each individual may find different tasks or processes more or less difficult than others and will work through the tasks or processes in his or her own idiosyncratic way. For example, to use Worden's (1991) task model, one of his tasks is "to work through the pain of grief" (p. 13). Some individuals may be able to accomplish this task, feeling the pain and finding ways over time, to release it. Others may have difficulty with this task, avoiding or suppressing pain. And each individual will find his or her own way to work through the pain. To some it may be affective ventilation—sharing their feelings with family and friends. Others, though, may use different ways to deal with the pain or loss, perhaps expending energy in some physical task or through cognitive strategies. The central point, though, remains—a variety of strategies may be helpful as individuals adapt to loss.

Cognitive strategies certainly can be helpful. Such strategies can include varied approaches. For example, Moos and Shaefer (1986) describe a series of adaptive strategies that are cognitive in nature. Among these strategies are:

- Logical analysis and mental preparation. In this strategy the crisis of loss is broken down into a series of small, manageable problems that can then be evaluated.
- Cognitive restructuring. Here the reality of the loss is accepted, but the individual focuses on favorable aspects such as how well they are coping or the transformative aspects of the loss.
- Cognitive avoidance or denial. These include strategies that deny, avoid, or minimize the loss. Other examples can include managing thoughts or selecting times and places where one avoids grief or uses diversion to avoid focusing on grief.
- Information seeking. Obtaining information allows the griever to understand and validate one's responses and to assess possible strategies to adapt to the loss.

Such cognitive strategies are used extensively by the bereaved. For example, many researchers have found these typical reactions by males (Cook, 1988; Brabent et al., 1992; Campbell & Silverman, 1996; Goodmen, 1996; Moss et al., 1997; Moss et al., 1997). Klass (1997), in his studies of grieving parents, also emphasized the critical importance of cognitive processes as he indicated how grieving parents continually maintained an inner representation of the dead child, which assisted them in maintaining a continued and therapeutic sense of connection to the child. Similarly, Calhoun and Tedeschi (1990) noted the wide use of cognitive restructuring as their sample took comfort in their ability to cope and even to grow as they faced loss. The use of cognitive-orientated adaptive strategies is common, then, among the bereaved.

Cognitive-orientated strategies can be helpful in a number of ways.

Neimeyer (1997a) and Attig (1996) emphasize that grief has strong cognitive components. To Neimeyer (1993, 1996, 1997a, 1997b), the central task in bereavement is "meaning-making" or reconstructing meaning. Losses may challenge earlier meanings, of ourselves and the person who died, as well as our perceptions of our world. In grief, then, we need to review and reconstruct these meanings. Similarly, Attig (1996) stresses that the central issue of loss is "relearning." Loss transforms one's world— the very fabric of life. In grief, then, one needs to learn new skills, review and "relearn" relationships with others—the deceased, as well as one's own sense of identify and spirituality.

Naturally, the judicious and skilled use of cognitive processes can facilitate meaning-making, allowing individuals to draw upon or develop spiritual strengths as they deal with the loss. As D. Klass stated, "almost every philosophical system, save British analytical thought, are examples of masculine grief" (March, 1998, personal communication). By that Klass means that much of philosophy represents cognitive attempts to construct the meaning of life in the face of death and loss. Moreover, cognitive-based adaptive strategies can facilitate other aspects of grief—allowing individuals to redefine and relearn relationships with self, the world, and others. As a client once stated: "Since Marie (his wife) died, I think lots about her. I do a lot for the grandkids because I know that's what she wanted, what she would have done. I keep thinking what would Marie have done or Marie would really like this. And it makes me feel good about the kids we raised and about myself."

Cognitive-based adaptive strategies provide other benefits. A loss creates myriad practical problems. One now needs to adjust to a new environment, which entails learning new skills, coping with loss-related difficulties, and coping with the mundane problems of everyday life. Cognitive skills can facilitate problem-solving, and they can provide opportunity to ventilate it. One of the critical recognitions that have emerged from critical incident stress theory (Figley, 1996) is that talking and thinking about loss can be as effective in ventilating and dissipating energy aroused by grief as affective-focused approaches.

It is little wonder, then, that research has indicated the effectiveness of cognitive-based strategies. Figley (1996), for example, found that simply telling and retelling the story often lowered trauma, and he noted that newer approaches to the treatment of post-traumatic stress disorder involve cognitive and physical interventions. Similarly, Powers and Wampold (1994) found that cognitive approaches were very successful in coping with loss, allowing grief to be validated, meaning reconstructed, and dosing periods of directly confronting the loss with other activities. Bonanno (1997) emphasized that cognitive approaches often worked better than affective processes, since they allowed one to function reasonably effectively and to meet ongoing responsibilities. This allowed individuals to maintain their sense of identity, in turn minimizing disruptions that might complicate their adjustment to loss, thereby reinforcing self-esteem and engendering support. Bonanno's research emphasized that those using a "positive bias," that is, a cognitive orientation, as a means to cope with loss actually had better outcomes than those who dealt with their loss by affective disclosure and ventilation of negative emotions (1997). In addition, those who disassociated with negative emotions had lower levels of grief. There was a short-term cost in more somatic symptoms at six months out from the loss, but these health differences were not apparent at 14 and 28 months. Naturally, such a cost may be significant for a medically frail population such as older widows, suggesting a need for alternate interventive approaches. Other researchers (Goodman et al., 1996; Moss et al., 1997; Moss et al., 1997) have noted both the presence of these cognitive strategies and their seeming effectiveness in their male samples. And Horowitz's (1970) work also emphasized the value of both cognitive and behavioral approaches.

But every strategy has limitations. Among the limitations of cognitive-based strategies is that the person employing them may be believed or be perceived by others to be cold and unfeeling. As Hochschild (1979) reminds us, every society has feeling rules that express a societal consensus on how one is to feel in a given situation. The feeling rules about grief often mandate overt affective expression. The absence of such overt affect can lead a person to redefine himself or herself, or lead others to define that person, as not grieving effectively or as being unfeeling, which may erode support, self-esteem, and adaptation to loss. Or in other cases, persons with an overly cognitive approach might find it difficult to be sensitive to the needs of other grievers. They may find it hard to understand their adaptive strategies or attempt to "solve" the problems of other individuals as they affectively ventilate.

☐ The Roles of Humor

Humor, too, represents a cognitive strategy. Humor offers a number of benefits including tension release. The following case illustrates that point.

> *"After my father died, there was that one difficult solemn moment at the funeral, you know, right before they close the casket and you go for your last look. After that we filed down to the limousine to the cemetery. No one said a word as the driver started following the hearse. Then all of a sudden my brother taps the driver on the shoulder. Now you have to understand that this was a large funeral home that had a number of funerals that day. My brother says to the driver seriously and quietly: "Is there another hearse in front of that one?" The driver, confused, answers con-*

fused "No. Why?" My brother deadpans "That is not my father's casket." The driver
absolutely panics and we all burst out laughing and talking as we reassure the
driver that he is following the correct hearse."

Not only does humor relieve tension (as it did in the case above), it provides opportunities to express emotion and stimulates memories. Often at funerals, sharing humorous stories about the deceased provides a way past the immediate memory of loss and pain, and allows attendees to acknowledge, even celebrate other legacies in the life of the deceased. And because humor reduces tensions and provides seen opportunities, it can often generate support. People are more drawn to those who respond to loss with a touch of laughter rather than a torrent of tears.

Humor provides other benefits as well. It can temporarily divert us from the pain. Humor can offer a sense of perspective that allows us to laugh at our fears and difficulties. In doing so, it can allow that positive sense of adapting that Bonanno (1997) associated with favorable overcomes. And it may even provide physiological benefits (Cousins, 1979) that can inoculate individuals experiencing a high level of stress and other negative physiological aspects of loss.

But the limits of humor are well illustrated by an episode on the sitcom "Home Improvement." In this episode Jill's (the mother) father dies. As her teenage sons prepare to join her for the funeral, the middle son, Randy, jokes about the death. "I know how to iron for a funeral—just set it on stiff." To his consternation, his brothers walk away from him in disgust. Later, in a quiet moment with his father, Randy confesses that he does not know why he does this. His father reassures him that it is a method of adapting that they share. But he offers sage advice "Don't make jokes around anybody sensitive—do it around me."

Many of the positive benefits of humor, like any other adaptive strategy, can be negated if used insensitively or excessively. There is a fine line between diverting pain, however tempered, and denying it. And while humor can generate and cultivate support, it also runs the risk of being off-putting, and strikes others as insensitive, thereby negating support. Tim's advice to Randy is sagacious—one has to know when to use it.

☐ Behaviorally Focused Strategies

Instrumental grievers will often make use of active adaptive strategies as well as cognitive approaches. Such adaptive strategies can be varied. For example, information seeking is both cognitive and active as it allows one a meaningful activity at a disorganized time. Problem-solving activity is another such strategy. Here, specific steps are taken to deal with one or more aspects of the crisis. For example, one may take comfort in planning and participating in the funeral. In another strategy, identifying alternative rewards, individuals either attempt to replace the loss or to find other sources of satisfaction to compensate it (see Moos & Shaefar, 1986).

Beyond these problem-focused strategies, sheer activity may be useful sometimes. This may have a symbolic relationship to the deceased. For example, one funeral director shared how two professional football players decided to handle the death of their father. They chose to physically dig the grave. Or in another case, a mother, after the death of her daughter, placed much of her energy in an annual award given in her daughter's memory. She raised funds, interviewed candidates, and had the public opportunity each year to remember her daughter.

Sometimes these actions may not be so overtly related to the loss. For example, in the film, "Basketball Diaries," the adolescents return from the funeral of a good friend and teammate, Bobby. They sit in a park unable to articulate their feelings of loss, each attempt ending in silence. But then their grief seems to come out in a furious game of basketball played in a dark playground under a drenching rain. A similar illustration occurred in a middle school after a student died in a car crash caused by a drunk driver. In the aftermath of the death many of the students openly wept and talked about their grief, while a number of the boys were mute. But later in gym, an aggressive game of dodge ball provided an opportunity for these boys to physically ventilate. As they lobbed the ball at one another, they made direct references to the crash and the driver.

Physical ventilation is one benefit of active strategies. As an old German-American pastor once shared in Idaho. "It's not just because the casket is heavy that six men lift it." In that environment, the opportunity for physical ventilation is welcome. It provides avenues for the discharge of the energy generated by grief.

But active strategies have other benefits as well. They allow one to "do something," reinforcing a sense of control in an otherwise hopeless time. Aaron, for example, was a social worker who worked with HIV-infected children in foster care. On his days off, he volunteered at an animal shelter. Here, he realized, he could assist in the adoption of pets that would not likely die within a short time after placement. In another illustration, Jim, a chaplain in a leukemia ward, donated platelets weekly, because it was something tangible he could do for the children in his ministry. One of the greatest benefits of prayer, beyond its spiritual efficacy, is that it offers a form of symbolic control in a seemingly uncontrollable situation (Doka & Davidson, 1998). Sometimes that control can be more than symbolic. Deathbed instructions, for example, can be seen as both an attempt to symbolically control the future as well as a real effort to problem-solve. For example, when Mike was dying he gave instructions to his wife about raising their young son. He also had a friend promise that he would assist in raising the child. These actions gave him comfort and reassurance that his son would be well taken care of after he died. We might add that even Christ on the cross gave instructions to his disciples and mother to care for one another.

At the time of the death, activity, too, can be helpful. Planning the funeral and engaging in ritual offer meaningful activity at a much-disorganized time. During the course of the grieving period, activity can also be helpful. Solving some of the day-to-day problems that arise as one deals with the loss can reinforce a sense of self-esteem, competence, and control. As one griever shared, "After Johnny died, I had to sell his house. I fixed it up some and handled all the details. It was funny—I felt kind of good about that—I could still handle stuff." Moreover, activities can provide structure in a seemingly disorganized time and offer opportunity for respite and diversion. This allows a person "time off" from active grieving. Sometimes it can allow one to assume a leadership role, assisting others who experience grief as more of an affective crisis. Such a role can generate support and enhance self-esteem.

And sometimes, these actions can not only solve an individual problem but address larger social issues as well. For example, Cindy Lightner responded to her child's death, caused by a drunk driver by founding Mothers Against Drunk Driving (MADD). MADD has played a significant role in changing the public perception of drunk driving as well as the laws that now address it. Similarly, much of the social concern about missing children arose from John Walsh's attempt to deal with the abduction and subsequent death of his young son, Adam. It is little wonder, then, that such adaptive strategies are often used (Moss et al., 1997; Moss et al., 1997; Brabert et al., 1992; Campbell & Silverman, 1996; Cook, 1988; Neugebauer, Raskin, Williams, Reimian, Goetz, & Gorman, 1992; Goodman et al., 1996), and that they are effective (Powers & Wampold, 1994; Horowitz, 1970; Figley, 1996; Bonanno, 1997).

But again, any strategy has its limitations. Active adaptive strategies may be used not only to engage and ventilate grief but also to divert and to deny grief. For dissonant grievers, particularly, activity may subvert their need to find more effective ways to adapt to their loss, as well as physically exhaust them.

Problem-solving approaches can be ineffective and sometimes complicate grief. For example, attempts to cope with the problems of loneliness may involve a premature attempt to replace the loss. Even avoiding such an extreme example, an instrumental grievers may attempt to join support groups that are primarily therapeutic merely for social contact.

In other cases the activity can complicate relationships with others. For example, sexual activity can be an attempt to create a sense of intimacy in an isolating time. But partners may not understand nor share that meaning. For example, when their child died, Ryan found sex to be a source of comfort for him, but his overtures troubled his wife who felt her own sexual desires decreased in her grief.

In addition, certain behaviors are, by themselves, problematic. For example, instrumental grievers may attempt to "resolve" issues generated by the loss by the use of drugs or alcohol. Or they may engage in acting out or other self-destructive behaviors.

☐ Affectively Focused Adaptive Strategies

The forgoing should not imply, in any way, that affectively oriented adaptive strategies are not as effective. Affective strategies such as affective ventilation and acceptance can be extremely helpful, both in generating support and in exploring and resolving emotional conflicts. Affective regulation—that is, choosing appropriate times and places to share or feel deep affect—is a critical strategy since it allows individuals to exercise elements of control over their affect, permitting them to function. It is often a key adaptive strategy in dissonant instrumental grievers who may strongly believe they should not show affect except at certain times or places when they find it safe and appropriate, such as in therapy or in self-help groups or when they are alone. But almost all grievers, including instrumental grievers, use this strategy to some degree. For even in instrumental grievers, affect is tempered, not absent.

As with other strategies, affective strategies have limitations as well. Excessive affect can limit support and impair effective functioning. Again, grieving can limit the time or place when grief is shared. As noted earlier, the grieving rules of American society tend to encourage affective ventilation early in the grieving period, while discouraging it later on. For example, ever since her sister died, Jean has found it difficult to remain composed. Even small events or little reminders have led to periods where she needs to cry. Many friends have begun to avoid her and her supervisor at work has written her up for "a lack of self-control." She is aware of these difficulties and her own sense of self-worth has suffered. Affective regulation can be problematic, as well, inhibiting grievers who really do need to affectively ventilate from doing so.

Thus, affective strategies, like all others, have positive and negative aspects. Used effectively, they can provide grievers with opportunities to explore and resolve feelings and to reach out for support. Doing so can assist grievers both in coming to terms with the loss and in reconstructing their lives in the face of that loss. But while more of the literature extols the value of affective expressiveness (e.g., Staudacher, 1991; Elmer, 1994;

Wolfelt, 1990), it is critical to remember that it is but one of a series of adaptive reactions, each with its unique strengths and limitations.

☐ Spiritually Focused Strategies

Spiritually focused strategies undoubtedly are the most analytically complex strategies, in that they are usually derivatives of cognitive, affective, or active strategies. For example, prayer can be a way to express emotion or process thoughts. And prayer allows one to do something, often when there are few other opportunities to do anything. The following cases illustrate the multifaceted nature of prayer, and, for that matter, other spiritually focused strategies.

> When my son first died, I still prayed but I would use my prayers to spew anger. "How could you do this to me?" I would rail against God daily" (34-year-old clergyman).
>
> When the doctor told me there was nothing more to do. I remember smiling and saying I can always pray (74-year-old widow).
>
> When I pray, I think about Bobby a lot. It gives me a chance to review what happened, to remind myself that his life and death were in God's hand's, and that I just did not have the power to save him (bereaved mother).

To Pergament (1997), this is one of the great strengths of religious or spiritually based strategies. The pathways of such strategies can utilize cognition, affect, or behavior. Like other forms of adaptive strategies, there are varied spiritual approaches that can entail a range of responses from deferring it to some higher power to collaborative approaches that emphasize using oneself as an instrument of one's own faith or prayer to those in which the person is totally self-directing. Pergament (1997) too, reminds us that, as with other strategies, spiritual strategies can be both helpful and harmful. For example, reframing a loss as God's will may be perceived by some as part of a design or plan that offers a sense of comfort, while others will see it as a vindictive punishment. Even spiritual or religious communities may be perceived as helpful or unhelpful.

This does not deny the critical importance of spiritual issues in loss and grief, nor the value of spiritual beliefs, practices, and rituals (see Doka 1993, Doka & Morgan, 1993). Loss and grief are fundamentally spiritual crises, since they evoke questions of meaning. As such, spiritually focused strategies will necessarily be utilized as individuals struggle with these spiritual concerns. The goals of the counselor or the person seeking to help himself or herself is to explore and understand how their use of these approaches reveals the underlying adaptive strategies they use and, as with other strategies, when they are helpful and when they are not.

☐ How Do You Know if a Person is Grieving?

Counselors often question how, if grief is not expressed in overt affect, they can determine whether or not an individual is, in fact, grieving. Might the lack of affect indicate denial or suppression? Two considerations may assist. The first is to assess activity. Individuals who can describe grief in some domain, that is, talk about ways they are thinking or behaving in response to the loss are demonstrating grief even if not in overt affect. In short, grievers will show some activity after a loss, but it may be in one or more domains. The absence of *any activity* may be an indication of more complicated responses, but the absence of significant affect may only point to the fact than an individual is an instrumental griever, actively using cognitive or behavioral strategies.

A second consideration is movement. As described earlier, grief is an unclear process, a roller coaster full of ups and downs. Significant amelioration may be experienced even within the first two years. Nevertheless, persons who are grieving ought to be able to describe the ways that they experience the process. And over time they should be able to indicate a lessening of intensity. In other words, while they still experience downs, these should be experienced as less intense, less long-lasting, and less frequent than was evident in the first two years.

Similarly, Webb (1993) offers a notion of disabling grief, referring to the degree that grief impairs normal functioning. Again, the level of impairment may vary in the grieving process, it may even increase once one moves beyond the initial shock of loss. But again, over time, persons should begin to function at levels similar to, or perhaps even better than, those earlier.

In summary, then, the fact that grievers are both doing something and conveying a sense of movement are clear signs that the person is grieving even if he or she does not fit some perceived stereotypes on how that person should grieve.

☐ Summation: Androgyny and Beyond

In recent years, there has been a concern to move toward androgynous perspectives (see Bem, 1981). The underlying notion, which has itself emerged from sections of the feminist and men's movements, is that both the feminine and masculine sides that exist within each individual should be embraced. Inherent in this idea is the perspective that one can learn much from both the feminine ability to recognize and to express feelings and the masculine ability to persevere in the midst of a crisis.

The therapeutic implication here is that counselors and individuals should cultivate alternative strengths. The feminine griever ought to be shown the value of cognitive and active approaches, while the instrumental griever ought to confront his or her underlying feelings, however difficult that is. It is argued that only by engaging both sides of oneself can one respond to loss in a holistic manner. Certainly those with the widest range of adaptive strategies are best able to surmount crises.

There is some support for this approach. For example, Stroebe (1997) found that men tended to benefit more from client-centered therapies, while women found value in more cognitive approaches. Yet since this research was based on gender rather than grieving styles, it is difficult to interpret. It may, in fact, indicate the value of androgynous approaches. Perhaps each benefited from exposure to less familiar, alternative approaches. Yet without evidence of the styles that these grievers initially presented, or full descriptions of the therapeutic process, alternative explanations also have weight. Perhaps these grievers leaned toward the dissonant part of the continuum. For example, a male dissonant griever who experiences grief as deep affect but is constrained by his perceptions that such feeling is inappropriate for a man to express, may find safe places to express feeling in a client-centered approach. Or the chosen therapeutic methods themselves may preclude a particular style. Cognitive-centered approaches do not preclude affective exploration and ventilation. In fact, some researchers have suggested a move beyond androgyny (Stillion & McDowell, 1997), urging both individuals and clinicians to ignore any hint of sexual stereotyping and to teach individuals the widest range of adaptive strategies as they seek to ameliorate grief.

Certainly, gender is but one factor that influences grief patterns. Just as surely, individuals as well as clinicians are urged to make careful assessment of one's own or a client's grieving style. In addition, it can also be affirmed that individuals with the widest range of strategies are more likely to adapt well.

Yet in other ways, one may part company with calls to androgyny (Bem, 1981) or even admonitions to move beyond androgyny (Stillion & McDowell, 1997). Bem's (1984) recognition that calls to androgyny can be "doubly incarcerating" has value. It is a reminder that such calls pose unrealistic and unfair demands on grievers.

Furthermore, such calls to androgyny or beyond are problematic in three ways. First, any careful assessment of an individual grieving style should not ignore factors such as gender, socialization, culture, or other variations that might influence the grief pattern. Certainly, understanding how these factors have influenced a grieving pattern can be useful to individuals and clinicians. For example, when Dave, a 15-year-old boy, heard the news of the death of his mother and younger sister in a car crash, he initially expressed little affect. But after time, his grades began to fall and he did exhibit acting-out behavior. He reluctantly agreed to counseling. In counseling, it became clear that throughout his life he experienced, both as the son of a military officer and as a student in a military academy, rigorous sex-role socialization. As a result, he learned to hide well the deep affect he did experience. Only by exploring these early factors was he able to acknowledge his level of affect and begin to grieve in a way more consistent with his experience of grief. But his older brother and father also recognized through similar exploration that their affect had always been tempered. True instrumental grievers, they benefited from more cognitive and active approaches.

Second, these cases that speak to androgyny and beyond ignore the fact that instrumental and intuitive grievers vary not only in the adaptive strategies they use but also in their very experience and expression of grief. To urge oneself or another to express feelings that are, in fact, not really a significant part of the grief experience is counter productive.

Finally, such calls ignore both the basic principle of self-help and counseling—lead with strengths. Crises are poor opportunities to attempt to comply to uncomfortable or unfamiliar approaches. One is better served by effectively employing the adaptive strategies that seem most natural.

10

CHAPTER

Strategies for Self-Help and Intervention: The Need for Interventive Intentionality

Many of the interventive strategies that have been developed for persons who are grieving are effective with a wide range of grievers, even those with different grieving patterns. The reason for that effectiveness is that these strategies allow grieving individuals to use them in ways that are compatible to their individual patterns. They allow grieving persons the ability to engage on a cognitive, affective, or behavioral level. One can express feelings or thoughts. In effectively using these strategies, counselors or grieving individuals ought to remember three critical aspects:

1. Be intentional. That is, understand what one is attempting to accomplish by the strategy that is used. For example, is one seeking to assist cognitive processing or empower the ventilation of feelings?
2. Choose comfortable modalities. Individuals are more likely to benefit when they are comfortable with the modality being used. For example, expressive therapies and the creative arts can be wonderfully effective in assisting persons who are grieving. But for someone who is uncomfortable with the arts, other approaches such as storytelling may be useful. However, persons who feel awkward in speaking may not find much value in storytelling as a therapeutic approach.
3. Build from strengths. These strategies work well because they allow a grieving individual to adapt to his or her pattern. They work best when

they illuminate and amplify the strengths of a given pattern rather than attempting to force an alternative approach. Journaling, for example, can be useful for many reasons. It can be used to assist in the reconstruction of meaning, to stimulate a continued bond, to ventilate feelings, or to allow meaningful activity. But to insist that a grieving individual with an instrumental pattern only use the journal to document feelings, both denies the value of such an exercise and creates resistance and frustration.

☐ Bibliotherapy

Bibliotherapy or the therapeutic use of self-help literature has grown in recent years. In fact, there is a wide range of self-help literature available. Some are first-hand, personalized accounts or grief, while others are written by professionals. Some are general, touching all types of loss (see Rando, 1991; Sanders, 1993), while others are written about a specific type of loss, such as the death or a child (Fitzgerald, 1992) or the death or a parent (e.g., Myers, 1988). Some, such as Golden's *Swallowed by a Snake* (1996) or Staudacher's *Men and Grief* (1991) are addressed to men, while others such as Caine's (1974) *Widow* are more suited to women. Some books may confront specific issues or concerns such as the spiritual (see Lewis, 1961; Kushner, 1981), while ignoring other concerns. In addition, there is a range of literature suitable for children.

In addition to books, there are a number of other print resources such as magazines like *Bereavement Magazine* or *Thanatos* or a newsletter such as *Journeys*. There are also a wide range of pamphlets, many of which may be available at funeral homes, hospitals, or hospices. In addition to these print resources, nonprint resources, such as self-help videos or audiotapes, are also available.

Bibliotherapy can have much value in general. It can offer grievers three major gifts. First, it can provide a sense of validation, normalizing feelings and reactions. Second, it can offer suggestions, options for adapting to varied issues that one faces in the grieving process. For example, Rando's book *How To Go Living When Someone You Love Dies* (1991) provides a variety of strategies for such practical problems as facing the holiday, reaching out for support, designing therapeutic rituals, and other problems that often accompany loss. Finally, bibliotherapy offers hope and reassurance to grievers that they, too, can survive their loss. It is little wonder that bibliotherapy has been found to be an effective tool in grief (Doka, 1990; Seogin, Jamison & Gochneaur, 1989).

Bibliotherapy may have special value to instrumental grievers. It is by its very nature cognitive and active. It is solitary. It allows dosing, that is, if the griever finds something too painful or difficult, he or she can set it aside for a while. And certainly it offers control. Grievers can choose the time and place that they use it.

Yet bibliotherapy should be treated as a prescription drug, that is, one should carefully assess what books may offer valued insights to a particular struggle. Not only do books vary in focus and orientation, they also vary in quality. More importantly, some, used uncritically or selected without forethought, may complicate grieving. For example, Kushner (1981) has a wonderfully written, sensitive book entitled *Why Bad Things Happen to Good People*. In it he addresses a frequent spiritual issue—if God is so good and so powerful, why did this loss occur? Many grievers may find solace in his notion that God allows the world to run itself—that while this power is distant, His mercy and goodness remain. But others may find that idea troubling, finding more comfort in Lewis's (1963) acceptance of that paradox, while acknowledging the unanswerable quality and mystery behind the question.

Similarly, dissonant instrumental grievers may find Staudacher's book, *Men and Grief* (1991), to offer both validation and permission to grieve using affective adaptive strategies. But those closer to the instrumental pole on the grieving continuum may find that her message invalidates their own adaptive strategies.

Happily, there is a range of resources available. One should simply choose well and read critically. The question is always a personal one—not "Are these ideas right?" but "Will they work for the grieving individual?"

☐ Online Resources

One of the remarkable events of the last quarter century has been the growth of personal computers and their use in a wide range or way. Given that context, it is unsurprising that they have become a resource for the bereaved.

Computers offer many online resources for grievers. Certainly a wide range of information on loss and grief is available through the Internet. Some informational resources provide referral to grief groups, organizations, or other available materials. There are interactive possibilities as well. Online grief groups, chat rooms, and E-mail offer opportunities to interact with other grievers. And some websites offer opportunities to memorialize, empowering cyberspace ritual.

Online resources can provide many of the benefits of bibliotherapy, as well as other advantages. They can be validating and offer suggestions for adapting as well as providing reassurances of hope. In addition, they may offer interpersonal support. Unlike many resources, the Internet is available 24 hours a day.

Instrumental grievers, in particular, may benefit since online resources are highly compatible to their grieving styles and strategies, particularly those that are cognitive and active, such as information seeking. These resources allow a certain degree of anonymity that may be lacking in other forms of interpersonal contact, while offering opportunities to connect with other grievers. Going online gives control to the griever allowing them to sign on or off or to not respond at all. Because of that, the griever retains the opportunity to dose pain and grief. Moreover, the very variety of online resources provides grievers opportunities to select a comfortable level of engagement as well as to choose what resources one accesses at any given point in his or her grief. Intuitive grievers and dissonant grievers, too, can find great value since it offers safe space for ventilation.

Yet online resources carry disadvantages as well. Quality varies more widely on the Internet than one would likely find in print and nonprint resources. Cyberspace is in many ways the final frontier. Because grievers can be vulnerable, it is essential to be wary of schemes that may seek to take advantage. Online resources can be a powerful tool, but again, they must be used with care.

☐ Creative Art

"Would you know my name if I saw you in heaven? Would it be the same if I saw you in heaven? I must be strong and carry on because I know I don't belong here in heaven." (Clapton, "Tears in Heaven")

When his three-year-old son died, Eric Clapton eulogized him in the beautiful and plaintive song "Tears in Heaven." Clapton's way of dealing with loss is just one example of using the creative arts as an adaptive strategy. Examples are as varied as the arts themselves. Native American groups have often included dance within their grieving rituals. Other examples include painting, music, photography, writing, storytelling, cinematography, and the use of videos, to name just a few. Journaling, or writing about one's feelings or thoughts is a well-established approach in grief counseling or self-help. John Gunther (1949) and Kent Koppelman (1994) each dealt with the loss of a son by writing extensive accounts of the life and death of the child. Another illustration, albeit fictional, is offered by S.E. Hinton's 1967 novel of class conflict among adolescents, *The Outsiders*. The book, written as the journal of Ponyboy, the adolescent protagonist, recounts the events leading to the deaths of two close friends. As this fictional journal continues, one has the sense of how healing writing the book must have been. In fact, research has supported the therapeutic value of such creative approaches. Both Lattanzi and Hale (1984) and Pennebaker, Keico-Glaser, and Glaser (1988) found that writing about trauma and loss was useful in ameliorating grief.

Creative arts can be useful for grievers with any grief strategy. They can allow affective ventilation or cognitive processing. All of these are active processes that allow a sense of interpretive control, allowing grievers symbolic control over a situation or loss that provides the grievers little actual control. They have other functions as well. Riches and Dawson (1998) noted that the use of photography by bereaved parents assisted them in remembering the life of the deceased child rather than the death, facilitated reminiscence with others, and introduced the child to others who did not know him, reinforcing a continued bond. Most current models of loss emphasize two functions in the grieving process: dealing with the loss and recreating a new life with a redefined relationship to the deceased (Worden, 1991; Stroebe & Schut, 1995). As Riches and Dawson (1998) affirm, creative arts can allow individuals outlets to fulfill both. And as time goes on, the creative expression can change as the grieving process continues (Harvey, Orbach, Weber, Merback, & Ait, 1992). For example, accounts and stories that are initially problematic or painful may later become more hopeful.

As with other strategies, creative arts should be used in a manner that is both intentional and prescriptive. Persons should use modalities that are comfortable for them. It makes little sense to encourage painting for someone who has little interest in it. Rather, it is worthwhile to assess which modes would be useful to the person. Similarly, these creative approaches often work best when they are reflective and amplify basic adaptive strategies. For example, intuitive grievers may find the arts to be effective approaches to ventilate affect, while instrumental grievers may use them to cognitively process memories. The goal remains to validate and respect the use of each form of creative expression.

☐ Ritual

The term *ritual* is one of those words that can have many different meanings. Any regularized activity can be said to be a ritual. For example, one can say that having coffee and reading the paper is one's regular morning ritual. But such usage trivializes the notion of ritual. Following Shorter (1996), we prefer to call such activities *ceremonies* or perhaps simply *habits* and reserve the term *ritual* to special acts that offer sacred meaning to events. As Grollman is apt to say, "Rituals make mountains out of moments" (tape series, 1997).

Rituals, then, can be a powerful tool in dealing with loss. Gennep (1960) reminds us that the power of rituals lies in the fact that they are *liminal*. By liminal, Gennep means that they strike us at the threshold of consciousness, speaking to both our conscious and subconscious simultaneously. Rando (1984), too, delineates many useful facets of ritual, which include allowing individuals to act, offering legitimization for physical and affective ventilation, delineating grief (i.e., limiting grief to a certain space and time), giving a sense of control (i.e., doing something at an otherwise uncontrollable event), providing an ongoing sense of connection to the loss, allowing space to safely confront ambivalent or confused feeling or thoughts, generating social support, and offering opportunities to find meaning in the loss by applying spiritual frameworks to that loss.

Rando (1984) reminds us that these therapeutic properties of ritual make it a highly useful tool throughout the entire experience of grief—from the illness through the funeral and beyond. And, in fact, research has supported the therapeutic role of ritual (e.g., Doka, 1984; Bolton & Camp, 1987, 1989; Reeves & Boersma, 1990; Gross & Klass, 1997).

Because rituals possess so many therapeutic properties, they can be valuable for many different types of grievers. Intuitive grievers can benefit from the opportunities rituals offer for affective ventilation. Instrumental grievers will appreciate the opportunities to act as well as to focus thoughts and assist in meaning-making.

Moreover, the fact that rituals provide a space for grievers, or as Golden (1994a) states, a container to hold grief, makes it highly compatible to grievers, either instrumental or dissonant, who seek to dose or limit their exposure to grief.

Naturally, funerals and other socially shared rituals can offer therapeutic opportunities to deal with grief. Planning and participating in funeral rituals can be very helpful to grievers (Doka, 1986). As the following case illustrates, instrumental grievers may particularly benefit.

> *When my father died, it was important for my brother and me to take charge of the funeral. Everything we did was intentional. We choose oak because that was his favorite wood. All the hymns we chose had meaning. We had a meal afterwards in his favorite restaurant. This had special meaning since he had, before he became real sick, wanted to take the whole family there. He was a newspaperman, so whenever I bought something, he would always say I should have come to him since he knew someone who gets it wholesale. My friend is a funeral director so he gave us a big discount. I figure Dad was thinking, "He finally learned that nobody pays retail." I think about the service often. It really helped* (40-year-old clergyman).

Other rituals, too, may have value. The Jewish ritual of kaddish, prayer said for a period of time after the loss, serves as an example. In the Orthodox tradition, only males counted toward the quorum. Thus, the prayer in effect offered an opportunity for males to come together in a ritual way for companionship and support.

But grievers may create rituals any time to deal with issues yet unresolved. Rituals provide a powerful tool to work on continuing issues. The first question to think through is what message one wants the ritual to convey. Van der Hart (1978), for example, building on the work of Gennep (1960), discusses two types of rituals. *Rituals of continuity* are rituals that emphasize, even in the midst of loss, the continuing connection. The AIDS quilt is an excellent example. Each panel reminds us that the individual remains part of the fabric of life and will not be forgotten. A friend offers another illustration. Every holiday his family ends the meal with a toast to an eccentric aunt with her favorite drink. This simple ritual becomes a wonderful way to recount all their favorite Aunt Carmen stories, even imparting them to a generation that barely knew her.

Rituals of transition (Van der Hart, 1978) offer another message. Here the theme is that one has entered a new place in one's journey through grief. The following case offers an illustration.

> Mary is a widow in her 40s, whose husband died seven years ago after a five-year, debilitating struggle with MS. Mary is at a point where she would like to take off her wedding ring and begin dating, but she seems unable to do so. In discussing her relationship with her counselor, it becomes clear that the ring has great meaning. Though the illness was very difficult for both, every night after a long day's struggle, when they lay in bed, they would put their ring fingers together and repeat their vows "in sickness and in health." The counselor acknowledged that she had put on the ring in a ritual that had great value, and both he and Mary agreed that it should be removed in another meaningful ritual. It was arranged that on Sunday afternoon, Mary and her friends and family gathered in the church where she and her husband had exchanged vows. The priest met her at the altar. There he repeated the vows, now in the past tense. "Were you faithful in sickness and in health, in good times and in bad?" he intoned. Mary could, in the presence of these witnesses, affirm that she had been. The priest then asked for the ring. As Mary later described, it came off "as if by magic." As planned, the priest arranged to have both rings interlocked and welded to her wedding picture. He returned it to her in a brief ritual of continuity.

Rituals can have other meanings as well. *Rituals of reconciliation* either ask for or extend forgiveness. A note at the Vietnam Memorial Wall provides a poignant example: "We did all that we could, I guess, but since you're here, it was not enough." *Rituals of affirmation* provide a complement to rituals of reconciliation. Rituals of affirmation simply provide ways to acknowledge legacies or say thanks. The following case provides an example:

> When my friend died, I took a special interest in Mark, his son. One day, I took him to a place where we had once fished. I had told him the story of how his dad had

angered me by always losing my fishing lures. On the trail down to the stream, we found an old rusted lure. Mark got a real kick out of that and said, "This was a gift from my dad." We ended up doing a ritual where we thanked his dad for bringing us together. As of that ritual, Mark decided to lose the lure.

In developing rituals, it is critical to remember four principles of planning:

1. Rituals always arise from the story. Each ritual should be individually planned. Think about what type of ritual is needed. What elements should be part of it and who should witness it? Some rituals may be private, others shared with a few. Some, like the ritual of the wedding ring, will be very public.
2. The elements used in a ritual should be both visible and symbolic. Since rituals are liminal, they should include elements that both can be seen, appealing to our conscious senses but moving beyond them. The ring is not only a piece of gold but also a symbol of commitment, just as the rusted lure symbolizes connection.
3. Rituals should be planned and processed. Before undertaking a ritual it is critical that it be carefully thought out. The powerful ritual around the wedding ring would have been far different if the priest had asked at that special moment when the ring was removed "Who gets it now?" Follow the planning through to the conclusion. After the ritual, individuals may need opportunities to process, or continue to think about, or talk about the event.
4. Rituals can be planned any time. While funeral, anniversaries, holidays, or special occasions offer times for ritual, one of the advantages of ritual is that it can be used whenever it meets a need.

☐ Self-Help and Support Groups

The value of self-help and support groups has long been established (Silverman, 1981, 1986). They can provide opportunities for education and ventilation, places to bond with supportive others, suggestions for adapting, and hope that one can survive the loss as others have done or seem to be doing. There may be other benefits as well. Lund (1999), for example, notes that individuals within a self-help group who perceive that they are helping others experience better grief outcomes themselves, perhaps because their own self-esteem is enhanced. And the very nature of mutual support reinforces a sense of the normality of the grief experience as well as furthering self-reliance.

Groups are not only an effective but also an efficient way of assisting grieving individuals. Many more persons can be helped within a group setting than through individual counseling. For these reasons, groups have become a staple of many bereavement outreach programs sponsored by varied agencies, such as hospices, funeral homes, larger self-help networks, or other organizations.

Groups can also vary in many ways. Some like The Compassionate Friends strongly emphasize self-help, keeping the professional's role minimal. Others are professionally led. Some are open-ended—individuals come and leave according to their own needs. Others ask for a specific commitment to attend a limited number of sessions. Once these sessions begin, others cannot join. Some are general, focusing on a wide variety of losses, while others are made up of individuals who have experienced a common loss such as the loss of a child or spouse. In some, such as Parents of Murdered Children, the focus is very narrow. Some, too, are part of larger groupings such as national or regional meetings; others simply are based in one community. Again, as with other interventions, the question is not which approach is best, but rather what best meets an individual's given need.

While groups have much value, they are not suitable for everyone. Some individuals whose needs for help are simply too overwhelming cannot prosper in a group environment. And, as discussed in Chapter 3, some individuals are very introverted. Here the "rule of reciprocity" may make them uncomfortable, since they may feel that they need to respond to the sharing of others. This may be particularly so in some groups where that more general rule is, in fact, a norm of the group. There is also the question of fit. Fit involves the somewhat tangible yet intangible way that the grieving individual experiences a sense of connection to the group. For example, when Bob died, he left his wife Lois quite well off since he was heavily insured. While Lois was devastated by the loss, she felt uncomfortable in the widows group where much of the discussion centered on the difficulty of surviving financially. With groups that have an intake process, issues of fit and appropriateness can be addressed prior to entry.

For many grieving persons with an intuitive pattern, groups can have a great value. They provide a safe, comfortable environment for sharing feelings. As such, they validate many of the difficult feelings that such individuals may be experiencing. And in addition to all the other benefits, they allow grieving individuals to identify and bond with supportive others who both share and understand their plan.

In other groups where the norm is not reinforced, some introverted individuals may experience great value in hearing their own sentiments expressed and in deriving other benefits of the group experience.

Dissonant grievers too, especially male dissonant grievers, may find great value in such groups as it gives them a safe place to validate and share their feelings. Joe, for example, has benefited much from one. A retired steamfitter in his 60s, he misses his late wife intensely. Joe believes that he needs to be tough and strong to hold his family together and support his daughter's grief. The support group provides a safe place for him to feel and share his loss. Each month as he tells different aspects of his story, his voice cracks and his eyes well with tears. But instead of the discomfort that such reactions cause when he is around friends and family, in the support group they engender empathy.

Can Grief Groups Work for Instrumental Grievers?

One of the questions often asked is whether groups work for instrumental grievers. Often this question says more about the needs of the person raising it than it does about the instrumental griever. Most traditional self-help groups, with their emphasis on self-disclosure and affective exploration, are a poor match with the characteristics of instrumental grievers. As Chapter 3 explored, instrumental grievers tend to be uncomfortable with self-disclosure and their tempered affect may be perceived as cold or resistant by other grievers. And instrumental grievers may look to utilize such groups for problem-solving approaches, striking facilitators and other group members as inappropriate or premature. For example, they may see such groups as opportunities for respite or socialization. Dan, a 52-year-old widower, provides one such example. After his wife died, he experienced both loneliness and problems in managing daily tasks around the house. He decided to attend a widow's group with the hope that he might "meet a nice widow." As he described it, he would often come late, hoping to minimize the "raw parts" of the meeting when people shared their feelings. And he wondered why his attempts to solve others' problems, for example telling a fellow member with anger "to run it off," seemed dismissed and unappreciated. "I always liked the 'coffee and cake part at the end best'," he stated.

Specifically for instrumental grievers we believe that some groups may be designed grievers. O'Neil (1994), for example, developed a network for widowers with school-aged children that provided information about resources as well as education about common problems. Men had the option to communicate in a variety of ways, including phone, fax, letter, or E-mail. Similar approaches that emphasize problem-solving or education could work with instrumental grievers, but such groups should remember the value of "truth in advertising." It does little good to advertise a group in such a manner to attract grievers uncomfortable with more traditional approaches as a way to slowly wean them into affective self-disclosure. For the reader who is an instrumental griever, a similar caution is offered. Be clear about what a group's approach and aims are, and assess whether this fits with your goals and needs.

☐ Conclusion

This chapter emphasized that there are many strategies that individuals can utilize as they deal with their grief. Effective strategies build upon, rather than deny, the strategies that grievers already count as strengths. The words of one person I once knew offer a wise conclusion. He was an older man who lived in my neighborhood, whose wife had died a few months earlier. In a chance meeting on the street, I asked him how he was doing. He thought he was doing well. But when he felt tense or lonely, he recounted, he often worked out or ran. Almost apologetically, he continued, reminding me that he had been a boxer earlier in life. "The one thing I learned in boxing was that you start with your strong hand."

11

Conclusion

In many ways, this project has been a journey which began with an interest in the way men grieve. It has subsequently opened up to larger patterns of grieving; ones that exist beyond gender. It would do well in the final section to summarize and briefly explore the implications for researchers, theorists, educators, clinicians and those experiencing grief.

To summarize:

- While grief is a very individual experience and the meaning of loss can vary significantly, individuals often exhibit patterns in the ways they experience, express, and adapt to loss.
- These patterns are a continuum; on one end are persons who tend to be instrumental in their grief, while on the other end are individuals who may be considered intuitive.
- Intuitive grievers experience grief primarily as waves of affect expressing this grief in a variety of ways, such as crying or ventilating affect. Finding appropriate ways to ventilate this affect is a useful adaptive strategy that facilitates their grieving process.
- Instrumental grievers experience grief in other ways. Affect is usually modulated and they tend to describe grief more in physical, behavioral, or cognitive manifestations. Expressions of grief tend to be active and cognitive. Useful adaptive strategies for instrumental grievers will be drawn from more cognitive and active approaches.
- Many individuals will experience changes in their patterns throughout

their life cycle. As individuals age their patterns are likely to move toward the center of the continuum, becoming more blended.

- There is a pattern that might be termed dissonant. Here there is dissonance between the way a person experiences grief and the manner in which that person expresses and adapts to grief. This usually occurs with an individual whose internal experience of grief is more intuitive, but who, for some reason or another (such as constraint), finds it difficult to express that emotion. Hence, some males may be dissonant, that is, experiencing grief as intense feelings they are constrained from expressing.
- These patterns are *related* to gender, albeit not *determined* by gender—at least in Western societies. Other factors—temperamental, cultural, historical, generational, perhaps even biological—as well as socialization and developmental experiences may affect an individual grieving pattern.
- Counselors need to carefully assess an individual's grieving patterns. Only then can counselors offer interventive strategies that are comparable with the way an individual grieves and build on that individual's strengths.
- Within family systems different grieving patterns can complicate one another's grief. Effective counseling can assist family members in identifying where they can find support they need while drawing upon the complementary strengths of individuals with other patterns.
- Differences in patterns are differences, not deficiencies. Each pattern, depending on the way it is utilized—as well as the societal expectations about grief—can complicate or facilitate the grieving process.

This approach suggests certain implications for theorists, researchers, educators, clinicians, as well as grieving individuals. In many ways, this is a new approach to grief theory, but one that takes seriously the understanding that grief is a multidimensional reaction consisting of multiple manifestations of grief. Grief is not just an affective experience, but one that touches the cognitive, spiritual, physical and behavioral realms. This approach also takes seriously the understanding of many current approaches, such as task models (see Worden, 1982), which show that there are varied ways for individuals to express grief and adapt to loss.

Finally, this approach reminds theorists of the valued linkages, models and insights that can be drawn from related disciplines such as psychology and sociology. There is a danger to the emergence of practice-oriented disciplines such as education, nursing, or thanatology. The danger is one of marginalization as a small circle of specialists teach and educate one another. Lest thanatology's models of the grieving process become too parochial, it is essential not to lose the connections with larger models and master concepts that provide linkages between and within one's discipline (see Corr and Doka, 1999).

This is a challenge to researchers as well: but hopefully there are other challenges offered by this work. First, there is a need to validate these assumptions of patterns and, if found, to assess the distribution of these patterns within given populations. Subsequent research could then consider the relationship of a pattern with a wide range of other variables, such as developmental factors, grieving outcomes, as well as associations with other assessments such as Myer-Briggs. In addition, a rough tool for assessment of a pattern was offered within this book. However, alternative approaches to assessment that are clearly validated are essential.

Finally, the journey taken in this book suggests to researchers that gender may not be as useful a variable as sometimes assumed. The extensive research cited here on gender simply seems to validate the old law of social physics—for every Ph.D. there is an opposite and opposing Ph.D. Perhaps this is because gender itself is related to a critical variable—pattern. Researchers, then, may wish to move beyond gender.

Educators and clinicians, too, may wish to examine carefully their own assumptions. As Sue and Sue (1990) note, there is an inherent bias in counseling, one that emphasizes the ventilation of feelings as a critical value. Not only does that lead to insensitivity to cultures that do not value emotional expressiveness as much, it disenfranchises those who express their grief in a different way. Educators and clinicians share a joint responsibility to validate the many ways that people grieve. It is a responsibility exercised in counseling sessions, classrooms, and community educational forums. It begins, too, in the education of counselors. Perhaps an emphasis is needed on both the value of exploring and validating counselors' own ways of dealing with loss, and on cultivating eclectic approaches that acknowledge the distinctive grieving patterns of their clients. Early in the public presentation of this material, one participant came up afterward to thank the presenter. The counselor stated how valuable he found the presentation and how much he could use the techniques shared. However, he concluded with an interesting statement: "How much easier it would be if these people could only get in touch with their feelings!" Educators and clinicians, too, need to see beyond gender and beyond our own biases.

In many ways this has been a personal journey as well as a professional one, clarifying earlier experiences and reactions. One author was part of a clinical pastoral education program, working with children with cancer. Each supervisory session spent considerable time exploring the comparative lack of affect that the supervisor noted in the student counselor. Each week, in tones of exasperation, the supervisor would ask, "What do you do with your feelings? How can you not grieve?" In reality much grieving was taking place, but it was expressed in other modes—biweekly donating of platelets, numerous journal entries, talking about the children, reading, and ultimately writing two master's theses based, in part, on the experience. How much more useful it would have been had the supervisor been able to identify that grief work and to explore its strengths and limitations. Similarly, the other author conducted a series of videotaped interviews with a sixteen-year-old female dying from an inoperable brain tumor. After the girl's death, he was asked by a graduate student in thanatology: "How can you continue to teach this stuff after what you've just been through?" It was pointed out that teaching was a way of expressing grief, just as delivering the teenager's eulogy had been.

Ultimately it is that identification, validation, and exploration of their pattern of grief that grieving individuals will find empowering and that will allow them to deal with that loss on their own terms, with their own unique strengths.

This book states that both instrumental and intuitive grievers are disenfranchised. Instrumental grievers are disenfranchised early in the grief process when the comparative absence of affective expression may make others believe they are untouched by the loss. Intuitive grievers may feel disenfranchised over time, when others seem to tire of their need to express and share their grief. Dissonant grievers as well may be disenfranchised when their own conceptions of their role of societal definitions of males and females constrain their expression of grief. Perhaps, as one understands these patterns of grief, and as one looks at grief beyond gender, these individuals may be disenfranchised no more.

APPENDIX

Item Analysis and Scoring of the Grief Pattern Inventory

The Grief Pattern Inventory contains 25 items with response choices ranged along a continuum: always, usually, sometimes, rarely, and never. This reflects the belief that patterns exist on a continuum from profoundly intuitive to intensely instrumental. What follows is a brief description of each question and/or the pattern suggested by a positive response.

1. *I am more emotional than most people I know.* The basis of the patterns lies in the individual's customary choice of feelings over thinking and vice versa. Positive = intuitive.
2. *It is easy for me to cry and show my feelings for others.* A willingness to disclose feelings is associated with the intuitive pattern. Positive = intuitive.
3. *Even though I have returned to my normal routine I still have strong and painful feelings about my loss.* Positive = intuitive.
4. *Even though I feel like crying, I do not cry in front of others.* This is the first of six questions where a positive response could reveal a tendency toward a dissonant response. Although this would usually point to an intuitive dissonant response, it could include instrumental grievers who have no other outlets for expressing whatever degree of feelings they experience. Positive = dissonant.
5. *Although I am grieving in my own way, others may think me cold and unfeeling.* Instrumental grievers are often perceived as lacking feelings. Positive = instrumental.

6. *I don't seem to get as upset as most other people I know.* Positive = instrumental.
7. *I feel overwhelmed by my feelings of grief.* Positive = intuitive.
8. *I appreciate when others encourage me to share my painful feelings with them.* While this could measure a griever's tendency towards introversion it is most likely an example of intuitive grieving. Positive = intuitive.
9. *I avoid highly emotional or "touchy-feely" situations of any kind.* Instrumental grievers rarely choose to place themselves in situations designed to elicit the experience and expression of feelings. Positive = instrumental.
10. *It is important to me that others view me as being in control.* This is especially important for intuitive grievers who may become image managers in the wake of a loss. Positive = dissonant.
11. *I have been told that I am avoiding my grief even though I don't think that I am.* Positive = instrumental.
12. *I have been controlling my painful feelings by drinking or using other prescription or nonprescription drugs.* Positive = dissonant.
13. *I believe that a bereavement support group is (would be) very helpful for me.* Positive = intuitive.
14. *I worry that I am not as upset by my loss as I should be and feel guilty that I don't have more intense feelings.* Penitent instrumental grievers feel unusually guilty about their lack of pain. Positive = dissonant.
15. *I resent efforts to get me to show feelings that I don't have.* Positive = instrumental.
16. *I think more about my loss than feel things about my loss.* Positive = instrumental.
17. *I believe it is important to be aware of, and in touch with, all of my feelings.* Positive = intuitive.
18. *I find that solving problems associated with my loss helps me.* Positive = instrumental.
19. *Although I can sometimes control my painful feelings, they return and overwhelm me.* Positive = intuitive.
20. *Since my loss, I feel like I'm pretending to be strong in front of most people.* Positive = dissonant.
21. *I find that I can't stop my grieving by thinking of other things.* Positive = intuitive.
22. *I have taken deliberate action to honor the memory of my loved one, even though I have not been as upset as most others who are grieving my loved one.* Positive = instrumental.
23. *Others seem surprised by my recovery from my loss.* Positive = instrumental.
24. *Although I took care of things immediately after my loved one's death, I was surprised when I eventually "crashed" and began to have intense, painful*

feelings. Even strongly intuitive grievers can sometimes manage certain post-death activities before being overwhelmed by their feelings. Positive = intuitive.

25. *I would describe myself as more intellectual about problems than emotional.* Positive = instrumental.

We again remind readers that the Grief Pattern Inventory is designed to augment other methods for assessing a client's grief. In addition, it is always a sound practice to readminister the GPI after several weeks have passed. Dissonant responses, in particular, are often temporary in nature. Finally, we would advise waiting at least two to three weeks after the death to begin evaluating patterns. Suggested guidelines for interpreting a griever's scores follows:

Key: A = +2 U = +1 S = 0 R = −1 N = −2.
Intuitive Pattern: Questions #1, 2, 3, 7, 8, 13, 17, 19, 22, 24.
Score: 16–20   Profoundly intuitive pattern
          11–15   Moderate intuitive pattern
           6–10   Blended intuitive pattern
          −5–+5   Blended balanced patterns.
Instrumental Pattern: Questions # 5, 6, 9, 11, 15, 16, 18, 22, 23, 25.
Score: 16–20   Profoundly instrumental pattern
          11–15   Moderate instrumental pattern
           6–10   Blended instrumental pattern
          −5–+5   Blended balanced pattern.
Dissonant Responses: Questions # 4, 10, 12, 14, 20.
Each dissonant response should be evaluated separately.

APPENDIX

Grief Pattern Inventory

Please respond to each of the following statements using the key below. If appropriate, choose the response that best describes you in the past 2 weeks.

KEY
A = ALWAYS
U = USUALLY
S = SOMETIMES
R = RARELY
N = NEVER.

Please circle the best response for you:

1. A U S R N I am more emotional than most people I know.
2. A U S R N It is easy for me to cry and show my feelings to others.
3. A U S R N Even though I have returned to my normal routine, I still have strong and painful feelings about my loss.
4. A U S R N Even though I feel like crying, I do not cry in front of others.
5. A U S R N Although I am grieving in my own way, others may think me cold and unfeeling.
6. A U S R N I don't seem to get as upset as most other people I know.

7. A U S R N   I feel overwhelmed by feelings of grief.

8. A U S R N   I appreciate when others encourage me to share my painful feelings with them.

9. A U S R N   I avoid highly emotional or "touchy-feely" situations of any kind.

10. A U S R N   It is important to me that others view me as being in control.

11. A U S R N   I have been told that I am avoiding my grief even though I don't think that I am.

12. A U S R N   I have been controlling my painful feelings by drinking or by using other prescription or non prescription drugs.

13. A U S R N   I believe that a bereavement support group is (would be) very helpful for me.

14. A U S R N   I worry that I am not as upset by my loss as I should be, and feel guilty that I don't have more intense feelings.

15. A U S R N   I resent efforts to get me to show feelings that I don't have.

16. A U S R N   I *think* more about my loss than *feel* things about my loss.

17. A U S R N   I believe it is very important to be aware of, and in touch with, all of my feelings.

18. A U S R N   I find that solving problems associated with my loss helps me.

19. A U S R N   Although I can sometimes control my painful feelings, they usually return and overwhelm me.

20. A U S R N   Since my loss, I feel like I'm just pretending to be strong in front of most people.

21. A U S R N   I find that I can't stop my grieving by thinking of other things.

22. A U S R N   I have taken deliberate action to honor the memory of my loved one, even though I have not been as upset as most others who are grieving my loved one.

23. A U S R N   Others seem surprised by my recovery from my loss.

24. A U S R N   Although I took care of things immediately after my loved one's death, I was surprised when I eventually "crashed" and began to have intense and painful feelings.

25. A U S R N   I would describe myself as more intellectual than emotional.

REFERENCES

Attig, T. (1996). *How we grieve: Relearning the world.* New York: Oxford University Press.

Barrett, R. (1997). Bereaved black children. In J. Morgan (Ed.), *Readings in thanatology* (pp. 403–420). Amityville, NY: Baywood.

Barnett, R., Biener, L., & Baruch, G. (Eds.). (1987). *Gender and stress.* New York: Free Press.

Bem, S. L. (1981). *The lenses of gender: Transforming the debate on sexual inequality.* New Haven, CT: Yale University Press.

Berger, P., & Luckmann, T. (1966). *The social construction of reality.* New York: Doubleday.

Berman, P. W. (1980). Are women more responsive than men to the young? A review of developmental and situational variables. *Psychological Bulletin, 88,* 668–695.

Biddle, L., & Walter, T. (1998). The emotional English & their queen of hearts. *The Forum Newsletter, 24*(5), 13–15.

Blauner, R. (1968). Death and the social structure. In M. Truzzi (Ed.), *Sociology and everyday life* (pp. 346–367). Englewood Cliffs, NJ: Prentice Hall.

Bly, R. (1990). *Iron John: A book about men.* New York: Vintage.

Boch Hughes, C., & Page-Lieberman, J. (1989). Fathers experiencing perinatal loss. *Death Studies, 13,* 537–556.

Bohannon, J. (1990). Grief responses of spouses following the death of a child: A longitudinal study. *Omega, 22,* 109–121.

Bohannon, J. E. (1991). Religiosity related to grief levels of bereaved mothers and fathers. *Omega, 23,* 153–159.

Bolton, C., & Camp, D. (1987). Funeral rituals and the facilitation of grief work. *Omega, 17,* 343–351.

Bolton, C., & Camp, D. (1989). The post-funeral ritual in bereavement counseling & grief work. *Journal of Gerontological Social Work, 13,* 49–59.

Bonanno, G. (1997). Examining the "grief work" approach to bereavement. Presentation to the Annual Meeting of the Association of Death Education and Counseling, Washington, DC.

Bonanno, G. A., Keltner, D., Holen, A., & Horowitz, M. J. (1995). When avoiding unpleasant emotions might not be such a bad thing: Verbal-autonomic response dissociation and midlife conjugal bereavement. *Journal of Personality and Social Psychology, 69,* 975–989.

Bonanno, G. A., & Singer, J. L. (1990). Repressor personality style: Theoretical and methodological implications for health and pathology. In J. L. Singer (Ed.), *Repression and dissociation* (pp. 435–470). Chicago: University of Chicago Press.

Bowlby J. (1980). *Loss, sadness and depression.* New York: Basic Books.

Brabert, S., Forsyth, C., & Melancon, C. (1992). Grieving men: Thoughts, feelings and behaviors following deaths of wives. *The Hospice Journal, 8*(4), 33–47.

Caine, L. (1974). *Widow.* New York: Bantam.

Calhoun, L., & Tedeschi, R. (1990). Positive aspects of critical problems: Recollections of grief. *Omega, 20,* 265–272.

Campbell, S., & Silverman, P. (1996). *Widower: When men are left alone.* Amityville, NY: Baywood.

Campos, J. J., Campos, R. G., & Barrett, K. C. (1989). Emergent themes in the study of emotional development and emotion regulation. *Developmental Psychology, 25,* 394–402.

Carroll, R., & Shaefer, S. (1994). Similarities and differences in spouses coping with SIDS. *Omega, 28,* 273–284.

Carverhill, P. (1995). Hearing men's voices: The lived experience of spousal bereavement. Presentation to the Kings College Conference on Death, Dying, and Bereavement. London, Canada.

Cherney, P., & Verhey, M. (1996). Grief among gay men associated with multiple losses from AIDS. *Death Studies, 20,* 115–132.

Clark, C. (1987). Sympathy, Biography, and Sympathy Margin. *American Journal of Sociology, 93,* 290–321.

Conway, V., & Feeney, J. (1997). Attachments and grief: A study of parental bereavement. *Journal of Family Studies, 3,* 36–42.

Cook, J. (1988). Dad's double binds: Rethinking father's bereavement from a men's studies perspective. *Journal of Contemporary Ethnography, 17,* 285–308.

Corr, C. (1992). A task based approach to coping with dying. *Omega, 24,* 81–94.

Corr, C. (1998). Enhancing the concept of disenfranchised grief. *Omega, 38,* 1–20.

Corr, C., & Corr, D. (2000). Anticipatory mourning and coping with dying: Similarities, differences, and suggested guidelines for helpers. In T. A. Rando (Ed.), *Clinical dimensions of anticipatory mourning: Theory and practice in working with the dying, their loved ones, and their caregivers.* Champaign, IL: Research Press.

Corr, C., Nabe, C., & Corr, D. (1997). *Death and dying: Life and living* (2nd Ed.). Pacific Grove, CA: Brooks/Cole.

Cousins, N. (1979). *Anatomy of an illness.* New York: Norton.

Davis, M. H. (1983). Measuring individual differences in empathy: Evidence for a multidimensional approach. *Journal of Personality and Social Psychology, 44,* 113–126.

Deffenbacher, J. L., Oetting, E. R., Thwaites, G. A., Lynch, R. S., Baker, D. A., Stark, R. S., Thacker, S., & Eiswerth-Cox, L. (1996). State-trait anger theory and the utility of the trait anger scale. *Journal of Counseling Psychology, 43,* 131–148.

Deutsch, H. (1937). Absence of grief. *Psychoanalytic Quarterly, 6,* 12–22.

DeVries, B., Dalla Lana, R., & Falek, V. (1994). Parental bereavement over the life course: A theoretical intersection and empirical review. *Omega, 29,* 47–70.

Doka, K. J. (1984). Expectation of death, participation in funeral arrangements, and grief adjustment. *Omega, 15,* 119–130.

Doka, K. J. (1987). Silent sorrow: Grief and the loss of significant others. *Death Studies, 11,* 455–469.

Doka, K. J. (1989a). *Disenfranchised grief: Recognizing hidden sorrow.* San Francisco: Jossey Bass.

Doka, K. J. (1989b). Grief. In R. Kastenbaum & B. Kastenbaum (Eds.), *The encyclopedia of death* (pp. 127–131). Phoenix, AZ: Oryx Press.

Doka, K. J. (1990). The therapeutic bookshelf. *Omega, 21,* 321–326.

Doka, K. J. (1993). *Living with life-threatening illness: A guide for patients, their families, and caregivers.* San Francisco: Jossey–Bass.

Doka, K. J., & Davidson, J. (1998). *Living with grief: Who we are, how we grieve.* Washington, DC: The Hospice Foundation of America.

Doka, K. J., & Martin, T. L. (1998). Masculine responses to loss: Clinical implications. *Journal of Family Studies, 4,* 143–158.

Doka, K. J., & Morgan, J. (1993). *Death and spirituality.* Amityville, NY: Baywood.

Douglas, J. (1990). Patterns of change following parent death in midlife adults. *Omega, 22,* 123–137.

Doyle, P. (1980). *Grief counseling and sudden death: A manual and guide.* Springfield, IL: Charles C. Thomas.

Elias, N. (1991). On human beings and their emotions: A process-sociological essay. In M. Featherstone, M. Hepworth, & B. Turner (Eds.), *The body: Social process and cultural theory* (pp. 103–125). London: Sage.

Elmer, L. (1994, May). *Grief does not compute.* Presentation to King's College Conference on Death Dying and Bereavement. London, Ontario.

Faschingbauer, T. R., Zissook, S., & DeVaul, R. (1987). The Texas revised inventory of grief. In S. Zissook (Ed.), *Biopsychosocial aspects of bereavement* (pp. 111–124). Washington, DC: American Psychiatric Press.

Fearon, I., McGrath, P., & Achat, H. (1996). Booboos: The study of everyday pain among young children. *Pain, 68,* 55–62.

Feinson, M. (1986). Aging widows and widowers: Are there mental health differences? *International Journal of Aging and Human Development, 23,* 241–255.

Festinger, L. (1957). *A theory of cognitive dissonance.* Stanford: Stanford University Press.

Figley, C. (1996). Traumatic death: Treatment implications. In K. Doka (Ed.), *Living with grief after sudden loss* (pp. 91–102). Washington, DC: Hospice Foundation of America.

Fox, N. A. (1989). Psychophysiological correlates of emotional reactivity during the first year of life. *Developmental Psychology, 25,* 364–372.

Freud, S. (1957). Mourning and melancholia. Standard edition (Vol. XIV). London: Hogarth. (Originally published 1917)

Fry, P. S. (1997). Grandparent's reactions to the death of a grandchild: An exploratory factor analysis study. *Omega, 35,* 119–140.

Futterman, A., Gallagher, D., Thompson, L., Lovett, S., & Gilewski, M. (1990). Retrospective assessment of marital adjustment and depression during the first two years of spousal adjustment. *Psychology of Aging, 5,* 277–283.

Gennep, A. (1960). *The rites of passage.* Chicago: University of Chicago Press.

Gilbar, O., & Dagan, A. (1995). Coping with loss: Differences between widows and widowers of deceased cancer patients. *Omega, 31,* 207–220.

Gilligan, C. (1982). *In a different voice.* Cambridge, MA: Harvard University Press.

Glick, L., Weiss, R., & Parkes, C. M. (1974). *The first year of bereavement.* New York: Wiley.

Goffman, E. (1959). *The presentation of self in everyday life.* Garden City, NY: Doubleday.

Goldbach, K., Dunn, D., Toedter, L., & Lasker, J. (1991). The effects of gestational age and gender on grief after pregnancy loss. *American Journal of Orthopsychiatry, G1,* 461–467.

Golden, T. (1994a). *A man's grief.* Privately published.

Golden, T. (1994b). *Different paths toward healing: The experience and healing of a man's grief.* Privately published.

Golden, T. (1994c). *Gender and cultural differences in grief.* Privately published pamphlet.

Golden, T. (1996). *Swallowed by a snake: The gift of the masculine side of healing.* Kensington, MD: Golden Healing.

Goodman, M., Black, H. K., & Rubinstein, R. L. (1996). Paternal bereavement in older men. *Omega, 33,* 303–322.

Gottlieb, L., Lang, A., & Amsei, R. (1996). The long-term effects of grief on marital intimacy following an infant's death. *Omega, 33,* 1–20.

Gray, J. (1992). *Men are from Mars, women are from Venus: A practical guide for improving communication and getting what you want in your relationship.* New York: Harper–Collins.

Gross, J. J., & Munoz, R. F. (1995). Emotion regulation and mental health. *Clinical Psychology: Science and Practice, 2,* 151–164.

Grollman, E. (1997). Coping with loss. In K. Doka (Ed.), *Clergy to clergy: A tape series.* Washington, DC: The Hospice Foundation of America.

Gunther, J. (1949). *Death be not proud: A memoir.* New York: Harper & Row.

Hansson, R. O., Carpenter, B. N., & Fairchild, S. K. (1993). Measurement issues in bereavement. In M. S. Stroebe, W. Stroebe, & R. S. Hansson (Eds.), *Handbook of bereavement: Theory, research, and intervention* (pp. 255–270). Cambridge, England: Cambridge University Press.

Harvey, J., Orbuch, T., Weber, A., Merback, N., & Ait, R. (1992). House of pain and hope: Accounts of loss. *Death Studies, 16,* 99–124.

Hegel, G. (1990). *Philosophy of history.* Amherst, NY: Prometheus Books.

Hetherington, E. M., Cox, M., & Cox, R. (1978). The aftermath of divorce. In J. H. Stevens, Jr., & M. Mathews (Eds.), *Mother-child father-child relations.* Washington, DC: National Association for the Education of Young Children.

Hinton, S. E. (1967). *The outsiders.* New York: Puffin.

Hochschild, A. R. (1979). Emotion work, feeling rules and social support. *American Journal of Sociology, 85*(Nov.), 551–573.

Horowitz, S. C. (1970). Strategies within hypnosis for reducing phobic behavior. *Journal of Abnormal Psychology, 75,* 104–112.

Hughes, C., & Fleming, D. (1991). Grief casualties on skid row. *Omega, 23,* 109–118.

Ice, T. (1995). The killing fields. In L. A. Despeider & A. L. Strickland (Eds.), *The path ahead: Readings in death and dying.* Mountain View, CA: Mayfield.

Izard, C. E. (1991). *The psychology of emotions.* New York: Plenum Press.

Jensen, M. R. (1987). *Psychobiological factors in the prognosis and treatment of neoplastic disorders.* Unpublished doctoral dissertation, Yale University, New Haven, CT.

Jung, C. G. (1920). *Psychological Types.* London: Rotledge & Kegan.

Kagan, J. (1994). On the nature of emotion. In N. A. Fox (Ed.), The development of emotion regulation. *Monographs of the Society for Research in Child Development, 59* (2–3, Serial No. 240).

Kalish, R., & Reynolds, D. (1981). *Death and ethnicity: A psychocultural study.* Amityville, NY: Baywood.

Kaminer, H., & Lavie, P. (1993). Sleep and dreams in well-adjusted and less adjusted Holocaust survivors. In M. S. Stroebe, W. Stroebe, & R. O. Hansson (Eds.), *Handbook of bereavement: Theory, research, and intervention* (pp. 331–348). Cambridge, England: Cambridge University Press.

Kastenbaum, R. (1971). Encountering death 1: From a distance. Paper presented at Mount Angel College, St. Benedict, Oregon.

Kavanaugh, R. E. (1972). *Facing Death.* Los Angeles: Nash.

Kavenaugh, S. (1997). Gender differences among parents who experience the death of an infant weighing less than 500 grams at birth. *Omega, 35,* 281–296.

Keen, S. (1991). *Fire in the belly: On being a man.* New York: Bantam.

Kelly, J. (1977). The aging male homosexual: Myth and reality. *The Gerontologist, 17,* 328–332.

Kimmel, D. (1978). Adult development and aging: A gay perspective. *The Journal of Social Issues, 34,* 113–131.

Klass, D. (1997). The deceased child in the psychic and social worlds of bereaved parents during the resolution of grief. *Death Studies, 21,* 147–175.

Klass, D. (1998). Private Communication.

Klass, D., Silverman, P., & Nickman, S. (1996). *Continuing bonds: New understandings of grief.* Washington, DC: Taylor & Francis.

Koppelman, K. (1994). *The fall of a sparrow.* Amityville, NY: Baywood.

Koriat, A., Melkman, R., Averill, J. R., & Lazarus, R. S. (1972). The self-control of emotional reactions to a stressful film. *Journal of Personality, 40,* 601–619.

Kushner, H. S. (1981). *Why do bad things happen to good people.* New York: Avon.

Lamb, M. E., & Urberg, K. A. (1978). The development of gender role and gender identity.

In M. E. Lamb (Ed.), *Social and personality development*. New York: Holt, Rinehart and Winston.

Lang, A., & Gottlieb, L. (1993). Marital intimacy after infant death. *Death Studies, 17*, 233–256.

Larsen, R. J., & Diener, E. (1987). Affect intensity as an individual difference characteristic: A review. *Journal of Research in Personality, 21*, 1–39.

Lattanzi, M., & Hale, M. (1984). Giving grief words: Writing during bereavement. *Omega, 15*, 46–52.

Lazarus, R. S. (1966). *Psychological stress and the coping process*. New York: McGraw–Hill.

Lazarus, R. S. (1991). Cognition and motivation in emotion. *American Psychologist, 46*, 352–367.

Lazarus, R. S., Averill, J. R., & Opton, E. M., Jr. (1970). Toward a cognitive theory of emotions. In M. Arnold (Ed.), *Feelings and emotions* (pp. 207–232). San Diego, CA: Academic Press.

Lazarus, R. S., & Folkman, S. (1984). *Stress, appraisal, and coping*. New York: Springer.

LeGrand, L. (1986). *Coping with separation and loss as a young adult*. Springfield, IL: Charles C. Thomas.

Lever, J. (1976). Sex differences in the games children play. *Social Problems, 23*, 478–487.

Lewis, C. S. (1963). *A grief observed*. New York: Bantam.

Lindeman, E. (1944). Symptomatology and management of acute grief. *American Journal of Psychiatry, 101*, 141–148.

Lund, D. (1999). Giving and receiving help during later life spousal bereavement. In J. Davidson & K. Doka, *Living with grief: At work, at school, at worship*. Washington, DC: The Hospice Foundation of America.

Lund, D., Caserta, M., & Diamond, M. (1993). The course of spousal bereavement in later life. In M. Stroebe, W. Stroebe, & R. Hansson (Eds.), *Handbook of bereavement: Theory, research, intervention*. Cambridge, UK: Cambridge University Press.

Maacoby, E. E., & Jacklin, C. N. (1974). *The psychology of sex differences*. Stanford: Stanford University Press.

Martin, J. (1988). Psychological consequences of AIDS-related bereavement among gay men. *Journal of Counsulting & Clinical Psychology, 51*, 856–862.

Martin, J., & Dean, L. (1993a). Bereavement following death from AIDS: Unique problems, reactions & special needs. In M. Strobe, W. Strobe, & R. Hansson (Eds.), *Handbook of bereavement: Theory, research, intervention* (pp. 317–330). Cambridge, UK: Cambridge University Press.

Martin, J., & Dean, L. (1993b). Effects of AIDS-related bereavement & HIV-related illness on psychological distress among gay men: A seven-year longitudinal study. *Journal of Consulting & Clinical Psycology, 61*, 94–103.

Martin, T. L., & Doka, K. J. (1996). Masculine grief. In K. J. Doka (Ed.), *Living with grief after sudden loss* (pp. 161–172). Washington, DC: Hospice Foundation of America.

Martin, T. L., & Doka, K. J. (1998). Revisiting masculine grief. In K. J. Doka & J. D. Davidson (Eds.), *Living with grief: Who we are, how we grieve* (pp. 133–142). Washington, DC: Hospice Foundation of America.

Marx, K. (1993). *Capital: A critique of political economy*. London: Penguin Classics.

McCrae, R. R., & Costa, P. T., Jr. (1989). Reinterpreting the Myers–Briggs type indicator from the perspective of the five-factor model of personality. *Journal of Personality, 57*, 17–40.

Meichenbaum, D. H. (1977). *Cognitive-behavior modification*. New York: Plenum.

Morgan, D. C. (1989). Adjusting to widowhood: Do social networks really make it easier? *The Gerontologist, 29*, 101–107.

Moos, R. H., & Shaefer, J. (1986). *Coping with life crises: An integrated approach*. New York: Plenum Press.

Morgan, D. L. (1989). Adjusting to widowhood: Do social networks really make it easier? *The Gerontologist, 29*, 101–107.

Moss, M., Resch, N., & Moss, S. (1977). The role of gender in middle age children's responses to parental death. *Omega, 36*, 43–65.

Moss, S., Rubinstein, R. L., & Moss, M. (1997). Middle-aged son's reactions to father's death. *Omega, 35*, 259–278.

Murphy, P., & Perry, K. (1988). Hidden grievers. *Death Studies, 12*, 451–462.

Myers, E. (1988). *When parents die: A guide for adults.* New York: Penguin Press.

Nadeau, J. (1998). *Families making sense of death.* Thousand Oaks, CA: Sage.

Neimeyer, R. (1993). An appraisal of constructivist psychotherapies. *Journal of Consulting and Clinical Psychology, 61*, 221–234.

Neimeyer, R. (1996). Process intervention for the constructivist psychotherapist. In H. Rosen & K. T. Kuchlwein (Eds.), *Constructing realities* (pp. 371–411). San Francisco: Jossey–Bass.

Neimeyer, R. (1997a). Meaning, reconstruction and the experience of chronic loss. In K. Doka with J. Davidson (Eds.), Living with grief: When loss is prolonged (pp. 159–176). Washington, DC: Taylor & Francis.

Neimeyer, R. (1997b, June). Presidental address, Association for Death Education and Conseling meeting, Washington, DC.

Neugebauer, R., Raskin, J., Williams, J., Reimien, R., Goetz, R., & Gorman, J. (1992). Bereavement reactions among homosexual men experiencing multiple losses in the AIDS epidemic. *American Journal of Psychology, 149*, 1374–1379.

Nord, D. (1990). Issues and implication in the counseling of survivors of multiple AIDS-related loss. *Death Studies, 20*, 389–413.

O'Neil, D. (1994, May) Home alone: Widowers with school age children, the need for a functional network. Presentation to the 12th annual Kings College Conference on Death, Aging and Bereavement. London, Ontario.

Osterweiss, M., Solomon, F., & Green, M. (Eds.). (1984). *Bereavement: Reactions, consequences and care.* Washington, DC: National Academy Press.

Parkes, C. M. (1987). *Bereavement: Studies of grief in adult life* (2nd ed.). Madison, CT: International Universities Press.

Parkes, C. M. (1996a). Genocide in Rwanda: Personal reflections. *Mortality, 1*, 95–110.

Parkes, C. M. (1996b). Conclusions II: Attachments and losses in cross-cultural perspective. In C. M. Parkes, P. Laugani, & B. Young (Eds.), *Death and bereavement across cultures* (pp. 233–243). London: Routledge.

Parkes, C. M., & Weiss, R. S. (1983). *Recovery from bereavement.* New York: Basic Books.

Paulhus, D. L., & Reid, D. B. (1991). Enhancement and denial in socially desirable responding. *Journal of Personality and Social Psychology, 60*, 307–317.

Pennebaker, J. W., Kiecott-Glaser, J., & Glaser, R. (1988). Disclosure of traumas and immune function: Health implications for psychotherapy. *Journal of Consulting and Clinical Psychology, 56*, 239–245.

Peppers, L., & Knapp, R. (1980). Maternal reactions to involuntary fetal infant death. *Psychiatry, 93*, 155–159.

Pergament, K. (1997). *The psychology of religion and coping: Theory, practice and research.* New York: Guilford Press.

Plante, T. G., & Schwartz, G. E. (1990). Defensive and repressive coping styles: Self-presentation, leisure activities, and assessment. *Journal of Research in Personality, 24*, 173–190.

Powers, L., & Wampold, B. (1994). Cognitive behavioral factors in adjustment to adult bereavement. *Death Studies, 18*, 1–24.

Prend, A. (1997). *Transcending loss: Understanding the lifelong impact of grief and how to make it meaningful.* New York: Berkley.

Rando, T. (1984). *Grief, dying, and death: Clinical interventions for caregivers.* Champaign, IL: Research Press.

Rando, T. (1986). The unique issues and impact of the death of a child. In T. Rando (Ed.), *The parental loss of a child* (pp. 5–44). Champaign, IL: Research Press.

Rando, T. A. (1988). *How to go on living when someone you love dies.* New York: Bantam Books.

Rando, T. (1993). *Treatment of complicated mourning.* Champaign, IL: Research Press.

Rando, T. A. (2000). Why study anticipatory mourning?: A justification of and introduction to clinical investigation of the phenomenon. In T. A. Rando (Ed.), *Clinical dimensions of anticipatory mourning: Theory and practice in working with the dying, their loved ones, and their caregivers.* Champaign, IL: Research Press.

Raphael, B. (1983). *The anatomy of bereavement.* New York: Basic Books.

Reeves, N., & Boersma, F. (1990). The therapeutic use of ritual in maladaptive grieving. *Omega, 20,* 281–291.

Reynolds, J. (1993). Grief and the culture of victimization. *The Forum,* (March/April), 9–11.

Riches, G., & Dawson, P. (1988). Lost children, living memories: The role of photographs in processes of grief and adjustment among bereaved parents. *Death Studies, 22,* 121–140.

Rosenblatt, P. (1993). Cross cultural variations in the experience, expression and understanding of grief. In D. P. Irish, K. F. Lundquist, & V. Jenkins (Eds.), *Ethnic variations in dying, death & grief: Diversity in universality* (pp. 13–20). Washington, DC: Taylor & Francis.

Rosenblatt, P. (1997). Grief in small-scale societals. In C. M. Parkes, P. Laugani, & B. Young (Eds.), *Death and bereavement across cultures* (pp. 27–51). London: Routledge.

Rosenblatt, P., Walsh, R., & Jackson, D. (1976). *Grief and mourning in cross-cultural perspective.* Washington, DC: HRDF Press.

Rothbart, M. (1991). Temperament: A developmental framework. In J. Strelau & A. Angleneitner (Eds.), *Explorations in temperament: International perspectives on theory and measurement* (pp. 61–74). New York: Plenum Press.

Rotundo, E. A. (1993). *American manhood: Transformations in masculinity from the revolution to the modern era.* New York: Basic Books.

Ryan, D. (1989). Raymond: Unquestioned grief. In K. Doka (Ed.), *Disenfranchised grief: Handling hidden sorrow* (pp. 127–134). Lexington, MA: Lexington Press.

Saarni, C. (1989). Children's understanding of strategic control of emotional expression in social transactions. In C. Saarni & P. L. Harris (Eds.), *Children's understanding of emotions* (pp. 181–208). New York: Cambridge University Press.

Sacco, R. L., Elkind, M., Boden-Albala, B., I-Feng, L., Kargman, D. E., Hauser, W. A., Shea, S., & Myunghee, C. P. (1999). The protective effect of moderate alcohol consumption on ischemic stroke. *Journal of the American Medical Association, 281,* 53–60.

Sanders, C. (1984). *Grief: The mourning after: Dealing with adult bereavement.* New York: Wiley.

Sanders, C. (1992). *Surviving grief and learning to live again.* New York: Wiley.

Sanders, C. (1993). Risk factors in bereavement outcome. In M. Stroebe, W. Stroebe, & R. Hansson (Eds.), *Handbook of bereavement: Theory, research, intervention* (pp. 255–267). Cambridge, UK: Cambridge University Press.

Sanders, C. M., Mauger, P. A., & Strong, P. A. (1985/1991). *A manual for the grief experience inventory.* Palo Alto, CA: Consulting Psychologists Press/Charlotte, NC: Center for the Study of Separation and Loss.

Schlenker, B. R. (1980). *Impression management: The self-concept, social identity, and interpersonal relations.* Monterey, CA: Brooks/Cole.

Schwab, R. (1990). Paternal and maternal coping with the death of a child. *Death Studies, 14,* 407–422.

Schwab, R. (1996). Gender differences in parental grief. *Death Studies, 20,* 103–113.

Schwartz, N. (1990). Feelings as information: Informational and motivational functions of affective states. In E. T. Higgins & E. M. Sorrentino (Eds.), *Handbook of motivation and cognition* (Vol. 2, pp. 527–561). New York: Guilford Press.

Seogin, F., Jamison, C., & Gochneaur, K. (1989). Comparative effects of cognitive and behavioral bibliography for mildly and moderately depressed older adults. *Journal of Consulting and Clinical Psychology, 17,* 403–407.

Sharkin, B. S. (1993). Anger and gender: Theory, research and implications. *Journal of Counseling and Development, 71,* 386–389.

Shorter, B. (1996). *Susceptible to the sacred: The psychological experience of ritual.* New York: Routledge.

Shuchter, S., & Zisook, S. (1993). The course of normal grief. In M. Stroebe, W. Stroebe, & R. Hansson (Eds.), *Handbook of bereavement: Theory, research, intervention* (pp. 23–43). Cambridge, UK: Cambridge University Press.

Silverman, P. R. (1981). *Helping women cope with grief.* Newbury Park, CA: Sage.

Silverman, P. R. (1986). *Widow to widow.* New York: Springer.

Silverman, P. R. (1988). Research as process: Exploring the meaning of widowhood. In R. Kastenbaum (Ed.), *Qualitative gerontology.* New York: Springer.

Silverman, S. (1997). Justice Joseph Story and death in early 19th century America. *Death Studies, 21,* 397–416.

Snyder, M. (1974). Self-monitoring of expressive behavior. *Journal of Personality and Social Psychology, 30,* 526–537.

Sorokin, P. (1937–41). *Social and cultural dynamics.* (Four Volumes). New York: American Book Company.

Spielberger, C. D. (1988). *State-trait anger expression inventory.* Orlando, FL: Psychological Assessment Presources.

Staudacher, C. (1991). *Men and grief.* Oakland, CA: New Harbinger Publications.

Stillion, J., & McDowell, G. (1997, June). Women's issues in grief. Presentation to the Association for Death Education and Caring Annual Meeting. Washington, DC.

Stroebe, M. (1997, June). Coping with bereavement: The sense and nonsense of science. Keynote, Association for Death Education and Counseling, Washington, DC.

Stroebe, M., & Schut, H. (1995, June 29). The dual process model of coping with loss. Paper to International Work Group. Oxford, England.

Stroebe, M., & Stroebe, W. (1983). Who suffers more: Sex differences in health risks of the widowed. *Psychological Bulletin, 93,* 279–301.

Stroebe, W., & Stroebe, M. (1993). Determinants of adjustment to bereavement in younger widows and widowers. In M. Stroebe, W. Stroebe, & R. Hansson (Eds.), *Handbook of bereavement: Theory, research, intervention* (pp. 208–226). Cambridge, UK: Cambridge University Press.

Sue, D. W., & Sue, D. (1990). *Counseling the culturally different: Theory and practice.* New York: Wiley.

Thomas, A., & Chess, S. (1977). *Temperament and development.* New York: Brunner/Mazel.

Thomas, A., & Chess, S. (1985). The behavioral study of temperament. In J. Strelau, F. Farley, & A. Gale (Eds.), *The biological basis of personality and behavior* (Vol. 1, pp. 213–226). Washington, DC: Hemisphere.

Thompson, N. (1995). Men and antisexism. *British Journal of Social Work, 25,* 459–475.

Thompson, R. A. (1994). Emotion regulation: A theme in search of a definition. In N. A. Fox (Ed.), The Development of emotion regulation: Biological and behavioral considerations. *Monographs of the Society for Research in Child Development, 59* (2–3, Serial No. 240).

Tudiver, F., Hilditch, J., Permaul, J. A., & McKendree, D. J. (1992). Does mutual help facilitate newly bereaved widowers? Report of a randomized controlled trial. *Evaluation and the Health Professions, 15,* 147–162.

Vachon, M. (1987). *Occupational stress in the care of the critically ill, dying, and bereaved.* New York: Hemisphere.

Vail, E. (1982). *A personal guide to living with loss.* New York: Wiley.

Van der Hart, O. (1978). *Rituals in psychotherapy: Transition and continuity.* New York: Irvington Press.

Van der Hart, O. (1988). *Coping with loss: The therapeutic use of leave-taking rituals.* New York: Irvington Press.

Viney, L., Henry, R., Walker, B., & Crooks, C. (1992). The psychological impact of multiple deaths from AIDS. *Omega, 24,* 151–163.

Walden, T. A., & Smith, M. C. (1997). Emotion regulation. *Motivation and Emotion, 21,* 7–25.

Webb, N. B. (1993). Helping bereaved children. New York: Guilford Press.

Weinberger, D. A., Schwartz, G. E., & Davidson, R. J. (1979). Low-anxious, high anxious, and repressive coping styles: Psychometric patterns and behavioral and physiological responses to stress. *Journal of Abnormal Psychology, 88,* 369–380.

Weiss, R. (1998). Issues in the study of loss and grief. In J. Harvey (Ed.), Perspectives on loss: A sourcebook (pp. 343–352). Philadephia: Brunner/Mazel.

Weisman, A. (1984). *The coping capacity: On the nature of being mortal.* New York: Human Science Press.

White, E. B. (1952). *Charlotte's web.* New York: Harper-Collins.

Wolfelt, A. (1990). Gender roles and grief: Why men's grief is naturally complicated. *Thanatos, 15*(3), 20–24.

Wolfenstein, M. (1966). How is mourning possible? *Psychoanalytic Study of the Child, 24,* 423–460.

Worden, W. (1991). *Grief counseling and grief therapy: A handbook of the mental health practitioner* (2nd ed.). New York: Springer.

Wortman, C., & Silver, R. (1989). The myths of coping with loss. *The Journal of Consulting and Clinical Psychology, 57,* 349–357.

BIBLIOGRAPHY

Alberts, M., Lyons, J., & Anderson, R. (1988). Relations of coping style and illness variables in ulcerative colitis. *Psychological Reports, 62,* 71–79.

Ashley, M. (1986). Being there with a dying son. *Public Welfare, 44,* 38–43.

Balk, D. (1996). Models of understanding adolescent coping with bereavement. *Death Studies, 20,* 367–387.

Balswick, J. (1988). *The inexpressive male.* Lexington, MA: Lexington Books.

Bernardo, F. M. (1985). Social networks and life preservation. *Death Studies, 9,* 37–50.

Bernardo, F. M., LaGreca, A. J., & Berardo, D. H. (1985). Individual lifestyles and survivorship: The role of habits, attitudes, and nutrition. *Death Studies, 9,* 5–22.

Betcher, W., & Pollack, W. (1993). *In a time of fallen heroes: The recreation of masculinity.* New York: Anthenum.

Bierthals, A., Prigerson, H., Fasiczka, A., Frank, E., Miller, M., & Reynolds, C. (1996). Gender differences in complicated grief among the elderly. *Omega, 32,* 303–317.

Brannon, R., & Dand, D. (1976). *The forty-nine percent majority: The male sex role.* Reading, MA: Addison–Wesley.

Braun, M., & Berg, D. (1994). Meaning reconstruction in the experience of parental bereavement. *Death Studies, 18,* 105–130.

Buckley, W. (1967). *Sociology and modern systems theory.* Englewood Cliffs, NJ: Prentice–Hall.

Carey, R. (1979). Weathering widowhood: Problems and adjustments of the widowed during the first year. *Omega, 10,* 163–172.

Carres, M., & Griffen, C. (Eds.). (1990). *Meanings of manhood: Construction of masculinity in Victorian America.* Chicago: University of Chicago Press.

Chenoweth, R., Tonge, J., & Armstrong, J. (1980). Suicide in Brisbane: A retrospective psycho-social study. Australia and New Zealand. *Journal of Psychiatry, 14,* 37–45.

Clarke, C. (1989). Sympathy biography and sympathy margin. *American Journal of Sociology, 93,* 290–321.

Clayton, P. (1979). The sequelae and non sequelae of conjugal bereavement. *American Journal of Psychiatry, 136,* 530–534.

Cleiren, M. (1993). *Bereavement and adaptation: A comparative study of the aftermath of death.* Washington, DC: Hemisphere.

Cochran, S., & Rabinowitz, F. (1996). Men, loss & psychotherapy. *Psychotherapy, 33,* 593–600.

Crossland, C. (1998). Working with widowed men. *Bereavement Care, 17*(2), 19–20.

Dulerman, L. (1975). *Gender and sex in society.* New York: Praeger.

Dyregrov. A., & Mattihiesen, S. (1987). Similarities and differences in mother's and father's grief following the death of an infant. *Scandinavian Journal of Psychology, 28,* 1–15.

Epstein, S. (1993). Bereavement from the perspective of cogntive-experiential self-therapy. In M. Stroebe, W. Stroebe, & R. Hansson (Eds.), *Handbook of bereavement: Theory, research, intervention* (pp. 112–125). Cambridge, UK: Cambridge University Press.

Forisha, B. (1978). *Sex roles and personal awareness.* Morristown, NJ: General Learning Press.

Gallup Organization. (1996). Knowledge and attitudes related to hospice care. Study conducted for National Hospice Organization, Washington, DC.

Gilbert, K. (1996). We've had the same loss, why don't we have the same grief: Loss and differential grief in families. *Death Studies, 20,* 269–283.

Golden, T. (1997). Men and grief. In J. Morgan (Ed.), *Readings in thanatology.* Amityville, NY: Baywood.

Good, G., Robertson, J., Fitzgerald, L., Stevens, M., & Bartels, K. M. (1966). The relation between masculine role conflict and psychological distress in male university counseling center clients. *Journal of Counseling and Development, 75,* 44–49.

Gray, R. (1988). Meaning of death: Implications for bereavement theory. *Death Studies, 12,* 309–318.

Gross, R. E., & Klass, D. (1997). Tibetan Buddhism and the resolution of grief: The Bardo–Thodell for the living and the grieving. *Death Studies, 21,* 377–398.

Hagemeister, A. K., & Rosenblatt, P. C. (1997). Grief and the sexual relationship of couples who have experienced a child's death. *Death Studies, 21,* 231–252.

Hendricks, J., & Hendricks, C. (1973). Defining the situation: Reflection of life styles in funeral eulogies. *Omega, 4,* 57–63.

Hogan, N., & Bak, D. (1990). Adolescent reaction to sibling death: Perception of mothers, fathers, and teenagers. *Nursing Research, 39,* 103–106.

Hogan, N., & Geenfield, D. (1991). Adolescent sibling bereavement: Symptomatology—a large community sample. *Journal of Adolescent Research, 6,* 97–112.

Hogan, N., Morse, J., & Tason, M. (1996). Toward an experiential theory of bereavement. *Omega, 33,* 43–66.

Irish, D., Lundquist, K. F., & Nelson, V. J. (1993). *Ethnic variations in dying, death and grief: Diversity in universality.* Washington, DC: Taylor & Francis.

Izard, C. E. (1981). *The psychology of emotions.* New York: Plenum Press.

Kalish, R., & Reynolds, D. (1976). *Death and ethnicity: A psychocultural study.* Los Angeles: University of California Press.

Klass, D. (1993). Solace and immortality: Bereaved parents continuing bond with their children. *Death Studies, 17,* 343–368.

Klass, D. (1998). *Developing a cross cultural model of grief: The state of the field.* Paper submitted to *Omega.*

Kugelmann, R. (1992). *Stress: The nature and history of engineered grief.* Westport, CT: Praeger.

Lee, R. (1979). Objective loss and counseling the bereaved. *NRIC National Reporter, 2,* 3.

Lopata, H. (1979). Grief work and identity reconstruction. In I. Gerber, A. Weiner, A. Kutscher, D. Battin, A. Arkis, & I. Goldberg (Eds.), *Perspectives on bereavement* (pp. 12–25). New York: Arno Press.

Lund, D., Caserta, M., & Dimond, M. (1986). Gender differences through two years of bereavement among the elderly. *The Gerontologist, 26,* 314–320.

Lund, D., Caserta, M., Dimond, M., & Gray, R. (1986). Impact of bereavement on the self-conceptions of older surviving spouses. *Symbolic Interactions, 9,* 235–244.

Lund, D., Diamond, M., Caserta, M., Johnson, R., Poulton, J., & Connelly, J. (1986). Identifying elderly with coping difficulties after two years of bereavement. *Omega, 16,* 213–224.

Lund, D., Diamond, M., & Juretich, M. (1985). Bereavement support groups for the elderly: Characteristics of potential participants. *Death Studies, 9,* 309–321.

Marshall, V. (1980). *Lost chapters: A sociology of aging and dying.* Monterey, CA: Brooks/Cole.

Martin, T. L. (1998). Taking it like a man [Review of the book *Widower: When men are left alone*]. *Omega, 38,* 325–327.

Marwit, S., & Carusa, S. (1998). Communicated support following loss: Examining the experiences of parental death and parental divorce in adolescence. *Death Studies, 22,* 237–255.

Pleck, J. (1982). *The myth of masculinity.* Cambridge, MA: MIT Press.

Rando, T. (1997). Living and learning the reality of a loved one's dying: Traumatic stress and cognitive processing in anticipatory grief. In K. Doka with J. Davidson (Eds.), *Living with grief: When illness is prolonged* (pp. 33–50). Washington, DC: Taylor & Francis.

Rodgers, B., & Cowles, K. (1991). The concept of grief: An analysis of classical and contemporary thought. *Death Studies, 15,* 443–448.

Rubinstein, R. (1986). The construction of a day by elderly widowers. *International Journal of Aging and Human Development, 23,* 161–174.

Scharlach, A., & Fuller-Thomson, E. (1994). Coping strategies following the death of an elderly parent. *Journal of Gerontology, 216,* 85–100.

Schatz, W. (1984). *Healing a father's grief.* Redmond, WA: Media Publishing Company.

Schneiden, J. (1994). *Finding my way: Healing and transformation through loss and grief.* Colfax, WI: Seasons Press.

Schwab, R. (1992). Effects of a child's death on the marital relationship: A preliminary study. *Death Studies, 16,* 91–134.

Schwab, R. (1997). Parental mourning and children's behavior. *Journal of Counseling and Development. 95,* 258–265.

Sonnemans, J., & Frijda, N. H. (1995). The determinants of subjective emotional intensity. *Cognition and Emotion, 9,* 483–506.

Stillion, J. (1985). *Death and the sexes.* Washington, DC: Hemisphere.

Stylianos, S., & Vachon, M. (1993). The role of social support in bereavement. In M. Stroebe, W. Stroebe, & R. Hansson (Eds.), *Handbook of bereavement: Theory, research, intervention* (pp. 397–410). Cambridge, UK: Cambridge University Press.

Tedeschi, R., & Hamilton, K. (1997). Support group experiences of bereaved fathers. *Catholic Cemetery,* May, 10–12.

Thoits, P. (1986). Social support as coping assistance. *Journal of Counseling and Clinical Psychology, 54,* 416–423.

Tudiver, F., Hildritch, J., & Permaul, J. (1991). A comparison of psychosocial characteristics of new widowers and married men. *Family Medicine, 23,* 501–505.

Walter, T. (1996). A new model of grief: Bereavement and biography. *Mortality, 1,* 7–25.

Weinberg, N. (1994). Self-blame, other blame and desire for revenge: Factors in recovery from bereavement. *Death Studies, 18,* 583–593.

INDEX